The Shopaholic's Guide to Buying Fashion and Beauty Online

Free Subscription Offer

www.thesiteguide.com

www.thesiteguide.com, described by Conde Nast's Glamour.com as 'the web's best shopping directory', is the online version of The Shopaholic's Guide to Buying Fashion and Beauty Online, where you'll find direct links through to all the website reviews, plus regular online shopping features and updates and news of the latest site launches.

We're delighted to offer you a year's free subscription to www.thesiteguide.com (normally £9.99) to thank you for purchasing this book. To take up this offer you need to click on to the site and subscribe. When you're prompted for a media code just use the password you'll find at the end of the introduction to Chapter 7: Handbag Temptation, and you'll be able to use the guide online.

'Thesiteguide.com is the most comprehensive shopping directory I've found on the web, and is also the first to report on fabulous new sites.'

Conde Nast

'A comprehensive guide to all the best shopping destinations on the web.'

Vogue mail

'This is a good shortcut to smart shopping'

The *Evening Standard*

'thesiteguide.com ... provides a discerning and easy to use guide to the best retail sites on the web.'

The Times

The Shopaholic's Guide to

Buying Fashion and Beauty
Online

Patricia Davidson

CAPSTONE

BICENTENNIAL
1807
WILEY
2007
BICENTENNIAL

Library of Congress Cataloging-in-Publication Data
Davidson, Patricia.
  The shopaholic's guide to buying fashion and beauty online / by Patricia Davidson.
    p. cm.
  Includes index.
  ISBN 978-1-84112-779-8 (pbk. : alk. paper)
  1. Clothing and dress--Purchasing--Great Britain--Guidebooks. 2. Teleshopping--Great
Britain--Guidebooks. I. Title.
  TT507.D348 2007
  381'.142--dc22
                                                                        2007011331

ISBN   978-184112-779-8

Anniversary Logo Design: Richard J. Pacifico

Set in Lucida Bright by Sparks (www.sparks.co.uk)
Printed and bound in Great Britain by TJ International Ltd, Padstow, Cornwall

Contents

Acknowledgements

My thanks to Andrew, Sholto and Calum for your enthusiasm about my new writing career, notwithstanding your wonderment about the number of hours I now spend at my computer. As always I'd like to thank Sally Smith at John Wiley, without whom this would never have happened, and Kate Hordern, my agent, for doing a continuously fantastic job.

I'd also like to thank Lee, Richard and Chris of E2E Solutions for creating a wonderful website for me – the fact that we're still working together after three years says a great deal more for your patience than for mine.

Finally (well, not quite), I'd like to thank Sue Douglas for her support and her belief in me over the years, particularly when mine was flagging. Everyone should be lucky enough to have such a mentor.

And really finally, to the real shopaholic in my family (apart from me, of course), my daughter Kirstie – you do it all so well.

About the Author

After twelve years in international designer fashion mail order, Patricia Davidson started www.thesiteguide.com, an online upmarket fashion, beauty and lifestyle website directory. Her first book, *The Shopaholic's Guide to Buying Online*, was published by Capstone in October 2006. Patricia is a regular contributor to Conde Nast's easyliving-magazine.com and has also been published on online shopping in other women's titles and national press. She lives in Buckinghamshire with her husband, three children and two dogs.

Introduction

You probably know by now that the web is a marvellous place to shop, that you can buy just about anything online and that searching is a complete bore. You may well have found the best places to buy your new camera, books, dvds and even your next washing machine.

Did you know, though, that the web is also a superb place to find your next little black dress, designer heels and essentials, such as gorgeous lingerie and swimwear, plus this season's lipstick fix?

Or that you can stock up on your favourite fragrance, shower gels, aromatherapy oils, scented candles and nail polish?

You can try on all the new season's styles at home (having read about the trends online) and then if you want to you can just slip them into their box and send them on their way back without having to worry about anyone asking you why you want to return them. You can also find out about all the new beauty products without having to go anywhere near a beauty counter and have a salesgirl try to push you into buying something you're not quite sure you want.

Now that fashion and beauty have established their proper places online it's possible, easy even, to buy your complete wardrobe without having to leave home. That's not to say that you want to buy everything online. You may, like me, enjoy both using the internet and browsing the shops, but if you don't like shopping, have very little time or live miles from great fashion and beauty stores, then this is definitely the place for you.

In this book you'll find all the fashion and beauty websites you could possibly want, from luxury, designer brand fashion (think Celine, Marni, Gucci and Diane von Furstenberg) to more affordable retailers such as Hobbs, Kew and Pantalon Chameleon.

You'll also find loads of advice on where to look up the trends, how to decide on what to buy (and what not to buy) online and ways of making online shopping easier and more fun than you ever thought it could be.

There are designers and retailers here you're bound to be familiar with, plus many that you probably won't have heard of, but they all have one thing in common: they've been handpicked to ensure that they offer extremely attractive, well-photographed ranges of clothing, accessories and beauty products on well laid out websites that are easy to navigate. They all offer a friendly and efficient service so that if you have a query or problem, there's someone to talk to. Most importantly, they use a secure server to give you peace of mind about buying from them on the web.

They're all just waiting to take your orders online at any time of day or night – so what are you waiting for?

Why Shop for Fashion and Beauty Products Online?

The first reason for shopping online is obvious: convenience. If you're constantly busy, working full time, with or without children and under pressure just to fit the essentials into everyday living, let alone being able to spend time browsing for clothes and beauty essentials (or treats), why not have everything come to you? Surely the convenience of online shopping is one of the best developments for the busy person to have hit for years? I certainly think so.

You can also place your order whenever you feel like it, whether it's four in the morning or eleven at night – 24-hour service is there, ready and waiting for you.

The second reason is time saving. No longer do you have to drive to the shops, find somewhere to park and then waste time putting up with that over-friendly assistant asking whether they can help you when what they're really saying is, can they sell you something? (And maybe I'm being unfair here but aren't some of them more interested in selling you *something* than in making sure it's perfect for you?)

You choose when you want to shop and how long you want to spend doing it. You choose what you want to buy quickly online to save time for special shopping in the stores. You free up your time to spend as you wish.

The third reason is choice. Unless you know exactly what you're looking for, in which case you're not interested in the kind of choice I'm talking about, it would simply not be possible to go round and find in the shops the kind of comprehensive selection you can see almost instantly online – even if you had a month, which most of us don't. You can look at as many or as few products as you wish and see the full details and specification for each and every one.

No, you can't feel and touch (as people keep saying to me) until the garments/products arrive at your door. But do you have the time to do all that feeling and touching in the stores? Thought not. Take advantage of the choice and do your trying on at home.

Finally, the fourth reason is price. Let me be clear here. I am not suggesting that you'll find the new season's ranges of clothes and accessories cheaper online than you will in the stores (although many retailers have online sales when they're still selling at full price offline – remember that). Don't expect to find your next up-to-the-minute pair of Jimmy Choo's cheaper on the website. You won't. You will, however, find excellent discounts at sale times from most fashion retailers and although you'll have to be quick, at least you won't be fighting your way through the crowds.

Beauty products are another matter entirely and you can find some very good prices. Browse through the sites and you'll soon find which are the best for buying the brand new ranges and colours and which are the best for discounts. Then always check there first, just in case your favoured brand and product is in stock for less.

Website Information

The best websites will give you clear and easy categories and customer information (delivery, returns, contact info) right on the home page so you don't have to waste time clicking through long Flash intros which slow down your search for that perfect product. After all, you're interested in buying from them, not seeing endless images for products you don't want.

Just take a look, for example, at www.eluxury.com and www.neiman-marcus.com, two top US websites offering every designer from Marc Jacobs to Manolo Blahnik, with Louis Vuitton and Christian Dior in between. There they are on the front page, ready and waiting for you to browse and buy, with clear information about delivery, returns and every other question you can think of just one click away. No 'clever' Flash intros, no extra home page; no nonsense, just straight to what you want to buy.

Using This Book

All the websites included in the guide have been looked at carefully not only for the service and products they offer but also for how easy the retailers make it for you to shop.

For almost every website you'll find something like the following:

Site Usability: ★★★★★	Based:	UK
Product Range: ★★★★★	Express Delivery Option? (UK)	Yes
Price Range: Medium	Gift Wrapping Option?	Yes
Delivery Area: Worldwide	Returns Procedure:	Down to you

In all cases the stars range from ★★★ to ★★★★★ – as explained below.

Site Usability

How quick and easy is it for you to click round the website and get to the products you're looking for? How quickly can you get to information on delivery, returns, whether or not gift wrapping is offered and how to contact the retailer? Are the pictures clear and attractive? Is there adequate information about every product offered?

Product Range

How much choice is there on the website? Fewer stars here do not mean a lower-quality product, just a smaller range.

Price Range

This is just a guide so you know what to expect.

Delivery Area

Does the retailer deliver to the UK, EU countries or worldwide?

Based

This tells you where the retailer is based, so you'll know straight away if you're going to be in for duty or extra shipping costs.

Express Delivery Option (UK)

Can you have your order tomorrow? Some websites are very quick anyway, but this is specifically for where next-day or express service is offered, usually within the country where the retailer is based.

Gift Wrapping Option

Do they or don't they?

Returns Procedure

'Down to you' means you pack it up and pay to send it back (unless your goods are faulty, in which case the retailer should pay for postage both ways). 'Free' means just that and they may even collect it from you. 'Complicated' means that they want you to call them and tell them you're sending your order back. This normally applies only where the product you've ordered is particularly valuable.

You'll find more about returns in Chapter 34.

Section 1
Fashion Fix

I f you have ever thought that buying clothes online is not for you (can't touch the fabric, can't really see what it looks like, might have to send it back), it's definitely time to think again.

Not only are excellent fashion websites arriving on the scene at regular intervals, from mainline designer brands to high street chains – some directly related to stores you probably already know and love and others totally new – but fashion retailers who launched a few years ago with fairly basic websites have got their acts together to offer clear and easy-to-use online services with great photos and each season's must-have clothes. Not only that, but many of them are excellent for reading up on the season's trends and working out which bits will be right for you.

'But ...' you may well be saying in answer to this, 'I like going shopping for clothes, trying them on, finding something special, getting that "I really need it now" buzz.' Well, so do I and I'd never suggest that buying clothes online is going to replace that great therapy of finding something gorgeous in the shops. However, there are a few excellent reasons for shopping for clothes online.

- Firstly, if you're really short of time and never manage to find what you're looking for 'out there' in the couple of hours you usually have on a Saturday afternoon.
- Secondly, you may live a distance away from the shops you'd really like to go to and ...
- Thirdly, there's the sheer choice of what you can find online – you'd need a huge amount of time to be able to see the range that's available on the web in the stores; frankly, it just wouldn't be possible. Online, you can flit from chic, modern Freda (Matches' own brand) to Gucci, River Island and Oasis (with a quick stopoff at Vogue to check up on the trends and make sure you're getting the right idea), all while you're sitting comfortably with a cup of coffee (or wine, of course). I'm sure you'll be really surprised at what's available.

Now that express delivery services, free postage and (sometimes) free returns are becoming the norm among the better online clothes retailers, making it easier than ever before and you *can* have it tomorrow, there's no longer any excuse not to give it a try.

Chapter 1

Luxury Fashion Brands

There's no doubt that this is an exciting time for luxury brands and the world wide web as they all begin to wake up to the fact that the online global marketplace is with us to stay, not as a threat but as a fabulous, glittering opportunity.

With brands such as Louis Vuitton, Christian Dior, Marni and Paul Smith taking the plunge and offering if not clothing; luxury shoes and handbags, watches, jewellery and gifts online, there's literally nothing you can't find at any price level and at some of the websites below, the sky really is the limit.

For more luxury brands visit the jewellery section, where you can invest in sublime diamonds, pearls and other precious stones from jewellers such as Tiffany, Boodles and Mikimoto.

Needless to say, you choose how much you spend, but one of the best things, to my mind, about these brands offering their wares online is that I no longer have to browse under the watchful eyes of superbly groomed shop assistants who, as I walk through the door, weigh me up (handbag, shoes, jacket) and know for a fact that I'm not going to be buying that £1000 handbag today - I just want to look. Now I can feast my eyes wherever and whenever I want for as long as I want at any time of day or night. So can you. Enjoy.

Sites to Visit

www.amandawakeley.com

Amanda Wakeley has launched her new website, where you can order from her luxuriously chic collection of dresses and separates, plus accessories such as shoes, belts and stoles. Everything here is in the highest quality fabric, beautifully made, and you can expect to find detailing such as beading, lace edging and silk satin trims.

Site Usability:	★★★★	Based:	UK
Product Range:	★★★★	Express Delivery Option? (UK)	No
Price Range:	Luxury	Gift Wrapping Option?	No
Delivery Area:	Worldwide	Returns Procedure:	Down to you

www.brownsfashion.com

The Browns website is not only very clear and easy to navigate but also offers a mouthwatering list of contemporary designers including Lanvin, Balenciaga, Missoni and Paul Smith, plus Dolce & Gabbanna, Roberto Cavalli, Ann Demeulemeister and Issa. There are several views of each item together with lots of essential information and size charts. Look here, too, for your next Luella (or Fendi or Marni) handbag fix or pair of heels (Christian Louboutin or Marc Jacobs).

Site Usability:	★★★	Based:	UK
Product Range:	★★★★	Express Delivery Option? (UK)	No
Price Range:	Luxury/Medium	Gift Wrapping Option?	No
Delivery Area:	Worldwide	Returns Procedure:	Down to you and complicated

www.burberry.com

Now you can buy from Burberry online through its beautifully designed website. You can browse the luxuriously photographed collections including Burberry Prorsum, Burberry London and the Icons Collection, then click through to Shop Online and choose from menswear, womenswear, bags and accessories. If you want to see what's coming next you can preview the new collections. Expect superb quality and gorgeous packaging.

Site Usability:	★★★★★	Based:	UK
Product Range:	★★★★★	Express Delivery Option? (UK)	Automatic
Price Range:	Luxury	Gift Wrapping Option?	No
Delivery Area:	UK but US site available	Returns Procedure:	Down to you and complicated

www.dior.com

At luxury brand Christian Dior's online boutique you can purchase from the range of covetable handbags, shoes and boots, small leather accessories, scarves, watches and fine jewellery. Prices are steep, as you would expect, but if you want to be carrying the latest version of the instantly recognisable Gaucho or My Dior handbag on your arm this season you'll no doubt be prepared. Dior has specific websites for overseas shipping so you need to check whether there is one for your country.

Site Usability:	★★★★	Based:	UK
Product Range:	★★★★★	Express Delivery Option? (UK)	Yes
Price Range:	Luxury	Gift Wrapping Option?	No, but beautiful packaging is standard
Delivery Area:	UK but US and other sites available	Returns Procedure:	Down to you and complicated

www.dvflondon.com

Diane von Furstenberg. How can you resist? Check out the latest arrivals in each new season's collection. Order one of her famous wrap dresses, skirts, tops or trousers and take a look at the catwalk pictures for this season or last. This is an innovative website and it may take a moment or two to learn how to navigate, but it'll be well worth the effort.

Site Usability:	★★★★	Based:	US
Product Range:	★★★	Express Delivery Option? (UK)	Yes
Price Range:	Luxury/Medium	Gift Wrapping Option?	Yes
Delivery Area:	Worldwide	Returns Procedure:	Down to you and complicated

www.escada.com

You'll probably be surprised at the range of clothes and accessories available on Escada's pretty website, where you'll find both the Escada and Escada Sport brands offering seriously beautiful and seriously expensive cocktail and evening dresses, skirts, jackets, shirts and knitwear, plus stylish sporty casual wear, handbags, belts, small leather goods and fragrance. They'll be happy to gift wrap and send your order out on your behalf – if you can bear to give away anything here.

Site Usability:	★★★★★	Based:	EU
Product Range:	★★★★★	Express Delivery Option? (UK)	Yes
Price Range:	Luxury	Gift Wrapping Option?	Yes
Delivery Area:	EU	Returns Procedure:	Contact them to arrange

www.forzieri.com

Florence-based Forzieri offers a wide range of products from some world-famous designers such as Gucci, Miu Miu, Dolce & Gabbana, Fendi and Gianfranco Ferre. You can choose from the highest quality leather jackets, shoes, bags, briefcases, wallets, gloves, scarves, belts, jewellery and other accessories, all for both men and women. It's a beautifully laid out website with clear pictures and they'll deliver fast all over the world.

Site Usability:	★★★★★	Based:	Italy
Product Range:	★★★★★	Express Delivery Option? (UK)	Yes
Price Range:	Luxury/Medium	Gift Wrapping Option?	Yes
Delivery Area:	Worldwide	Returns Procedure:	Down to you

www.lineafashion.com

Linea started life as a boutique in London's Hampstead, offering designer-wear from around the world. The shop is now online, with the range clearly photographed so you can see each item properly. Included are collections from international designers such as Blumarine, Celine, Etro, Gharani Strok, Juicy Couture, Missoni and Emanuel Ungaro, plus handbags and shoes by Hogan, Tods and Celine. If you're in a buying mood, this could be a dangerous site to visit.

Site Usability:	★★★★★	Based:	UK
Product Range:	★★★★★	Express Delivery Option? (UK)	Yes
Price Range:	Luxury/Medium	Gift Wrapping Option?	No
Delivery Area:	Worldwide	Returns Procedure:	Down to you and complicated

www.luisaviaroma.com

This excellent luxury online boutique is based, not surprisingly, at No 3 Via Roma, Florence, Italy. It offers worldwide shipping on a wonderful range of designers, including Burberry, Chloe, Balenciaga, Lanvin, Narcisco Rodruigez, Roberto Cavalli and Missoni. Prices are exactly as you would expect them to be, but there are several clear views of each item – the range is exceptional.

Site Usability:	★★★★★	Based:	Italy
Product Range:	★★★★★	Express Delivery Option? (UK)	No
Price Range:	Luxury/Medium	Gift Wrapping Option?	No
Delivery Area:	Worldwide	Returns Procedure:	Down to you

www.marni.com

Luxury brand Marni has launched its high-tech 'virtual store' where all the garments seem to be hanging in mid-air. Everything is clearly photographed and you can see several views of each. Register with the site so that you can create 'My Style Notes', where you can view all the pieces you've selected together in one place and then see whether you can resist putting them all in your basket. Be warned – most items don't go beyond size 44/12. This really is high-fashion online shopping at its best, so take time to look round.

Site Usability:	★★★★★	Based:	UK
Product Range:	★★★★	Express Delivery Option? (UK)	Yes
Price Range:	Luxury	Gift Wrapping Option?	No
Delivery Area:	Worldwide	Returns Procedure:	Down to you

www.matchesfashion.com

Designer boutique Matches is famous for offering a unique, personal service together with a mouthwatering choice of designers such as Dolce & Gabbana, Bottega Veneta, Chloe, Christian Louboutin, Lanvin, Marc Jacobs, Missoni and Stella McCartney. You can now find this excellent service and the full range of designers online, where you can place your order directly through the website or search through the entire season's Lookbook, then call for availability when you find something you like. They'll be delighted to help you choose the essential pieces for each season.

Site Usability:	★★★★★	Based:	UK
Product Range:	★★★★	Express Delivery Option? (UK)	Yes
Price Range:	Luxury	Gift Wrapping Option?	Yes
Delivery Area:	Worldwide	Returns Procedure:	Down to you

www.net-a-porter.com

This is the über-fashionista's website, where you'll find the most impressive range of designer clothes and accessories available online and a retailer that's becoming increasingly well known for its clever buying, excellent service and attractive packaging. So if you're looking for something special with a designer label, such as Marc Jacobs, Alexander McQueen, Burberry, Roland Mouret, Alberta Feretti, Marni, Jimmy Choo or Paul Smith (the list goes on and on), you should definitely have a look here.

Site Usability:	★★★★★	Based:	UK
Product Range:	★★★★★	Express Delivery Option? (UK)	Yes
Price Range:	Luxury	Gift Wrapping Option?	Yes
Delivery Area:	Worldwide	Returns Procedure:	Free using their DHL service

www.paulsmith.co.uk

One of the most successful and internationally well-known British designers, with several collections including Paul Smith Black, Jeans and Fragrance, his website is, as you would probably expect, different and idiosyncratic. Here you'll find a selection of his jeans, shoes, knitwear, T-shirts and accessories, plus a small amount of tailoring, and there are several clear views of each item. This is also a great place for gifts for Paul Smith fans.

Site Usability:	★★★★★	Based:	UK
Product Range:	★★★★	Express Delivery Option? (UK)	Yes
Price Range:	Luxury/Medium	Gift Wrapping Option?	Yes
Delivery Area:	Worldwide	Returns Procedure:	Down to you

www.shoptommy.co.uk

Yes, US brand Tommy Hilfiger is now online, offering an excellent selection of modern daywear and accessories from cashmere/cotton cable knitwear, jeans and winter jackets and coats to bags and wallets, snow boots and shoes and chic skiwear. There's also a gift section and the option of gift boxing for all items. This is a really easy website to shop from and a must to have a look at if you want to add some new casual wear to your wardrobe.

Site Usability:	★★★★★	Based:	UK
Product Range:	★★★★	Express Delivery Option? (UK)	No
Price Range:	Medium	Gift Wrapping Option?	Yes
Delivery Area:	Worldwide	Returns Procedure:	Down to you

www.zenggi.com

Keep your credit cards firmly locked away when you start to look at this Netherlands-based website as the temptation levels are extremely high. Zenggi is a new online luxury clothing and accessories store offering a chic, high-quality, covetable range. When you click on an item you can see a stylish model pic showing your chosen piece and how to accessorise it. Gift packaging is standard.

Site Usability:	★★★★★	Based:	Netherlands
Product Range:	★★★★	Express Delivery Option? (UK)	No
Price Range:	Luxury	Gift Wrapping Option?	Yes
Delivery Area:	EU	Returns Procedure:	Down to you

Chapter 2

Fashion Online

Boutique Bliss   Modern Fashion Retailers

The High Street

This is the place where it's hard to know where to stop, where traditional mail-order retailers, offline stores coming online, independent boutiques and the fast-moving high street stores online all blend together to form just one thing: choice.

Fashion is one of the fastest growing areas of online shopping – yes, really – mainly because now that most of us have broadband connections at home, pictures are becoming clearer and larger and colours more true. At the same time we're becoming used to buying all sorts of other products online so we're giving it a try. Forget the 'but I really need to see and touch it' dilemma; we're all busy so much of the time with kids, work and travel that to be able to browse through and buy such a marvellous choice of fashion without having to go anywhere is a real treat. That top from River Island, that cashmere sweater from Lands' End, that pair of ballet flats from Plumo. Thanks very much, I'll take them all and I'd like them delivered tomorrow. Just a few clicks is all it takes. Trust me.

I'm not saying (and never will) that online shopping can replace the pleasure of those relaxing and therapeutic times choosing things in the stores. Now, however, you can choose how much you want to buy online, save that time and then buy some of the more special, fitted pieces 'out there'. I know I do.

Boutique Bliss

I have to confess that I'm not an expert offline boutique shopper. Tempted by a gorgeous window I'll frequently be drawn in by an artfully laid-out 'must-have' jacket, bag, belt or pair of shoes, only to find that the average size is an 8 for most of the clothing on the rails, that a size 12 is considered 'outsize' and they don't have any left anyway.

So for me this is boutique heaven where the prettiest clothes and accessories mingle, usually beautifully photographed and offered together with indulgent pampering products and lovely gift ideas. Most online boutiques will gift wrap for you, many ship worldwide and some will express your order so that you can have it tomorrow.

There's quite a range here, from small boutiques such as Anusha, Max Oliver and Plumo to My Wardrobe and Jeanne Petitt, which, in a clever, boutique-style atmosphere, sell a wide range of premium brands such as Nicole Farhi, Tocca and Betty Jackson. Take a good look at them all and you'll get an idea of how great online boutique browsing can be.

Sites to Visit

www.allegrahicks.com

This is, as you would expect, a beautifully designed website offering some unusual and contemporary clothes and accessories designed by Allegra Hicks, who specialises in translating oriental themes into western styles using strong organic patterns and colour. Her fashion collection is aimed at the woman who travels a lot and needs stylish clothes that work in many climates and travel and pack easily.

Site Usability:	★★★★	Based:	UK
Product Range:	★★★★	Express Delivery Option? (UK)	No
Price Range:	Luxury	Gift Wrapping Option	No
Delivery Area:	Worldwide	Returns Procedure:	Down to you

www.anusha.co.uk

Here's a boudoir-style online boutique where you can buy pretty and indulgent designer pieces from clothes, luxurious loungewear, vintage-inspired jewellery and unique accessories to pampering gifts. Your order will be wrapped in layers of fuchsia tissue paper and finished off with a feather butterfly and chocolate-brown Anusha label. So come here for a treat for yourself or for perfect presents. They deliver worldwide and in the UK you need to allow five to seven days.

Site Usability:	★★★★	Based:	UK
Product Range:	★★★	Express Delivery Option? (UK)	Yes
Price Range:	Medium	Gift Wrapping Option?	Yes
Delivery Area:	Worldwide	Returns Procedure:	Down to you

www.boxinthepost.com

Box in the Post is a fashion mail-order service and website boutique, delivering everything in a stylish yet simple box. Launched in spring 2005, Box promises 'non-high street', original yet stunning clothes, a friendly and efficient service and a personal touch to its customers. Run as a chic boutique, stock is updated all the time throughout the season, so keep coming back to find something new.

Site Usability:	★★★★	Based:	UK
Product Range:	★★★	Express Delivery Option? (UK)	No
Price Range:	Medium	Gift Wrapping Option	No
Delivery Area:	Worldwide	Returns Procedure:	Down to you

www.jeannepetitt.com

This is an excellent boutique to have a look round. It offers brands such as Nicole Farhi, Edina Ronay, Pink Soda, Temperley and Yves St Laurent, accessories by Emma Hope and J&M Davidson, jewellery by Angie Gooderham and Tataborello and fragrance by Annick Goutal and Rosine. The pictures are clear and simple and you can enlarge them to see the detail. Prices, needless to say, are at the designer end.

Site Usability:	★★★★	Based:	UK
Product Range:	★★★★	Express Delivery Option? (UK)	Yes
Price Range:	Luxury/Medium	Gift Wrapping Option	Yes
Delivery Area:	Worldwide	Returns Procedure:	Down to you

www.max-oliver.co.uk

If you're in the mood for a visit to a small but beautiful boutique where you'll find unusual, personally chosen clothes, accessories and homewares you probably won't find anywhere else, then stop here. Max Oliver is quite simply a treasure trove of French and vintage-inspired pieces including dresses, skirts, jackets and coats, cushions, crockery and accessories. However, there are never large quantities of anything, so if you see something you like, snap it up fast.

Site Usability:	★★★	Based:	UK
Product Range:	★★★	Express Delivery Option? (UK)	No
Price Range:	Medium	Gift Wrapping Option?	No
Delivery Area:	Worldwide	Returns Procedure:	Down to you

www.my-wardrobe.com

This is a well laid out designer clothing and accessories website (with lots of designers you'll have found it difficult to buy online before), including items by FrostFrench, Cacharel, Ann Louise Roswald, Sara Berman, Tocca and See by Chloe. For each item you can see several different views, plus a close-up of details such as embroidery and prints. You will find description and commentary under 'My Advice'. When you spot something you like, they'll recommend other items to go with it.

Site Usability:	★★★★★	Based:	UK
Product Range:	★★★★	Express Delivery Option? (UK)	Yes
Price Range:	Luxury/Medium	Gift Wrapping Option?	Automatic
Delivery Area:	Worldwide	Returns Procedure:	Free of charge

www.pantalonchameleon.com

You'll discover colourful, dressy, modern and fun clothing from this unusual London boutique offering an individual collection you won't find anywhere else. It's particularly good if you have a special event to go to and you like long, pretty skirts, which they match with embroidered tops and knitwear and some stunning shoes. You can finish off your outfit from the selection of beaded jewellery and other small accessories.

Site Usability:	★★★★★	Based:	UK
Product Range:	★★★★	Express Delivery Option? (UK)	Yes
Price Range:	Medium	Gift Wrapping Option?	No
Delivery Area:	Worldwide	Returns Procedure:	Down to you

www.plumo.co.uk

At Plumo you'll always find something different and interesting, from a gold-trimmed basket to a floral print tote. They also offer homewares, clothes and accessories including shoes and jewellery. It's not a huge collection but beautifully edited to be feminine and chic at the same time. There are some lovely gift ideas here as well and express delivery and gift wrapping are just two of the services offered.

Site Usability:	★★★★	Based:	UK
Product Range:	★★★	Express Delivery Option? (UK)	Yes
Price Range:	Medium	Gift Wrapping Option?	Yes
Delivery Area:	Worldwide	Returns Procedure:	Down to you

www.pocket-venus.net

Youthful, happy and alluring is the signature style of Pocket Venus, where you'll find bespoke prints, flattering shapes and unusual embellishments combined to create chic separates and dresses with a vintage feel. Think hand embroidered, slim silk organza dresses, pin tucked silk chiffon shirts and cotton voile sundresses and you'll get the idea. Although it's a small collection there are some really unusual and attractive clothes so you should definitely take a look.

Site Usability:	★★★★	Based:	UK
Product Range:	★★★	Express Delivery Option?	(UK) Yes worldwide
Price Range:	Medium	Gift Wrapping Option?	No
Delivery Area:	Worldwide	Returns Procedure:	Down to you within seven days

www.shopatanna.co.uk

With stores based in London, Norfolk and Suffolk, Anna is an innovative boutique offering clothes and accessories by Betty Jackson, Seven, Issa London, Orla Kiely, Gharani Strock and lesser-known designers such as Day and Noa

Noa. It's an eclectic and modern collection combining elegance and quirkiness and designers are being added all the time, so keep checking back.

Site Usability:	★★★★★	Based:	UK
Product Range:	★★★★	Express Delivery Option? (UK)	Yes
Price Range:	Luxury/Medium	Gift Wrapping Option?	Yes
Delivery Area:	Worldwide	Returns Procedure:	Down to you

www.valentineandfrench.co.uk

At the Valentine and French boutique there's a treasure trove of accessories, home treats and gift ideas such as glamorous clutch bags, unusual and beautifully fragranced body products, cashmere separates and pretty jewellery. This is an attractive website and you'll discover all the products under headings such as 'Stepping Out', 'Staying In', 'Little Pleasures' and 'Jewellery Box'.

Site Usability:	★★★★	Based:	UK
Product Range:	★★★	Express Delivery Option? (UK)	No
Price Range:	Medium	Gift Wrapping Option?	No
Delivery Area:	Worldwide	Returns Procedure:	Down to you

Modern Fashion Retailers

Here you'll find lots of brands you've heard of, such as Agnes b, Hobbs, Boden and Laura Ashley, plus some you may be discovering for the first time, like Evisu, Freda (Matches' own brand) and APC.

There's an enormously varied choice here, from chic separates and classic daywear to full-length evening gowns from retailers originally based as bricks-and-mortar stores or mail-order catalogues. Then there are the web-only retailers such as Boden, Poetry and Wrap, which have easily navigable websites with service levels that simply get better and better. They all have one thing in common wherever they started from – they've made it online and their sales can only grow. Think that right now we're already spending £1 out of every £10 online and you'll get the idea.

Unlike the US, where just about every brand has an online presence, the UK is still far behind. Those who haven't yet made it on to the web will surely lose out.

Sites to Visit

www.agnesb.com

You may not like the music they play on this unusual but cleverly designed website, but you can still buy your perfect fitted white shirts, superbly designed T-shirts and chic trousers from this famous French designer offering addictive quality and cut. It isn't the easiest site to use if you want to place a quick order, but if you're an Agnes b addict (and there are many of them), this is the place to be.

Site Usability:	★★★	Based:	France
Product Range:	★★★★	Express Delivery Option? (UK)	Yes
Price Range:	Medium	Gift Wrapping Option?	No
Delivery Area:	EU	Returns Procedure:	Down to you

www.apc.fr

You will need quite a fast broadband connection to get the best out of this unusually designed French website offering high-quality and well-priced chic designer separates. Collections are offered as complete 'looks' from the outerwear to the basics, after which you click on the individual items to buy. You'll find each new season's essentials here as well as the jeans and accessories collections for men, women and children.

Site Usability:	★★★	Based:	France
Product Range:	★★★★	Express Delivery Option? (UK)	Yes
Price Range:	Medium/Very Good Value	Gift Wrapping Option?	No
Delivery Area:	Worldwide	Returns Procedure:	Down to you

www.artigiano.co.uk

At Artigiano you could buy your whole wardrobe without even visiting another website. The emphasis is fairly classic, with easy rather than very fitted shapes and standard sizing (not small). You'll find lovely fine and chunky knitwear, excellent T-shirts and tops, trousers in a selection of styles and fabrics and unique jackets and outerwear you can't buy anywhere else. There's some very good leather and suede as well. The collection is updated four times a year.

Site Usability: ★★★★★	Based:	UK
Product Range: ★★★★★	Express Delivery Option? (UK)	Yes
Price Range: Medium	Gift Wrapping Option?	Yes
Delivery Area: Worldwide	Returns Procedure:	Free using Royal Mail

www.boden.co.uk

It would be surprising if you hadn't already seen the Boden catalogue. It's everywhere, with Johnnie Boden's inimitable style (and commentary) all over it. Provided you like his colourful style, the clothes have their own relaxed appeal which is popular with a lot of people. If you're into minimalist chic black, don't go there. If you like your pinks, blues, greens and reds, then certainly have a browse. There's a mini Boden and menswear as well.

Site Usability: ★★★★	Based:	UK
Product Range: ★★★★	Express Delivery Option? (UK)	Yes
Price Range: Medium	Gift Wrapping Option?	No
Delivery Area: Worldwide	Returns Procedure:	Down to you

www.eveningdresses.co.uk

This is a large collection of classic, elegant, full-length and cocktail dresses ranging in price from around £150 to £700. The main collection shown is held in stock and provided they have your chosen colour and size, they'll rush it to you by express delivery. So the next time you have a special event to go to and no time to shop, you don't need to panic. Alongside their own collection they offer dresses by Alfred Sung and Dessy which can take longer to deliver.

Site Usability: ★★★★	Based:	UK
Product Range: ★★★★	Express Delivery Option? (UK)	Yes if dress is in stock
Price Range: Luxury/Medium	Gift Wrapping Option?	No
Delivery Area: Worldwide	Returns Procedure:	Down to you

www.evisu.com

Evisu is the brainchild of Japanese jean junkie Yamane, who came up with the idea in the 1980s of using reconditioned sewing machines and making new 'vintage-style' jeans with old Japanese handicraft traditions. Every pair of Evisu jeans is made from 100 per cent Japanese indigo dyed denim and features 23 details, which makes each pair unique. In the fun and different online store there are all the Evisu ranges, including Heritage, EV Genes, Mens Mainline, Evisu (European Edition), Kizzu and Shoos.

Site Usability:	★★★★	Based:	UK
Product Range:	★★★	Express Delivery Option? (UK)	No
Price Range:	Luxury/Medium	Gift Wrapping Option?	No
Delivery Area:	Worldwide	Returns Procedure:	Down to you

www.fredafashion.com

You'll no doubt be delighted to know that top designer store Matches of Wimbledon has launched its own collection online, with a beautifully finished and wearable selection of each season's essentials, including chic coats, jackets, skirts, trousers, tops and knitwear, all in line with fashion's latest trends and all of which you'll probably want to buy immediately. Sizes are from 8 to 14.

Site Usability:	★★★★	Based:	UK
Product Range:	★★★★	Express Delivery Option? (UK)	Yes
Price Range:	Luxury/Medium	Gift Wrapping Option?	Automatic
Delivery Area:	Worldwide	Returns Procedure:	Down to you

www.hobbs.co.uk

You may well have shopped at Hobbs already for beautifully cut workwear, chic evening wear or casual separates (not to mention the wide collection of shoes). You'll no doubt be pleased to learn that the company is now offering an ordering facility on its website. All the items are put together as outfits so you can see what works together. Wherever you click you'll get the details for that particular piece, whether it's a scarf, dress, cardigan or pair of shoes, together with the size and colour choices. It's an excellent collection and delivery takes about three days.

Site Usability:	★★★★★	Based:	UK
Product Range:	★★★★	Express Delivery Option? (UK)	No
Price Range:	Luxury/Medium	Gift Wrapping Option?	No
Delivery Area:	UK	Returns Procedure:	Down to you

www.landsend.co.uk

This leading catalogue company originated in the US and offers a wide range of high-quality, well-priced clothing for men and women. Signature collections include stylish co-ordinates, casual wear, linen wear, swimwear, outerwear, cashmere and footwear, with lots of essentials for your new season's wardrobe. Many products are available in extended ranges to fit and flatter plus and petite sizes. First-class customer service is backed by a no-quibble money-back guarantee and free delivery on your first order.

Site Usability:	★★★★★	Based:	UK (this website)
Product Range:	★★★★★	Express Delivery Option? (UK)	Yes
Price Range:	Very Good Value	Gift Wrapping Option?	Yes
Delivery Area:	Worldwide	Returns Procedure:	Down to you

www.lauraashley.com

Becoming more up to date by the day (although retaining some of the feminine influences we've come to associate this longstanding retailer with), Laura Ashley offers some really good tops and knitwear, shirts, skirts, trousers and accessories. Alongside this, and possibly the strongest part of the website, is the home accessories and furniture section, where you can choose everything from pretty gift ideas to handcrafted cabinet furniture, as well as getting lots of decorating advice.

Site Usability:	★★★	Based:	UK
Product Range:	★★★	Express Delivery Option? (UK)	No
Price Range:	Medium/Very Good Value	Gift Wrapping Option?	No
Delivery Area:	UK (there are global sites as well)	Returns Procedure:	Down to you

www.no-one.co.uk

No-One is a boutique based in Hoxton, East London and on its website you can find on-trend (or even beyond-trend, if there is such a thing) dresses, separates and accessories for girls and boys from a collection of cool, cutting-edge designers such as Mine, Karen Walker, Louise Amstrap and Cheap Monday. There's absolutely nothing classic here, but if you like to be ahead, fashion-wise, you should take a look.

Site Usability:	★★★★	Based:	UK
Product Range:	★★★	Express Delivery Option? (UK)	No
Price Range:	Luxury/Medium	Gift Wrapping Option	No
Delivery Area:	Worldwide	Returns Procedure:	Down to you

www.orvis.co.uk

Originally a company specialising in fishing equipment, Orvis has developed its brand to offer a full clothing and accessories range for men and women. You'll find a high-quality classic range here from Donegal tweed jackets to quilted, microfibre coats plus knitwear, shirts, polos, T-shirts and accessories, all in a wide choice of colours. There's hardwearing footwear here too, plus the Barbour Collection.

Site Usability:	★★★★★	Based:	UK (this website)
Product Range:	★★★★★	Express Delivery Option? (UK)	Yes
Price Range:	Medium	Gift Wrapping Option?	Yes
Delivery Area:	Worldwide	Returns Procedure:	Down to you

www.peruvianconnection.com

Each season Peruvian Connection offers a richly photographed collection of ethnic-style separates (with some classics) using Peruvian alpaca and jewel-coloured pima cotton. The look is elegant, matching the unusually coloured tops and fine knitwear with gorgeously patterned skirts. The site also offers specialist art knit jackets and sweaters, beaded jewellery, scarves and bags. You'll find excellent quality and in some cases quite steep prices.

Site Usability:	★★★★★	Based:	UK
Product Range:	★★★★	Express Delivery Option? (UK)	Yes
Price Range:	Luxury/Medium	Gift Wrapping Option?	Yes
Delivery Area:	Worldwide	Returns Procedure:	Down to you

www.planet.co.uk

I'm sure you've heard of this brand but if it's not one you normally shop from offline you should stop now and take a quick look round here. They've made it very easy to see everything that's offered and tell you straight away all the sizes that are available. Styles tend to be classic and there are quite a lot of (high-quality) man-made fabrics, but it's a very good range, particularly for the jackets and outerwear.

Site Usability:	★★★★	Based:	UK
Product Range:	★★★★	Express Delivery Option? (UK)	Yes
Price Range:	Medium	Gift Wrapping Option?	No
Delivery Area:	UK	Returns Procedure:	Down to you

www.poetrycollection.co.uk

Poetry is a new, fresh collection of clothing online, offering a good selection of tops, fine knitwear, tailoring, pretty skirts and dresses in a modern range of colours and all using mainly natural fibres. The prices are reasonable and sizes go from 10 to 24 in just about everything. This is a beautifully photographed and easy-to-use website, and you can see several pictures of everything offered.

Site Usability:	★★★★★	Based:	UK
Product Range:	★★★★	Express Delivery Option? (UK)	Yes
Price Range:	Medium	Gift Wrapping Option?	No
Delivery Area:	EU	Returns Procedure:	Down to you

www.precis.co.uk

If you're under 5'3" tall and prefer not to have to make lots of alterations to your new clothes, then this is the place for you. Precis offers ranges with names such as 'Left Bank' and 'Coco Boutique' and in each there are separates that work very well together. If you prefer you can also select by type of clothing – coats, jackets or trousers, for example – and sizing goes from 8 to 18.

Site Usability:	★★★★	Based:	UK
Product Range:	★★★★	Express Delivery Option? (UK)	Yes
Price Range:	Medium	Gift Wrapping Option?	No
Delivery Area:	UK	Returns Procedure:	Down to you

www.thelinenpress.co.uk

As far as linen clothing goes I think there are two sorts of people: those who love it and those who don't. It is a pain to iron and always creases the minute you put it on, but at least you can now find linen that washes beautifully and doesn't shrink as it used to. The Linen Press has a range of men's and women's clothing in soft, wearable twill weave, fine garment washed linen, natural cotton stretch baby cord and fleecy pure cotton.

Site Usability: ★★★	Based:	UK
Product Range: ★★★	Express Delivery Option? (UK)	No
Price Range: Medium	Gift Wrapping Option?	No
Delivery Area: Worldwide	Returns Procedure:	Down to you

www.toastbypost.co.uk

Toast has long been well known for simple, beautifully made clothes in natural colours and natural fabrics. The range of separates includes skirts, tops, knitwear and trousers, plus nightwear and gowns, beachwear and a small collection of bed linen. Don't expect lots of bright colours here, you won't find them. This designer is about quiet, easy style. The photographs are beautiful and they offer still-life pictures as well as model pics, which is extremely helpful.

Site Usability: ★★★★	Based:	UK
Product Range: ★★★	Express Delivery Option? (UK)	Yes
Price Range: Medium	Gift Wrapping Option?	Yes
Delivery Area: Worldwide	Returns Procedure:	Down to you

www.wallcatalogue.com

If you haven't already heard of Wall but you like beautifully made, easy-to-wear clothing in unusual fabrics, you should take a good look at this well-photographed website. It's a very different and attractive range of modern flattering separates in muted colours such as barley, oyster, pale grey and black, of course, for winter. The clothes aren't inexpensive, but you're buying into real quality and the service is excellent.

Site Usability: ★★★★★	Based:	UK
Product Range: ★★★★	Express Delivery Option? (UK)	No
Price Range: Medium	Gift Wrapping Option?	No
Delivery Area: Worldwide	Returns Procedure:	Down to you

www.wraponline.co.uk

At Wrap you'll find modern separates in each season's colours attractively photographed on real models, so you can not only see the clothes clearly but there's lots of atmosphere too. There's always a good selection of tops, knitwear, trousers and skirts using mainly natural yarns such as cotton, silk and cashmere. You can see how they all work together and also tell at a glance whether what you want to order is in stock or not. Check out the new accessory range of casual bags and belts. There are separate websites for the UK, USA and Germany.

Site Usability:	★★★★	Based:	UK
Product Range:	★★★★	Express Delivery Option? (UK)	Yes
Price Range:	Medium	Gift Wrapping Option?	No
Delivery Area:	Worldwide	Returns Procedure:	Down to you

The High Street

For fun, well-priced and right up-to-the-minute clothes and accessories, stop off here. Even if this isn't the place you'll choose to put together your new season's wardrobe, you should have a good look, as nowhere is better at interpreting the trends in a user-friendly fashion than the online high street stores.

Not only do they outline the current trends, different looks, colours and ideas much better than most of the middle-range fashion retailers, they're also great at telling you how to create the new looks, which bag to buy in which colour at each stage of the season, the must-have shoes, and the essential belts and chic jewels that establish the fact that you definitely know what you're doing.

Once you've made your new wardrobe wish list, you can choose to make your purchases here or elsewhere, or do a bit of both. With the addition of brands such as Oasis, All Saints and Urban Outfitters, there's never been a better place to get it right.

Sites to Visit

www.allsaintsshop.co.uk

All Saints offers up-to-the-minute styling totally in line with each season's different looks on its funky urban appeal website. There are lots of well-photographed views of every item available, including both model shots and basic product close-ups. Sizing goes from 6 to 14 in most items (although expect general sizing to be on the small size). You can shop by collection or by item and see straight away what's available in your size.

Site Usability:	★★★★	Based:	UK
Product Range:	★★★	Express Delivery Option? (UK)	No
Price Range:	Medium	Gift Wrapping Option?	No
Delivery Area:	Worldwide	Returns Procedure:	Down to you

www.debenhams.com

When I look at some of the 'trend' clothing offered by Debenhams, and in particular its 'Designers for Debenhams' section (think Betty Jackson, Jasper Conran, Ben de Lisi, John Rocha, etc.), and even though I'm well aware that I'm not getting the quality of fabric or make I'd get if I bought the real thing, I simply can't resist. Ok, so maybe you'll wear some of the items for only one season, but if you fancy trying a new trend this is a very good place to buy for men, women and children.

Site Usability:	★★★★	Based:	UK
Product Range:	★★★★★	Express Delivery Option? (UK)	No
Price Range:	Very Good Value	Gift Wrapping Option?	No
Delivery Area:	UK	Returns Procedure:	Down to you

www.dorothyperkins.co.uk

Dorothy Perkins' clothes and accessories are modern and amazingly well priced. They use some natural and some man-made fabrics and sizing goes from 8 to 22 for most items. You'll find wearable new looks each season, plus some colourful knits, tops and accessories. Take a good look at the start of the season if you're likely to want something here, as once a product has sold out it probably won't be replaced, however new styles are offered online each week.

Site Usability:	★★★★	Based:	UK
Product Range:	★★★	Express Delivery Option? (UK)	Yes
Price Range:	Very Good Value	Gift Wrapping Option?	No
Delivery Area:	UK	Returns Procedure:	Down to you

www.fcukbuymail.co.uk

This is a company where the words young, funky and high street come immediately to mind. Alongside the fashion pieces you can find some very good basics, in particular the knitwear and T-shirts, which are well priced, good quality and available in a range of colours. French Connection is definitely not cheap, but it delivers up-to-the-minute styling for men and women and is well worth taking a look at for modern additions to your wardrobe.

Site Usability:	★★★★	Based:	UK
Product Range:	★★★★	Express Delivery Option? (UK)	Yes
Price Range:	Medium	Gift Wrapping Option?	No
Delivery Area:	Worldwide	Returns Procedure:	Use the free service

www.ilovejeans.co.uk

You'll find just five brands here – Made in Heaven, Ruby, !IT, Hudson and NYDJ. But there's a good range of styles and washes and lots of information on fit – essential if you're going to splash out on a pair of designer jeans online. Prices range from around £70 to £140. The site aims to stock all items offered so they can be shipped out to you within 48 hours.

Site Usability:	★★★★	Based:	UK
Product Range:	★★★	Express Delivery Option? (UK)	No
Price Range:	Medium	Gift Wrapping Option?	No
Delivery Area:	Worldwide	Returns Procedure:	Down to you

www.jeans-direct.com

If you're a fan of wearing jeans, you should take a look at this website, where there's a wide choice by Levi, Ben Sherman, Wrangler, Diesel and Duchesse. Personally I think you really have to know your size in each brand to be sure you won't have to send them back, but obviously you can try lots of different styles at home which is a great benefit if you'd rather try on your jeans in private than in a public changing room.

Site Usability: ★★★	Based:	UK
Product Range: ★★★	Express Delivery Option? (UK)	No
Price Range: Medium	Gift Wrapping Option?	No
Delivery Area: EU	Returns Procedure:	Down to you

www.kew-online.com

From the same family as Jigsaw, Kew offers modern, versatile, well-priced separates in a wide choice of colours and styles. There's a good selection on this website, with some great tops and fine knitwear, plus easy jackets and skirts. It sometimes takes quite a while for each new season's collection to be available online, so be patient – it'll be worth it.

Site Usability: ★★★★	Based:	UK
Product Range: ★★★★	Express Delivery Option? (UK)	Yes
Price Range: Medium/Very Good Value	Gift Wrapping Option?	No
Delivery Area: Worldwide (call for details)	Returns Procedure:	Down to you

www.layer-up.co.uk

Here's a new, young brand-driven retailer offering labels such as Chilli Pepper, Fever, Looking Glass and MbyM. There is an excellent trend section where they've put all the looks together so you can see exactly what you need to buy. This is great teen/high street shopping in a clear and easy-to-use format.

Site Usability: ★★★★	Based:	UK
Product Range: ★★★★	Express Delivery Option? (UK)	Yes
Price Range: Medium	Gift Wrapping Option?	No
Delivery Area: Worldwide	Returns Procedure:	Down to you

www.mango.com

Spanish label Mango offers inexpensive, up-to-the-minute clothes and ac-cessories which it will ship to you just about anywhere in the world. This clever, modern website shows you everything at a glance. With jackets at around €60 and T-shirts from around €13, you can find plenty here to help you get the latest look without breaking the bank. Delivery is from Spain but is usually extremely quick.

Site Usability:	★★★★	Based:	Spain
Product Range:	★★★★★	Express Delivery Option? (UK)	No
Price Range:	Very Good Value	Gift Wrapping Option?	No
Delivery Area:	Worldwide	Returns Procedure:	Down to you

www.marksandspencer.com

You've probably already shopped from Marks & Spencer's huge online range of just about everything clothing related, from outerwear, tailoring, casual wear and accessories to lingerie, swimwear, shoes – the list just goes on and on. What's really great about this website now is that the special collections are available, such as Autograph, Per Una and Limited Collection, where you can shop from the more contemporary designs too.

Site Usability:	★★★★★	Express Delivery Option? (UK)	Yes
Product Range:	★★★★★	Gift Wrapping Option?	No
Price Range:	Medium/Very Good Value	Returns Procedure:	Free to store or the Freepost service
Delivery Area:	UK		

www.missselfridge.co.uk

An integral part of the high street since the 1960s, Miss Selfridge has always been a mainstay for young, modern style. There's nothing quiet about the clothes on offer but plenty of information and guidance on how to put together the latest looks and the background to the trends. They do go up to a size 16, but most of the clothes are designed for smaller sizes. Delivery is to the UK only, with express delivery for just £1 more than the standard service.

Site Usability:	★★★★	Express Delivery Option? (UK)	Yes
Product Range:	★★★★	Gift Wrapping Option?	No
Price Range:	Very Good Value	Returns Procedure:	Freepost or to the stores but
Delivery Area:	UK		complicated
Based:	UK		

www.monsoon.co.uk

With its well-known presence on the high street, almost everyone has heard of Monsoon. It offers attractive, not inexpensive but still good-value clothing, including some extremely wearable and different occasionwear. Sizing in a lot of cases goes up to a 20. The childrenswear selection is smaller but excellent, with delightful clothes, mainly for younger girls, including candy-coloured skirts and tops, sugar-striped swimwear and the prettiest party wear.

Site Usability:	★★★★★	Based:	UK
Product Range:	★★★★	Express Delivery Option? (UK)	No
Price Range:	Medium/Very Good Value	Gift Wrapping Option?	No
Delivery Area:	UK	Returns Procedure:	Down to you

www.oasis-stores.com

The new Oasis website allows you to shop simply and easily by garment, where you can zoom right in to every detail and find all the information on sizing and fabric you could need. Sizing goes up to a 16. Alternatively you can shop by trend, where all the relevant pieces are brought together for you, or visit the new, glamorous Vintage collection. The site is really easy to buy from. Delivery is UK only.

Site Usability:	★★★★★	Based:	UK
Product Range:	★★★★	Express Delivery Option? (UK)	No
Price Range:	Medium/Very Good Value	Gift Wrapping Option?	No
Delivery Area:	UK	Returns Procedure:	Down to you

www.principles.co.uk

With an easier-to-wear selection than some of the high street retailers, Principles offers a stylish, well-priced collection of separates, dresses and coats on its attractively designed website. The site clearly shows some of the season's trends and pieces have been picked out to complement each other for each look. You'll find dresses, skirts, tops, jeans, knitwear, some very attractive tailoring and occasionwear and a petite collection which goes from size 6 to 16.

Site Usability: ★★★★	Based:	UK
Product Range: ★★★★	Express Delivery Option? (UK)	Yes
Price Range: Very Good Value	Gift Wrapping Option?	No
Delivery Area: UK		

www.riverisland.com

If you're looking for the latest combat trousers, sparkly, decorated jeans or flirty tops (and you're no larger than a size 12, sorry), take a look here. They seem to get more modern each season, but there are some coats, parkas and jackets that fashion addicts of all ages would wear. There is also a casual, modern menswear collection. The site is quick and easy to use and the help desk, with all the delivery information, is excellent.

Site Usability: ★★★★★	Based:	UK
Product Range: ★★★★	Express Delivery Option? (UK)	Yes
Price Range: Medium	Gift Wrapping Option?	No
Delivery Area: UK	Returns Procedure:	Down to you

www.savagelondon.com

For T-shirt collectors this is the place to be, with T-shirts and tops of all shapes and sizes and an enormous range of colours. But here's the main point – you get to customise your T-shirt, top or hoody specifically for you (or whoever you want to give one to). Just select your design, choose your style (raw edge, long sleeve, etc.), then the colour. On some you can choose the text or word as well. The website is very busy but the instructions are clear once you get the hang of how things work.

Site Usability: ★★★★	Based:	UK
Product Range: ★★★★	Express Delivery Option? (UK)	No
Price Range: Medium	Gift Wrapping Option?	No
Delivery Area: Worldwide	Returns Procedure:	Down to you

www.tedbaker.co.uk

Expanding global brand Ted Baker offers well-made and innovative clothing on their modern, well photographed and easy-to-navigate website, for men, women and kids. Don't expect cheap here, you won't find it. What you will find is up-to-the-minute, mainly understated fashion, totally in line with each season's trends. Also swimwear, underwear, watches, accessories and fragrance.

Site Usability:	★★★	Based:	UK
Product Range:	★★★	Express Delivery Option? (UK)	No
Price Range:	Medium	Gift Wrapping Option?	No
Delivery Area:	Worldwide	Returns Procedure:	Down to you

www.topshop.co.uk

This is the place to go if you want the latest fashions at the best prices and definitely the place to go if you can't stand the scrum of the shops. Can't afford Marc Jacobs or Miu Miu? Go straight to Top Shop and if you can't bear the heaving crowds in the store, desperately seeking the last pair of the latest and absolutely must-have heels in your size, you can order them online and have them sent to you by express delivery. A fashionista could surely ask for no more than this.

Site Usability:	★★★★	Based:	UK
Product Range:	★★★★★	Express Delivery Option? (UK)	Yes
Price Range:	Very Good Value	Gift Wrapping Option?	Yes
Delivery Area:	UK	Returns Procedure:	Down to you

www.urbanoutfitters.co.uk

Fast-growing US-based brand Urban Outfitters' website is clearly targeted directly at its 18–30-year-old audience – check out a wide range of chic, 'urban-styled' clothes and accessories for girls and boys. There's designer-wear from Alice McCall and See by Chloe, an eclectic, well-priced range of separates, hosiery, scarves and gloves, right through to shoes, jewellery and underwear. Get the look now.

Site Usability:	★★★★★	Based:	UK
Product Range:	★★★★★	Express Delivery Option? (UK)	Yes
Price Range:	Medium	Gift Wrapping Option?	Yes
Delivery Area:	UK	Returns Procedure:	Down to you

www.wallis-fashion.com

Wallis offers a small selection from its stores on the website and just about everything goes up to a size 20, so styles on the whole are easier to wear for most people. There is clear information about each and every product, right down to washing information, fabric content and sizing. The site also tells you about each season's looks and how to put them together. It aims for 48-hour delivery in the UK, with the option of express delivery.

Site Usability:	★★★★★	Based:	UK
Product Range:	★★★	Express Delivery Option? (UK)	Yes
Price Range:	Medium/Very Good Value	Gift Wrapping Option?	No
Delivery Area:	UK	Returns Procedure:	Freepost or return to store

www.warehouse.co.uk

Shop online at Warehouse for the latest trends and stylish must-haves. You'll find excellent seasonal collections as well as Warehouse Maternity, Denim and the Spotlight collection – a glam range of pieces for special occasions. The website is user-friendly and it delivers to all UK and ROI addresses. You can also subscribe to its e-newsletter to be kept up to date with what's new online and be the first to know about the latest news and promotions. Log on now and get shopping.

Site Usability:	★★★★	Based:	UK
Product Range:	★★★	Express Delivery Option? (UK)	Yes
Price Range:	Very Good Value	Gift Wrapping Option?	No
Delivery Area:	UK	Returns Procedure:	Freepost or return to store

Chapter 3

The Knitwear Store

In most cases what you'll find here are cashmere retailers at different levels of quality (and, of course, different prices). As with most things, you get what you pay for – invest in a luxurious piece of Belinda Robertson or Emma Jane Knight cashmere and you'll be buying into a 'designer luxury' level which you're unlikely to find elsewhere. Buy cheap and cheerful from the websites here and you'll still get a quality product but a different type of cashmere and you can't expect it to be the same.

You'll also find excellent knitwear at some of the fashion retailers in the previous chapter, from cashmere to merino and from fine to chunky knits, so they're all worth having a look through. If it's not cashmere you're after but you want high-quality knitwear, take a look at John Smedley, the long-established brand that creates beautiful pieces that will last you season after season – investments certainly and definitely worth it.

Sites to Visit

www.anonymousclothing.com

Knitwear? Underwear? Clothing? I'm not really certain where this collection belongs as the way I think of it is as the place for those fine knit, lace trimmed tops, camis and cardis, so I thought you could read about it here. You're bound to have seen them; now you can buy all of these online in a range of sometimes quite unusual colours and with pointelle details and different shaped necklines, plus there's a new selection of tunics and dresses.

Site Usability: ★★★★	Express Delivery Option?	(UK) Yes
Product Range: ★★★	Gift Wrapping Option?	Yes
Price Range: Medium	Returns Procedure:	Email first for returns code then down
Delivery Area: Worldwide		to you
Based: UK		

www.belindarobertson.com

Award-winning Belinda Dickson is a knitwear designer whose international reputation for quality, colour and modern eclectic style has earned her the affectionate title of 'Queen of Cashmere'. On her website you'll find her two different labels, the White Label collection, offering affordable but beautifully designed cashmere, and her signature 'Cashmere Couture' range of the finest cashmere, made exclusively in Scotland and sparkling with Swarovski crystals and satin trims, all available in up to 120 colours.

Site Usability: ★★★★	Based:	UK
Product Range: ★★★★	Express Delivery Option? (UK)	Yes
Price Range: Luxury/Medium	Gift Wrapping Option?	Yes
Delivery Area: Worldwide	Returns Procedure:	Down to you

www.brora.co.uk

Brora was established in 1992 with the aim of offering classic, fine-quality Scottish cashmere with a contemporary twist, at prices that give real value for money. Although the pieces are not the cheapest, they come in some of the best quality available and in designs and a selection of colours that you won't find anywhere else. The pictures are beautifully clear and you'll find them hard to resist. The collection extends to men, children and babies.

Site Usability: ★★★★★	Based:	UK
Product Range: ★★★★	Express Delivery Option? (UK)	Yes
Price Range: Luxury/Medium	Gift Wrapping Option?	Yes
Delivery Area: Worldwide	Returns Procedure:	Down to you

www.cashmere.co.uk

Purely Cashmere is one of Scotland's longest-standing online cashmere retailers. It offers high-quality single-, two- and three-ply knits for men and women in a good range of colours and there's a combination of truly classic designs and modern styles, plus some luxurious throws for the home. The site also sells cashmere care products such as Cashmere Wash and clear zipped bags for storing and travelling.

Site Usability: ★★★★		Based:	UK
Product Range: ★★★		Express Delivery Option? (UK)	Yes, if an item is in stock
Price Range:	Luxury/Medium	Gift Wrapping Option?	No
Delivery Area:	Worldwide	Returns Procedure:	Down to you

www.claireid.com

This is a site with a really different, fun and quirky feel offering modern pure cotton knitwear in unusual styles and a good range of colours. There's also a made-to-measure service, plus a colour advisory service. Some of the pictures are at strange angles which makes it hard to see the products clearly, but everything is designed to be easy to wear and sizing goes from 8 to 24, so whatever your size or shape (or if you're expecting) you may well find something.

Site Usability: ★★★★		Based:	UK
Product Range: ★★★		Express Delivery Option? (UK)	No
Price Range:	Medium	Gift Wrapping Option?	No
Delivery Area:	Worldwide	Returns Procedure:	Down to you

www.crumpetengland.com

Crumpet offers a small range of quite expensive but beautiful and modern cashmere, ranging from fine, almost lingerie-inspired pieces to chunky knits. Most items are available in a range of the new season's colours and all are beautifully photographed. There are plenty of places to find your everyday cashmere classics: you'll find something special and different here, so take a look.

Site Usability: ★★★★		Based:	UK
Product Range: ★★★		Express Delivery Option? (UK)	No
Price Range:	Luxury/Medium	Gift Wrapping Option?	No
Delivery Area:	Worldwide	Returns Procedure:	Down to you

www.designsoncashmere.com

This company is based in Edinburgh and offers real Scottish, mostly two-ply cashmere, so the prices will be more than on some other websites offering single-ply cashmere sourced overseas. The styles are mostly classic and the range of colours isn't huge, but if you want your cashmere to come from Scotland, this could be the place to buy. They'll ship to you all over the world, shipping is free (worldwide) and the site has a currency converter if you're ordering from overseas.

Site Usability:	★★★★	Based:	UK
Product Range:	★★★	Express Delivery Option? (UK)	No, but worldwide delivery is free
Price Range:	Luxury/Medium	Gift Wrapping Option?	No
Delivery Area:	Worldwide	Returns Procedure:	Down to you

www.ejk.biz

If you're looking to invest in a new piece of cashmere but want something slightly different, then here's the place to look. Emma Jane Knight's collection is uniquely detailed, high quality (and high-end priced), with cashmere sweaters, wraps and jackets in a good range of colours. You need to download and fill in the order form or call them to order.

Site Usability:	★★★★	Based:	UK
Product Range:	★★★	Express Delivery Option? (UK)	No
Price Range:	Luxury	Gift Wrapping Option?	No
Delivery Area:	Worldwide	Returns Procedure:	Down to you

www.eric-bompard.com

French knitwear retailer Eric Bompard offers a pretty and unusual collection with chic styling and some different colours. Remember to click for the English version in the bottom right-hand corner unless your French is very good. They have some attractive designs in a wide range of colours that you won't find anywhere else, so do have a look here. They'll ship to anywhere in the EU and you need to allow 6 to 8 days for delivery.

Site Usability:	★★★★★	Based:	France
Product Range:	★★★★	Express Delivery Option? (UK)	No
Price Range:	Medium	Gift Wrapping Option?	No
Delivery Area:	EU	Returns Procedure:	Down to you

www.johnsmedley.com

John Smedley is a family-owned business established in 1784 which specialises in the highest-quality fine-gauge knitwear. It's definitely expensive but unbeatable for quality and fit. Whether you want a simple shell to wear underneath a jacket or a modern-cut fine merino cableknit top with the perfect neckline and three-quarter sleeves, it's better to buy just one piece from here than several cheaper versions. Buy two if you can. You really won't regret it.

Site Usability:	★★★★	Based:	UK
Product Range:	★★★	Express Delivery Option? (UK)	No
Price Range:	Luxury/Medium	Gift Wrapping Option?	No
Delivery Area:	Worldwide	Returns Procedure:	Down to you

www.purecollection.com

This is chic, high-quality cashmere in a wide range of styles, with the emphasis on modern shapes and the new season's colours. Alongside the less expensive range, the site offers 'Superfine' cashmere at a higher price which is perfect for layering or wearing on its own. The delivery and service are excellent and the prices are very good too. If you want something particular in a hurry, call to make sure it's in stock and you can have it the next day.

Site Usability:	★★★★★	Based:	UK
Product Range:	★★★★	Express Delivery Option? (UK)	Yes
Price Range:	Luxury/Medium	Gift Wrapping Option?	Yes
Delivery Area:	Worldwide	Returns Procedure:	Free

www.spiritoftheandes.co.uk

Spirit of the Andes offers a good selection of fitted and chunky knitwear in Pima cotton and the finest baby alpaca yarn. The styling and photography are very classic, so this is not the place if you're looking for something with a modern twist. However, the quality is high and there's an excellent choice of colours. Sizing is from small to extra large.

Site Usability:	★★★★	Based:	UK
Product Range:	★★★	Express Delivery Option? (UK)	No
Price Range:	Medium	Gift Wrapping Option?	No
Delivery Area:	Worldwide	Returns Procedure:	Free

Chapter 4

Tall and Plus Sizes

I t's essential when you're choosing larger-sized clothes that you go to a retailer who really understands what they're doing, rather than one simply offering you larger sizes in their normal ranges.

There aren't so many at the designer(ish) end of the market at the moment, although I'm sure that's going to change. Two of the best currently are Cinnamon Fashion, which offers continental ranges up to size 34, and Spirito (part of Artigiano) – offering its own range.

There are also several excellent US-based websites which I've listed below and which are included in the Shop America section of this book. Don't be put off by the thought of buying from the US – provided you don't go for anything too fitted you can use their size charts to find the right one for you and delivery is usually unbelievably fast.

Sites to Visit

www.cinnamonfashion.co.uk

Cinnamon specialises in clothing for sizes 16 to 34 and stocks casual wear, tailoring and occasionwear, plus sportswear and swimwear. You'll find lots of continental brands such as Chalou, Melli Mel, Doris Streich, Yoek, Samoon and BS Casuals, plus designers such as Kirsten Krog and Charles and Patricia Leicester. They're happy if you call them for advice on what works with what and will deliver to you anywhere in the world. Contact them to request express delivery.

Site Usability:	★★★★	Based:	UK
Product Range:	★★★	Express Delivery Option? (UK)	Yes
Price Range:	Medium	Gift Wrapping Option?	No
Delivery Area:	Worldwide	Returns Procedure:	Down to you

www.grayandosbourn.co.uk

This is an excellent selection of designer separates from labels such as Basler and Gerry Weber, plus their own well-priced Gray and Osbourn range. Most items are available in sizes 12 to 22 and some go up to 26. The range is essentially classic but in tune with each season and you can dress here from holiday/cruise, country weekends, smart tailoring, tops and accessories to chic evening wear. Delivery is by courier within 7–10 days, UK and Channel Islands only.

Site Usability:	★★★★★	Based:	UK
Product Range:	★★★★	Express Delivery Option? (UK)	No
Price Range:	Luxury/Medium	Gift Wrapping Option?	No
Delivery Area:	UK	Returns Procedure:	Down to you

www.longtallsally.co.uk

As someone who's always been quite a bit shorter than they'd really like to be, when I click on to this modern, stylish website I always wish that it offered clothes I could wear as well (foolish, I know, but there it is). Here you'll find a range of clothes for women over 5ft 7in, from casual to smart and everything in between, as well as swimwear, maternity wear, shoes and accessories. Everything is beautifully photographed. They'll ship worldwide and offer an express service to the UK.

Site Usability:	★★★★	Based:	UK
Product Range:	★★★★	Express Delivery Option? (UK)	Yes
Price Range:	Medium	Gift Wrapping Option?	No
Delivery Area:	Worldwide		

www.pennyplain.co.uk

Penny Plain (who you've probably already heard of) has a good, clear website, where you can order clothes which go from size 10 to size 26. The collection of separates, dresses and evening wear is essentially classic and combines pretty fabrics with reasonable (although definitely not cheap) prices. There's a small range of attractive shoes as well.

Site Usability:	★★★★★	Based:	UK
Product Range:	★★★★	Express Delivery Option? (UK)	Yes, but expensive
Price Range:	Medium	Gift Wrapping Option?	No
Delivery Area:	Worldwide	Returns Procedure:	Down to you

www.rowlandsclothing.co.uk

The first Rowlands shop opened in Bath in 1983 with the aim of providing a range of high-quality, reasonably priced, smart-casual classic country clothing. From its successful mail order catalogue Rowlands has now put its collection online with a simple, easy-to-use website offering smart coats and jackets, dresses and a selection of separates from day to evening. Sizing is 10 to 22 (24 for some items). They aim to deliver within 7 to 10 days.

Site Usability:	★★★★	Based:	UK
Product Range:	★★★★	Express Delivery Option? (UK)	No
Price Range:	Medium	Gift Wrapping Option?	No
Delivery Area:	UK	Returns Procedure:	Down to you

www.silhouettes.com

Silhouettes is an excellent, US-based fashion retailer offering collections in sizes 14 to 38 (UK equivalent 16/18 to 40/42). To make sure you order the correct size you need to use the size chart, which gives everything in inches.

You'll find smart separates, tailoring, dresses and outerwear. Because you'll be ordering from the US I suggest that you don't go for anything too fitted.

Site Usability:	★★★★	Based:	US
Product Range:	★★★★	Express Delivery Option? (UK)	Yes, worldwide
Price Range:	Medium	Gift Wrapping Option?	No
Delivery Area:	Worldwide	Returns Procedure:	Down to you

www.spirito.co.uk

This is the top end of the online plus-size clothing ranges, with a high-quality selection in sizes 10 to 20, including smart daywear, knitwear, casual wear and evening wear. Everything is beautifully made in Italy and smartly photographed to make you really want to buy, as you would expect from Artigiano's sister company. Shoes, accessories and jewellery are from the main Artigiano ranges and footwear goes up to a size 9.

Site Usability:	★★★★★	Based:	UK
Product Range:	★★★★	Express Delivery Option? (UK)	Yes
Price Range:	Medium	Gift Wrapping Option?	No
Delivery Area:	Worldwide	Returns Procedure:	Free with Royal Mail

Also visit these websites for tall and plus-size clothing:

Website address	You'll find it in:
www.dorothyperkins.co.uk	The High Street
www.principles.co.uk	The High Street
www.wallis-fashion.com	The High Street
www.llbean.com	Shop America
www.eddiebaur.com	Shop America
www.landsend.com	Modern Fashion Retailers
www.claireid.com	The Knitwear Store
www.poetrycollection.co.uk	Modern Fashion Retailers
www.marksandspencer.com	Modern Fashion Retailers

Chapter 5

Shop America

If you don't have time to go out looking round the shops and you can't find it online where you are, why not consider making your next purchase from the US, but without the jet lag, of course.

Ordering is normally very easy – you will incur extra delivery charges but you won't pay US tax. You will probably have to pay duty, but you'll still find the prices are competitive. In this section I have included only sites that ship internationally. The speed at which your order will reach you may well surprise you, with FedEx and UPS taking just a couple of days to anywhere in the world.

Just a word of advice. If you're not sure about the size you're ordering, go up. You're much less likely to have to send something back if it's slightly too big than if it's too small.

For clothing size conversions, US clothes are usually one but can sometimes be two sizes down from the UK. So a US 8 will be a UK 10 or 12. The only way to be sure about clothing measurements is to look at the size guides, measure yourself, then allow a bit. Here are the US/UK/Europe sizing conversions for reference.

Women's clothing size conversions

US	UK	France	Germany	Italy
6	8	36	34	40
8	10	38	36	42
10	12	40	38	44
12	14	42	40	46
14	16	44	42	48
16	18	46	44	50
18	20	50	46	52

Women's shoe size conversions

UK	3.5	4	4.5	5	5.5	6	6.5	7	7.5	8	8.5
EU	36.5	37	37.5	38	38.5	39	40	41	42	43	43.5
US	6	6.5	7	7.5	8	8.5	9	9.5	10	10.5	11

Men's shoe size conversions

UK	7	7.5	8	8.5	9	9.5	10	10.5	11	11.5	12
EU	40.5	41	42	42.5	43	44	44.5	45	46	46.5	47
US	7.5	8	8.5	9	9.5	10	10.5	11	11.5	12	12.5

Sites to Visit

www.abercrombie.com

This is where the young chic American denim brigade shop for their jeans, jackets and tees. The style is very 'Casual Luxury' and they even call it that. Take a look around if you can tear yourself away from the outstanding photographs of the most beautiful models (mostly men). Prices are good and delivery is speedy. The quality is excellent. Sizing is *small*, particularly for fitted items, so if in any doubt go up a size. Of course, you can now shop in their Savile Row, London, store, but if you can't get there...

Site Usability:	★★★★★	Based:	US
Product Range:	★★★	Express Delivery Option? (UK)	No
Price Range:	Medium	Gift Wrapping Option?	No
Delivery Area:	Worldwide	Returns Procedure:	Down to you

www.ae.com

Not as expensive as Abercrombie (and not quite so well known, particularly over here), American Eagle offers a wide selection of colourful, young, casual clothing which is extremely popular across the pond and I wish they were just down the road here, too. Think preppy striped shirts, humorous and sporty T-shirts and great jeans, hoodies and jackets, plus some camis and underwear and a good range of shoes. Orders are delivered by air to international addresses via United States Postal Service (USPS) Global Express Mail within 5 to 14 business days.

Site Usability:	★★★★★	Based:	US
Product Range:	★★★★	Express Delivery Option? (UK)	No
Price Range:	Medium/Very Good Value	Gift Wrapping Option?	No
Delivery Area:	Worldwide	Returns Procedure:	Down to you

www.brooksbrothers.com

Here you'll find quite expensive, beautifully made classic clothes for both men and women. The quality really is excellent and for a perfect classic cardigan or pair of trousers you'll be hard put to find anywhere better, particularly if you've tried them and know their look. The website is beautifully photographed, easy to navigate and delivery is speedy.

Site Usability:	★★★★★	Based:	US
Product Range:	★★★★★	Express Delivery Option? (UK)	No
Price Range:	Luxury/Medium	Gift Wrapping Option?	No
Delivery Area:	Worldwide	Returns Procedure:	Down to you

www.eddiebaur.com

Eddie Baur is one of those American companies that show how it really should be done. It's attractive to look at, easy to navigate and full of great products at good prices (not cheap but good value). No wonder *Vogue US* picks some of its products as the 'must-haves' of the season regularly.

From clothing to swimwear, performance walking boots, accessories and some superb sporting luggage, you won't go wrong here.

Site Usability: ★★★★★	Based:	US
Product Range: ★★★★★	Express Delivery Option? (UK)	No
Price Range: Medium/Very Good Value	Gift Wrapping Option?	No
Delivery Area: Worldwide	Returns Procedure:	Down to you

www.goclothing.com

You have been warned. There's so much to look at on this website that it takes a while to load. You'll almost certainly discover something you like, from C & C California T-shirts to funky belts and bags and a whole host of clothing labels, including allen b jeans, Tracy Reese, Cathering Malandrino, Lilly Pulitzer and a lot you've probably never heard of.

Site Usability: ★★★★	Based:	US
Product Range: ★★★★★	Express Delivery Option? (UK)	No
Price Range: Luxury/Medium	Gift Wrapping Option?	Yes
Delivery Area: Worldwide	Returns Procedure:	Down to you

www.grahamkandiah.com

If you're going anywhere hot in the near future you have to take a look at this website. Choose from the most attractive sarongs, kaftans, wraps and bikinis, plus T-shirts and totes, all in a wonderful treasure trove of fabrics with names such as Tiger, Riviera, South Beach, Jungle, Havana and Bahia. And it's quick and easy to order.

Site Usability: ★★★★	Based:	US
Product Range: ★★★	Express Delivery Option? (UK)	No
Price Range: Medium	Gift Wrapping Option?	Yes
Delivery Area: Worldwide	Returns Procedure:	Down to you

www.llbean.com

You'll be hard put to see a more comprehensive collection of well-priced, quality clothing, including outerwear, fleeces, shirts, trousers and snow sport clothing, luggage, outdoor gear, swimwear, footwear and accessories. L.L. Bean is particularly good for its cold-weather shirts, which are extremely reasonable. Have a browse. It's hard to get away without buying something.

Site Usability:	★★★★★	Based:	US
Product Range:	★★★★★	Express Delivery Option? (UK)	No
Price Range:	Medium/Very Good Value	Gift Wrapping Option?	No
Delivery Area:	Worldwide	Returns Procedure:	Down to you

www.neimanmarcus.com

Every designer from YSL to Marc Jacobs and accessories from Manolo Blahnik to Tods are offered at this top-level US store. The website is brilliantly laid out, showing beautiful modern pictures of absolutely everything. The downside is you'll have to pay duty on top of the designer prices (if you're not based in the US), but it's worth having a look at some of the American designers and well worth checking out the trends from season to season.

Site Usability:	★★★★★	Based:	US
Product Range:	★★★★★	Express Delivery Option? (UK)	No
Price Range:	Luxury/Medium	Gift Wrapping Option?	Yes
Delivery Area:	Worldwide	Returns Procedure:	Down to you

www.shopbop.com

Here is just about the full collection from Juicy Couture, including the velour and cashmere collections, plus brands such as Diane von Furstenberg, Chip and Pepper, Marc by Marc Jacobs and Seven for all Mankind: great brands you can find here but would really have to search for elsewhere. The site offers standard UPS delivery plus the worldwide express service which will take only 2 to 3 days.

Site Usability:	★★★★★	Based:	USA
Product Range:	★★★★★	Express Delivery Option? (UK)	No
Price Range:	Luxury/Medium	Gift Wrapping Option?	No
Delivery Area:	Worldwide	Returns Procedure:	Down to you

www.sillysports.co.uk

Now you can buy your Abercrombie and Fitch T-shirts and American Eagle shorts from one online retailer. And despite the fact that it is based in Florida, they say you shouldn't be charged duty and all prices here are in sterling. Other brands on offer include Converse, Hollister (A & F again), K-Swiss and Timberland.

Site Usability: ★★★★	Based:	USA
Product Range: ★★★★	Express Delivery Option? (UK)	No
Price Range: Medium	Gift Wrapping Option?	No
Delivery Area: Worldwide	Returns Procedure:	Down to you

www.sundancecatalog.com

Inspired (and initiated) by Robert Redford, Sundance is a truly American catalogue which has now become a worldwide online store. You'll discover wonderful jewellery by American craftsmen and a wide range of high-quality classic American clothing, including shirts, tops, tees, skirts and trousers, ranch-style boots, home accessories (gorgeous quilts and throws) and lots of ideas for gifts.

Site Usability: ★★★★★	Based:	USA
Product Range: ★★★★★	Express Delivery Option? (UK)	No
Price Range: Luxury/Medium	Gift Wrapping Option?	Yes
Delivery Area: Worldwide	Returns Procedure:	Down to you

www.swimwearboutique.com

This is an excellent swimwear boutique offering great labels such as Gottex and Gideon Oberson, which, for some reason, are almost impossible to buy in the UK. When you're placing your order you'll notice that one of the clever features of the site is the 'availability' box which shows up as soon as you've chosen your style, size and colour and tells you when you can have your order. Note that you'll have to pay duty if you're outside the US.

Site Usability: ★★★★★	Based:	US
Product Range: ★★★★	Express Delivery Option? (UK)	No
Price Range: Medium	Gift Wrapping Option?	No
Delivery Area: Worldwide	Returns Procedure:	Down to you

www.travelsmith.com

This US-based website must be the ultimate online travel clothing store. It offers a comprehensive and well-priced range of travel clothing and accessories for men and women, from outerwear including washable suede, tailoring and safari jackets, to easy-care separates, hats, swimwear and luggage. You can't place your order directly online for international delivery, but you can fax it to them.

Site Usability:	★★★★★	Based:	US
Product Range:	★★★★★	Express Delivery Option? (UK)	No
Price Range:	Medium	Gift Wrapping Option?	No
Delivery Area:	Worldwide	Returns Procedure:	Down to you

www.trunkltd.com

For T-shirt addicts only. This funky US-based website sells collectible T-shirts, camis and jackets emblazoned with classic rock-and-roll art – think The Beatles, Alice Cooper, Blondie, Frank Zappa, Fleetwood Mac and Janis Joplin. Be careful before you get too excited, though – some of these, embellished with Swarovski crystals, are definitely collectors' items, with steep prices to match.

Site Usability:	★★★★	Based:	USA
Product Range:	★★★★	Express Delivery Option? (UK)	No
Price Range:	Luxury/Medium	Gift Wrapping Option?	No
Delivery Area:	Worldwide	Returns Procedure:	Down to you

www.victoriassecret.com

The US-based mail-order lingerie company that uses world-famous models. Seductive pictures of bronzed beauties don't detract from the fact that this is quite possibly the best selection of lingerie in the world and with such good prices you'll probably want to buy here.

Site Usability:	★★★★★	Based:	US
Product Range:	★★★★★	Express Delivery Option? (UK)	No
Price Range:	Very Good Value	Gift Wrapping Option?	Yes
Delivery Area:	Worldwide	Returns Procedure:	Down to you

Chapter 6

Sportswear to Look Great in

Whether you're looking for something to wear every day in the gym (hmmm...) or just some comfortable clothes to relax in, you've come to the right place.

That famous velour tracksuit's still out there, although now available in some wonderfully wild and wacky colours, but there are lots of other options that will take you to the gym, your Pilates class, yoga and back for an evening in front of the box.

You'll find hoodies, zip-front jackets, wrap tops and vests, plus excellent soft pants in different styles at many of the places below and across a range of prices. I've also included retailers such as Joules and Jack Wills – wonderful polo shirts and fleeces – Wildlife Online (which offers brands such as Amor Lux, Kipling and Musto) and Puma, which must surely have the most comfortable sport/casual trainers available (and I know, I'm a collector).

Sites to Visit

www.adidas-shop.co.uk

Up until now you've had to go to a general sports store to find Adidas foot-wear and clothing. Now with this new, modern-design website you can look at everything in one place. Much better than that, though, you can read up on all the latest sports innovations from this famous brand. You'll find sports clothing and footwear for men, women and kids, plus the Adidas by Stella McCartney line.

Site Usability:	★★★★★	Based:	UK
Product Range:	★★★★	Express Delivery Option? (UK)	Yes
Price Range:	Medium	Gift Wrapping Option?	No
Delivery Area:	UK	Returns Procedure:	Down to you

www.asquith.ltd.uk

If you haven't yet given up on your New Year's resolution of getting fitter, or you want something to stimulate you into getting on with it, have a look here. Asquith offers an unusual collection of clothes for yoga, Pilates (and yes, lounging around) in a lovely selection of colours, including candy, coral, aqua and dewberry. You can choose from wrap tops, capri pants, camisoles and T-shirts. There's excellent information about each item, from what it's made of to sizing and washing instructions.

Site Usability:	★★★★	Based:	UK
Product Range:	★★★	Express Delivery Option? (UK)	Yes
Price Range:	Medium	Gift Wrapping Option?	No
Delivery Area:	Worldwide	Returns Procedure:	Down to you

www.blacks.co.uk

If you or any member of your family have ever done any camping, walking, hiking or climbing you'll probably already have visited Blacks, where they offer a well-priced (rather than 'designer') range of clothing and accesso-ries and good-value skiwear in season. You can buy waterproof jackets and trousers, lots of fleeces, tents, poles, footwear and socks and great gifts such as Cybalite torches, Kick and Huntsman knives and tools and Garmin compasses.

Site Usability:	★★★★★	Express Delivery Option? (UK)	No
Product Range:	★★★★	Gift Wrapping Option?	No
Price Range:	Medium	Returns Procedure:	Down to you
Delivery Area:	UK		

www.crewclothing.co.uk

This is an attractive and modern website with a constantly expanding range, offering all the Crew gear. Choose from the full collection of sailing-inspired clothing as well as hard-wearing footwear, faux fur jackets and gilets in winter, together with excellent travel bags, gloves, hats and socks. The site offers standard and next-day UK delivery and same-day in central London if you order by 12pm. They'll also ship worldwide.

Site Usability:	★★★★★	Based:	UK
Product Range:	★★★	Express Delivery Option? (UK)	Yes
Price Range:	Medium	Gift Wrapping Option?	No
Delivery Area:	Worldwide	Returns Procedure:	Down to you

www.elliegray.com

This is an excellent sportswear destination, whether you're looking for exercise clothes for the gym or just for relaxing in. Offering brands USA Pro, Pure Lime, Deha and their own, you'll find a selection of hoodies and jackets, sweatshirts, pants, outerwear, sports bras and accessories in a good range of colours and styles. Everything is easy to see and descrbed in detail and, even better, you can immediately see what's in stock.

Site Usability:	★★★★★	Based:	UK
Product Range:	★★★	Express Delivery Option? (UK)	Yes
Price Range:	Luxury/Medium/Very Good Value	Gift Wrapping Option?	No
Delivery Area:	Worldwide	Returns Procedure:	Down to you

www.figleaves.com

Figleaves' collection of activewear now includes designers such as Calvin Klein, Puma, Elle, Candida Faria, Venice Beach and Tommy Hilfiger and the range is growing all the time. You'll find bright colours and good shapes with lots of stretch included. If you haven't tried the service before, you should certainly give it a go as it really is excellent and worldwide shipping is free. As Figleaves' main area of business is lingerie, you'll be able to buy your sports bras here as well.

Site Usability:	★★★★★	Based:	UK
Product Range:	★★★★	Express Delivery Option? (UK)	Yes
Price Range:	Luxury/Medium/Very Good Value	Gift Wrapping Option?	Yes
Delivery Area:	Worldwide	Returns Procedure:	Use their returns service

www.jackwills.co.uk

If you're missing your Abercrombie/American Eagle fix this year you should take a look at this website, offering 'cool' and idiosyncratic sportswear, including jeans, hoodies, fun printed T-shirts, polo shirts and accessories for girls and guys. Annoyingly you can't find the delivery details until you start to place an order. However, this is a well laid out site with clear product pictures, so take a look.

Site Usability:	★★★★	Based:	UK
Product Range:	★★★	Express Delivery Option? (UK)	Yes
Price Range:	Medium/Very Good Value	Gift Wrapping Option?	No
Delivery Area:	Worldwide	Returns Procedure:	Use their returns service

www.jdsports.co.uk

As one of the largest UK sports retailers there is, as you'd expect, a huge range of sports shoes on this website, including Nike, Puma, Reebok, Lacoste and Adidas. The clothing ranges are also extensive and taken from the same brands, while the ordering system is easy to use. With each pair of shoes (or each item of clothing) you will be shown other items to go with. They aim to make delivery within five working days of receipt of your order.

Site Usability:	★★★★★	Express Delivery Option? (UK)	No
Product Range:	★★★★	Gift Wrapping Option?	No
Price Range:	Medium	Returns Procedure:	Down to you
Delivery Area:	UK		

www.joulesclothing.com

Joules is a clothing website with a difference. Beautifully photographed and well laid out, there are some fun sporty separates for just about everyone, provided you like stripes and colours (although lots of items are available in black/jet as well). It's aimed mainly at the riding fraternity, although many of the clothes, particularly the jackets and fleeces, have a much wider appeal.

Site Usability:	★★★★	Express Delivery Option? (UK)	Yes — call them
Product Range:	★★★★	Gift Wrapping Option?	No
Price Range:	Medium	Returns Procedure:	Down to you
Delivery Area:	Worldwide		

www.nomadtravel.co.uk

The next time you feel like taking off on safari or into the jungle, take a look at this website, which offers a well-selected range of efficient and well-priced travel clothing. There are lightweight trousers, zip-offs and vented shirts, base layer fleeces and thermals. You will also find lots of advice on travel health, depending on where you're going, with particular information on malaria and travelling with children. You can place your order for delivery to the EU online, and elsewhere by contacting the site. They offer 48-hour delivery in the UK.

Site Usability:	★★★★★	Express Delivery Option? (UK)	48-hour service
Product Range:	★★★★	Gift Wrapping Option?	No
Price Range:	Medium	Returns Procedure:	Down to you
Delivery Area:	Worldwide		

www.puma.com

Puma has launched its own website, so it can offer its full range to you online. As a great fan of the unbelievably comfortable footwear (so comfortable I've become an addict), this is great news. Whereas on most sports websites you'll find just a small part of the range, here you can choose from all the styles and all the colourways. Delivery is within 1 to 3 days unless you select Royal Mail Special Delivery, in which case you can have your order the day after you place it.

Site Usability:	★★★★★	Based:	UK
Product Range:	★★★★	Express Delivery Option? (UK)	Yes
Price Range:	Medium	Gift Wrapping Option?	No
Delivery Area:	EU most countries	Returns Procedure:	Down to you

www.sheactive.co.uk

Here's a website just for women, covering sports such as fitness, cycling, rock climbing, skiing and swimming. The site doesn't offer any products that are adaptations of men's sportswear and just goes for the best that's been specifically designed for women. There's a good selection, whether you're a dedicated sportswoman or just want the look. Brands include Puma, Adidas, Berghaus, Bolle, Helly Hansen and Salomon.

Site Usability:	★★★★★	Based:	UK
Product Range:	★★★★	Express Delivery Option? (UK)	Yes
Price Range:	Medium	Gift Wrapping Option?	No
Delivery Area:	Worldwide	Returns Procedure:	Free of charge

www.shoe-shop.com

Puma, Asics, Nike, Adidas and Reebok are just some of the many brands you can choose from on this site, whatever your sport. If you're a lounge lizard and simply want to look modern (and like being comfortable), you'll find all the latest styles here too. The site does sell other types of shoes, but its strength is definitely at the sporty end. Beware of wearing your sports shoes too much though – you'll never be happy in your killer heels again.

Site Usability:	★★★★★	Based:	UK
Product Range:	★★★★★	Express Delivery Option? (UK)	No
Price Range:	Medium	Gift Wrapping Option?	No
Delivery Area:	Worldwide	Returns Procedure:	Down to you but select their good-value returns-paid option

www.sport-e.com

Part of Littlewoods Online, this is the place to find discounted sports shoes by Nike, Adidas, Puma, Reebok, Converse and Lacoste. There's also a good selection of sportswear, sports bras and sports equipment. Delivery is free if you spend over £100 and returns are free as well, so if you really don't want to spend too much but you still like to have that 'designer' look, you may well find your answer here.

Site Usability:	★★★★★	Based:	UK
Product Range:	★★★★	Express Delivery Option? (UK)	No
Price Range:	Medium/Very Good Value	Gift Wrapping Option?	No
Delivery Area:	UK	Returns Procedure:	Free of charge

www.sportswoman.co.uk

Don't visit this website unless you're feeling energetic (although it could push you in the right direction). Here you can see, beautifully photographed, the Casall range of sportswear, which includes basic activewear, tennis, running, yoga, Pilates and golf clothing, plus underwear and accessories such as socks, waterbottles and kit bags. In the excercise equipment and accessories section there are gym balls, ab rollers and gloves and more will be added soon.

Site Usability:	★★★★★	Based:	UK
Product Range:	★★★★★	Express Delivery Option? (UK)	Yes
Price Range:	Medium	Gift Wrapping Option?	No
Delivery Area:	UK	Returns Procedure:	Down to you

www.sweatybetty.com

Another website to get you going, where you can choose from an excellent and stylish range of clothes for the gym and for yoga, available in basic colours such as black, grey and pink. It also offers sleek (and minimal) beachwear, chic and well-priced skiwear, plus accessories such as leg and arm warmers and books on yoga. Postage is free on UK orders over £50.

Site Usability:	★★★★	Based:	UK
Product Range:	★★★	Express Delivery Option? (UK)	No
Price Range:	Medium	Gift Wrapping Option?	No
Delivery Area:	Worldwide	Returns Procedure:	Down to you

www.travellinglight.co.uk

Order your hot-weather travel clothing here at any time of the year. There's an excellent range for men and women if you're planning to go trekking or on safari, plus smart/classic, easy-to-wear separates, tailoring and evening wear. In the casual wear section there are shorts, bermudas and capri pants, plus lots of tops and T-shirts. You'll also find accessories such as lightweight luggage, Bolle and Oakley sunglasses and sun hats.

Site Usability:	★★★★★	Based:	UK
Product Range:	★★★★	Express Delivery Option? (UK)	Yes
Price Range:	Medium	Gift Wrapping Option?	No
Delivery Area:	Worldwide	Returns Procedure:	Free of charge

www.whitestuff.com

This young, urban clothing company sells casual sporty lightweight gear in the summer months for guys and girls and trendy skiwear in the winter (hence the name). There are colour options for just about all the clothes, from the Flawless tee to the Java Jive pant, and you can see straight away what's available in stock or what you'll have to wait for. This isn't a huge collection but it's fun and well-priced and definitely worth a look.

Site Usability:	★★★★	Based:	UK
Product Range:	★★★	Express Delivery Option? (UK)	Yes
Price Range:	Medium/Very Good Value	Gift Wrapping Option?	No
Delivery Area:	Worldwide	Returns Procedure:	Freepost or return to store

www.wildlifeonline.com

Wildlife Clothing offers a range of leisurewear, footwear and accessories for people with active lifestyles. It brings together a selection of products from international brands such as Armor Lux from Brittany, Camper and Hispanitas footwear from Spain, Dockers, Merrell and Sebago from the United States, Oska from Germany, Kipling from Belgium and Joules, Jack Wills, Quayside, Orla Kiely, Musto and Seasalt from the UK. Allow 7 to 10 days for delivery, although they aim to despatch all items much faster.

Site Usability:	★★★★★	Based:	UK
Product Range:	★★★★	Express Delivery Option? (UK)	No
Price Range:	Luxury/Medium	Gift Wrapping Option?	Yes
Delivery Area:	Worldwide	Returns Procedure:	Down to you

Chapter 7

Handbag Temptation

The A List   Carry These Without Breaking the Bank

Bag a Bargain

I have to admit it – this is probably my favourite place for web shopping as anyone who knows me will tell you that I'm a handbag addict (collector, I like to call it, but others will tell you differently, I'm sure).

My main reason for being so enthusiastic about handbag shopping is quite simple. Carry the right handbag and you can definitely dress for less. Your handbag says so much about you – immediately people look at you they can tell whether you have any idea about style and what's going on in fashion because your bag is one of the first things they take in. I'm not talking about forking out £1000 for the latest Gucci, but just the right colour, fittings and shape say so much more than you think about your overall look. If in doubt take a look at the people around you, then go shop.

You'll find three sections here – all equal temptation. Start off with a browse through The A List where, if you buy, your bank manager might not speak to you for a while (mine definitely wouldn't), but you'll be investing in true 'superbrand', designer, covetable, must-have pieces from famous labels such as Louis Vuitton, Dior, Celine and Gucci. Take a good look and see what this season's 'now' handbag looks like and be tempted if the mood takes you.

Then go through to Carry These without Breaking the Bank (sorry, that's long I know, but I'm sure you get the idea) where there are plenty of chic and high-quality handbags that you can buy each season and enjoy carrying in the latest colours: hot orange, pink and blue as well as the favourite neutrals.

After that take a look at Bag a Bargain and no, I'm not talking about cheap handbags here but Fendi, Gucci and Dior for less. The real thing, from resellers who won't be offering you the latest, new season's designs but classics and overstocks from seasons past. It's well worth having a look at these websites as you can often buy something really great at a good discounts. Just a word here – please don't even think of buying fake 'replica' bags online, you're bound to be disappointed by the quality. My advice is also not to buy branded handbags on an auction website unless you're absolutely sure what you're doing. I personally wouldn't do it. There are all the quality/fake/delivery issues plus the security of your payment. The web is a really wonderful place to shop, but it can be a minefield too.
** Your siteguide.com password is SG011. Please use this as the media code when subscribing for your free year's login.

The A List

www.anyahindmarch.com

Anya Hindmarch's collection of beautiful, unique and sometimes quirky handbags and small accessories has long been a favourite of glossy magazine fashion editors. They're totally different and very special, always carrying her signature bow logo somewhere, whether on her clever picture bags or the richly coloured, leather-tassled Marissa. Her chic bespoke Ebury handbag is available in several colourways and is made to order only, with your personalised inscription inside.

Site Usability:	★★★★	Based:	UK
Product Range:	★★★	Express Delivery Option? (UK)	No
Price Range:	Luxury	Gift Wrapping Option?	No
Delivery Area:	Worldwide	Returns Procedure:	Down to you

www.forzieri.com

Italian company Forzieri offers handbags and wallets by Dolce & Gabbana, Prada, Tods, Gucci and Burberry, plus superb leather and shearling jackets, a stylish shoe collection, gloves, leather travel bags and other accessories. There's also a wide choice of reasonably priced, high-quality Italian brands.

Very good descriptions are given about all the products, plus lots of different views so you know exactly what you're buying.

Site Usability:	★★★★★	Based:	Italy
Product Range:	★★★★★	Express Delivery Option? (UK)	Yes
Price Range:	Luxury/Medium	Gift Wrapping Option?	Yes
Delivery Area:	Worldwide	Returns Procedure:	Down to you

www.gucci.com

Leading the way for 'superbrand' designers to come online, Gucci has opened up its website for online accessory orders. As you would expect, the site is modern and beautiful (and heartstoppingly expensive) and the products irresistible. You can buy handbags, luggage, men's and women's shoes and gifts, such as keyrings and lighters. Don't expect the site to offer clothes, at least not for a while, as the fit would be very difficult and returns far too high.

Site Usability:	★★★★★	Express Delivery Option? (UK)	Yes
Product Range:	★★★★★	Gift Wrapping Option?	Yes/Automatic
Price Range:	Luxury	Returns Procedure:	Down to you
Delivery Area:	Worldwide, most places		

www.jandmdavidson.com

J & M Davidson designs and produces beautiful quality and extremely expensive leather goods and clothing, together with handbags and small accessories in lovely leathers and different colours. The website is quite simple and the pictures small and not as good as they could be, but don't be fooled. Anything you buy from this site will be designer quality, superbly made and will last you a long time.

Site Usability:	★★★	Based:	UK
Product Range:	★★★★	Express Delivery Option? (UK)	No
Price Range:	Luxury	Gift Wrapping Option?	No
Delivery Area:	Worldwide	Returns Procedure:	Down to you

www.louisvuitton.com

Louis Vuitton's unmistakable, covetable (and luxuriously expensive) handbags are now available online through its quick and clear website. So you don't have to go into one of its stores any more and ask for help and information – you'll find everything you could possibly need to know here, such as interior details, care and sizing. Once you've selected your country you'll find which styles are available to you. Simply choose the design you like and go shop.

Site Usability:	★★★★★	Based:	UK
Product Range:	★★★★★	Express Delivery Option? (UK)	Yes
Price Range:	Luxury	Gift Wrapping Option	Automatic
Delivery Area:	Worldwide	Returns Procedure:	Down to you

www.luluguinness.com

'Be a glamour girl, put on your lipstick' is the phrase welcoming you to this elegant website. Exquisite handbags and accessories from British designer Lulu Guinness can be shipped to you wherever you are. With unique styling, sometimes quirky, sometimes just plain gorgeous, and a selection of cosmetic bags in stylish prints to take you anywhere, this is a website you should take a look at if you're in the mood for a treat or special gift.

Site Usability:	★★★★	Based:	UK
Product Range:	★★★	Express Delivery Option? (UK)	No
Price Range:	Luxury/Medium	Gift Wrapping Option?	No, but everything is beautifully
Delivery Area:	Worldwide		packaged

www.mulberry.com

Mulberry is a truly British luxury brand with an extensive line of highly crafted bags which combine stylish, standout design with the finest leathers and highly wrought detailing. Stuart Vevers, Design Director, has used Mulberry's 1970s' bohemian roots as a reference point in many of his designs and styles like the Bayswater, Emmy and Brooke have become covetable fashion classics for consumers and celebrities alike. Buy one if you can.

Site Usability:	★★★★★	Based:	UK
Product Range:	★★★★	Express Delivery Option? (UK)	No
Price Range:	Luxury	Gift Wrapping Option?	No
Delivery Area:	Worldwide	Returns Procedure:	Down to you

www.smythson.com

For over a century Smythson has been famous as the Bond Street purveyor of top-quality personalised stationery and accessories, including diaries, leather journals, albums, frames and gold-edged place cards. It also have a luxurious collection of handbags, briefcases, wallets and small leather goods at totally frightening prices. You can use the online personalised stationery service or call to order on 020 7629 8558. They'll send you a sample pack from which you can choose your paper and style. Just let them know your choice and you're away.

Site Usability:	★★★★★	Based:	UK
Product Range:	★★★★	Express Delivery Option? (UK)	No
Price Range:	Luxury	Gift Wrapping Option?	No
Delivery Area:	Worldwide	Returns Procedure:	Down to you

www.tannerkrolle.co.uk

Tanner Krolle, launched in 1856, is one of London's oldest and finest luxury leather goods houses and all of the brand's bespoke bridle leather pieces are still handcrafted in London. In addition to its traditional luggage, Tanner Krolle produces beautiful handbags, shoes and small leather goods. You need to call 020 7823 1688 to order and you can expect excellent service.

Site Usability:	★★★★	Based:	UK
Product Range:	★★★	Express Delivery Option? (UK)	Yes
Price Range:	Luxury	Gift Wrapping Option?	No, but luxury packaging is standard
Delivery Area:	Worldwide	Returns Procedure:	Down to you

Also visit these websites for luxury handbags:

Website address	You'll find them in:
www.net-a-porter.com	Luxury Fashion Brands
	Miu Miu
	Chloe
	Bottega Veneta
	Marc Jacobs
	Juicy Couture
	Stella McCartney
	Celine

	Fendi
	Jimmy Choo
	Missoni
	Roberto Cavalli

www.paulsmith.co.uk   Luxury Fashion Brands

www.lineafashion.com   Luxury Fashion Brands
                          Tod's
                          Cesare Paciotti
                          Missoni

www.brownsfashion.com   Luxury Fashion Brands
                          Chloe
                          Fendi
                          Marni
                          Luella
                          Bottega Veneta
                          V.B.H

Carry These Without Breaking the Bank

Sites to Visit

www.alicecaroline.co.uk

Not your usual range of handbags and jewellery here but something just a little bit different to tempt you when you want a new colourful fix but don't want to shell out the earth. There are fabric bags which would be perfect for summer and evenings, with oriental and funky prints such as Glamour Girls and Shoes, pretty gemstone, silver and gold jewellery. They would all make great gifts for style-conscious girls.

Site Usability: ★★★★	Based:	UK
Product Range: ★★★	Express Delivery Option? (UK)	Yes – call them
Price Range: Medium	Gift Wrapping Option?	No
Delivery Area: Worldwide	Returns Procedure:	Down to you

www.angeljackson.co.uk

From the glamorous Ultimate Day Bag in black, cocoa, green or gold to the woven leather Polanski, you'll find an irresistible collection of extremely well-priced and well-made handbags here, plus weekenders, purses and day to evening clutches. You can see all the items in detail with close-up and different-view photographs. Call for mail order until the online shopping facility is up and running.

Site Usability:	★★★	Based:	UK
Product Range:	★★★	Express Delivery Option? (UK)	No
Price Range:	Medium	Gift Wrapping Option?	No
Delivery Area:	Worldwide	Returns Procedure:	Down to you

www.belenechandia.com

Here are soft leather handbags by accessory label Belen Echandia in a choice of colours, with names such as Rock Me, Hold Me and Take Me Away. Choose your style of handbag, check out the measurements and detailing and then use the semi-bespoke service to select your favourite leather, from croc finish to metallics and brights to neutrals. These are definitely at the luxury end of the market, with prices starting at about £200, but they are a unique investment that will last you for years.

Site Usability:	★★★★	Based:	UK
Product Range:	★★★	Express Delivery Option? (UK)	Yes
Price Range:	Luxury	Gift Wrapping Option?	Yes
Delivery Area:	Worldwide	Returns Procedure:	Down to you

www.billamberg.com

From Bill Amberg's London studio the accessories team design a seasonal collection of modern bags and luggage in carefully selected fine leathers and suedes, with names such as Rocket Bag, Trafalgar Tote and Supernatural. You won't find his full range online, just a small collection, which also gives you a good idea of his individual style. You can also buy jewellery boxes and briefcases here along with his range for the shooting enthusiast.

Site Usability:	★★★	Based:	US
Product Range:	★★★	Express Delivery Option? (UK)	No
Price Range:	Luxury	Gift Wrapping Option?	No
Delivery Area:	Worldwide	Returns Procedure:	Down to you

www.bravida.co.uk

Bravida offers a collection of simple, stylish handbags made by Italian craftsmen in high-quality leather. You may not be buying into a famous brand, but many of the handbags are really chic and with prices starting at around £130 they're good value. There are contemporary and classic bags, plus a small collection of wallets. They'll ship worldwide and offer an express service.

Site Usability:	★★★	Based:	UK
Product Range:	★★★	Express Delivery Option? (UK)	Yes
Price Range:	Medium/Very Good Value	Gift Wrapping Option?	No
Delivery Area:	Worldwide	Returns Procedure:	Down to you

www.guessboutique.co.uk

There's an amazing range here of US brand Guess's bags and watches, all reasonably priced, so you can buy into a totally up-to-date look without breaking the bank (unless you buy several, of course). Check in the New Arrivals section to see what the latest items are. But be warned – once started you'll probably want to spend at lot of time as there's so much to see and choose from.

Site Usability:	★★★★★	Based:	UK
Product Range:	★★★★★	Express Delivery Option? (UK)	Yes
Price Range:	Medium/Very Good Value	Gift Wrapping Option?	No
Delivery Area:	Worldwide	Returns Procedure:	Down to you

www.ignesbags.com

The next time you feel the urge for a new handbag, take a look at ignesbags.com, where you can find unique designs in unusual South American leathers. This is a small, high-quality collection priced mostly at between £150 and £200 and ranging from large day bags to small, idiosyncratic evening bags with chain handles. Contact them if you want to order from outside the EU.

Site Usability: ★★★★	Based:	UK
Product Range: ★★★	Express Delivery Option? (UK)	No
Price Range: Medium/Very Good Value	Gift Wrapping Option?	No
Delivery Area: Worldwide	Returns Procedure:	Down to you

www.julieslaterandson.co.uk

You can certainly find these products on other websites (passport covers, address books, purses, luggage tags and the like), however you'd have to search long and hard to find the colour ranges offered here, which include pistachio, aubergine, meadow blue, hot pink and carnation. Everything is beautifully pictured in detail so you'll know exactly what you're ordering.

Site Usability: ★★★★	Based:	UK
Product Range: ★★★	Express Delivery Option? (UK)	Yes
Price Range: Medium	Gift Wrapping Option	Yes
Delivery Area: Worldwide	Returns Procedure:	Down to you

www.kanishkabags.co.uk

This is a lovely, ethnically inspired collection of clothes and accessories and you're unlikely to find it in the shops. You'll discover beaded and quilted handbags, straw totes in the summer, unusual and well-priced jewellery, beautifully embroidered and colour-woven shawls, plus beaded silk and cotton kaftans. So if you like something unique and unusual, you may find it here.

Site Usability: ★★★	Based:	UK
Product Range: ★★★	Express Delivery Option? (UK)	No
Price Range: Medium	Gift Wrapping Option?	No
Delivery Area: Worldwide	Returns Procedure:	Down to you

www.lizcox.com

Liz Cox offers a very British collection of bags and luggage using exclusive fabrics, bridle and saddle leathers, and she's well known for her use of exotic patterns and innovative designs. Her shops are based in Bath and Notting Hill, London. Now you can buy a selection of her range online. Prices are definitely not cheap, so make sure you're a colourful patterned bag sort of person before you invest (although you can buy her gorgeous leather bags here as well).

Site Usability:	★★★	Express Delivery Option? (UK)		Call them
Product Range:	★★★	Gift Wrapping Option?		Call them
Price Range:	Medium	Returns Procedure:		Down to you but you need to tell them first
Delivery Area:	Worldwide			
Based:	UK			

www.ollieandnic.com

Ollie & Nic offer a stylish and chic range of accessorises at excellent prices including pretty bags for day, evening and holiday, umbrellas, sunglasses, scarves, brooches and other accessories. The collection is very seasonal with new products being introduced all the time and each season will have a specific theme so you can visit this website regularly and you'll never be bored. There are very good gift ideas here for anyone who collects accessories, particularly in the winter season.

Site Usability:	★★★★	Based:	UK
Product Range:	★★★	Express Delivery Option? (UK)	No
Price Range:	Medium	Gift Wrapping Option?	No
Delivery Area:	Worldwide	Returns Procedure:	Down to you

www.orlakiely.com

Orla Kiely designs unique, instantly recognisable clothes and accessories, using bold and colourful patterns that are always fresh and appealing. On her website there is a small selection from her ready-to-wear clothing range, but a much wider choice of her unusual, attractive and highly functional accessories, including handbags, purses and luggage.

Site Usability:	★★★★	Based:	UK
Product Range:	★★★	Express Delivery Option? (UK)	No
Price Range:	Medium	Gift Wrapping Option?	No
Delivery Area:	Worldwide	Returns Procedure:	Down to you

www.osprey-london.co.uk

For many years Osprey has created beautifully crafted handbags and small leather accessories in high-quality leathers, all designed by Graeme Ellisdon in Florence. The range includes classic and business handbags, but think modern business, so although they'll take all the papers you need to carry, they look like great bags as well. There is also the London Collection of contemporary bags in tune with what's happening each season.

Site Usability: ★★★★	Based:	UK
Product Range: ★★★	Express Delivery Option? (UK)	Yes
Price Range: Luxury/Medium	Gift Wrapping Option?	No
Delivery Area: Worldwide	Returns Procedure:	Down to you

www.pierotucci.com

I'm sure you'd agree with me that if you really had your choice you'd be on that plane to Florence to choose your next Italian leather handbag, wallet or fur-trimmed pair of gloves. However, if that's just not possible you should have a look at this Florence-based website, where you can choose from classic, beautifully made Italian styling. They offer UPS express shipping to anywhere in the world.

Site Usability: ★★★★	Based:	Italy
Product Range: ★★★★	Express Delivery Option? (UK)	Yes
Price Range: Luxury/Medium	Gift Wrapping Option?	No
Delivery Area: Worldwide	Returns Procedure:	Down to you

www.tabitha.uk.com

At Tabitha you can see some covetable, not overpriced but unusual bags and accessories in a choice of coloured leathers and metallics. There's lots of choice, from the studded Angel Bag to the chic Go Less Lightly bag with loads of pockets and buckles. My favourite is the Lost Weekend Bag, simply irresistible in ice white glazed leather. To order you need to complete the online form and email it back to them.

Site Usability: ★★★★	Based:	UK
Product Range: ★★★	Express Delivery Option? (UK)	No
Price Range: Medium	Gift Wrapping Option?	No
Delivery Area: Worldwide	Returns Procedure:	Down to you

Bag a Bargain

Sites to Visit

www.blitzbags.co.uk

From the same family as Blitz Watches and Jewellery comes the new website Blitz Bags, where you can buy handbags and accessories by Chloe, Chanel, Burberry, Dior, D&G, Fendi, Prada and more. There's usually a good selection which is constantly changing and the website is extremely easy to use.

Site Usability:	★★★★	Based:	UK
Product Range:	★★★★	Express Delivery Option? (UK)	Yes
Price Range:	Luxury/Medium	Gift Wrapping Option?	Yes
Delivery Area:	EU	Returns Procedure:	Down to you

www.branded.net

Handbags, wallets and purses by Gucci, Christian Dior, Fendi, Dolce & Gabbana and Prada are on offer here, all at discounted prices and from recent seasons' collections. The site is based in London and will ship all over the world. You always have to be careful when buying discounted designer labels in case they're not the real thing; however, there are a number of resellers at present, particularly in Italy, which are able to sell on ends of lines and overstocks of real designer products and these are what you'll find here.

Site Usability:	★★★★	Based:	UK
Product Range:	★★★★	Express Delivery Option? (UK)	No
Price Range:	Luxury/Medium	Gift Wrapping Option?	Yes
Delivery Area:	Worldwide	Returns Procedure:	Down to you

www.handbagcrush.co.uk

This company buys from designer resellers to offer you authentic handbags and accessories from designers such as Gucci, Prada, Fendi and Versace. It clearly states the RRP (which I always suggest you should check if you can), plus the discount on offer, and there are detailed pictures and lots of information. Worth having a look.

Site Usability: ★★★★	Based:	UK
Product Range: ★★★★	Express Delivery Option? (UK)	Yes
Price Range: Luxury/Medium	Gift Wrapping Option?	No
Delivery Area: Worldwide	Returns Procedure:	Down to you

www.yoox.com

At Yoox you'll find end-of-season designer pieces at good discounts – usually 50% off the designer's original price. It's a huge site and there are lots of designer clothes and accessories, so it's best to have some sort of idea of what you're looking for before you start. Click on your favourite designer, search for a specific type of item and you're away.

Site Usability: ★★★★★	Based:	USA but use UK website
Product Range: ★★★★★	Express Delivery Option? (UK)	Yes
Price Range: Luxury/Medium	Gift Wrapping Option?	Yes
Delivery Area: Worldwide, but click on the country for delivery to see that range	Returns Procedure:	Free, but there's a $5 restocking fee per item

Chapter 8

Kick Your Heels

Luxury Heels   Affordable Heels

Ok, I'll admit it, this is another area I'm truly dedicated to. There are several designer shoe shops here I go through longingly at the start of each season, only to be distracted with children shopping dilemmas – rugby boots, new uniform, kit for uni... I'm sure you know what I mean – not to mention car problems, fridge problems and dog problems: the list is endless.

Anyway, back to shoes and less moaning. Like handbags, there are wonderful premium-brand shoes online from designers such as Jimmy Choo, Gina, Emma Hope and Christian Louboutin where you're going to be paying upwards of £250 a pair (if you're lucky).

There are also excellent, lower-priced collections at places like vivaladiva.com, Pantalon Chameleon and Boden. If it's a well-priced pair of chic killer heels you're after, you could go to Moda in Pelle, Kurt Geiger or Faith, for example. You can see everything clearly online, delivery is fast and they're right up with the trends (although you can take it as far as you like – no need to buy those 9cm platforms unless you really want to).

Like handbags, shoes say so much about you. You may not be aware how much your whole look is affected by what you're wearing on your feet, but everyone else is, so buy something reasonably modern and definitely chic, make sure that, if you're wearing trousers, they're the right length and don't wear *anything* that isn't – too-short trousers are one of my personal hates, they look so old fashioned – then take a look at yourself in the mirror and admire the difference.

Just in case you're in doubt, here are the size conversions for UK, European and US women's shoes:

Women's shoe size conversions										
UK	3.5	4	4.5	5	5.5	6	6.5	7	7.5	8	8.5
EU	36.5	37	37.5	38	38.5	39	40	41	42	43	43.5
US	6	6.5	7	7.5	8	8.5	9	9.5	10	10.5	11

Luxury Heels

Sites to Visit

www.gina.com

Gina was established in 1954 and named after Gina Lollobridgida. Now it's run by the three Kurdash brothers (the sons of the founder, Mehmet Kurdash), who continue to design exquisite shoes, so if you want the couture look and a seriously special pair, click no further. Here you'll find a truly wonderful collection of beautiful, sexy shoes in the softest leather and with out-to-lunch and dinner heels. There's a price to match as you would expect, but the shoes are definitely worth it and they'll last a long time. There's also a small selection of handbags.

Site Usability:	★★★★	Based:	UK
Product Range:	★★★★	Express Delivery Option? (UK)	No
Price Range:	Luxury	Gift Wrapping Option?	No
Delivery Area:	Worldwide	Returns Procedure:	Down to you

www.jimmychoo.com

Needless to say, the new Jimmy Choo website is beautifully and provocatively designed and makes you want to browse right through, even though the prices are quite frightening in most cases, to say the least. This is always a covetable collection, including diamante-encrusted sandals, killer-heel peep-toe slides, gorgeous boots and wonderful, right-on-trend handbags.

Site Usability:	★★★★★	Based:	UK
Product Range:	★★★★★	Express Delivery Option? (UK)	Yes
Price Range:	Luxury	Gift Wrapping Option?	Automatic
Delivery Area:	Worldwide	Returns Procedure:	Down to you

Also visit these websites for luxury heels:

Website address	You'll find them in:
www.brownsfashion.com	Luxury Fashion Brands Jill Sander Lanvin Christian Louboutin Salvatore Ferragamo Dries van Noten Dolce & Gabbana
www.net-a-porter.com	Luxury Fashion Brands Miu Miu Chloe Christian Louboutin Jimmy Choo Missoni Roberto Cavalli
www.paulsmith.co.uk	Luxury Fashion Brands
www.lineafashion.com	Luxury Fashion Brands Tod's Cesare Paciotti Missoni
www.gucci.com	Handbag Temptation/The A List
www.vivaladiva.com	Kick Your Heels/ Affordable Heels Lulu Guinness Beatrix Ong Christian Dior Sergio Rossi

Affordable Heels

Sites to Visit

www.bucklesandbows.co.uk

If you're considering investing in a pair of boots but you have the common problem of most boots being too tight on the calf, have a look at this extremely quick website. First measure the widest part of your calf, then click on the boots you like and check which size you should take. Prices are around £100. They offer next-day delivery and they'll ship worldwide.

Site Usability:	★★★★★	Based:	UK
Product Range:	★★★	Express Delivery Option? (UK)	Yes
Price Range:	Medium	Gift Wrapping Option?	No
Delivery Area:	Worldwide	Returns Procedure:	Down to you

www.dune.co.uk

Here you can buy from a range of trendy, affordable and stylish shoes and accessories, including glitzy sandals, dressy pumps and flats, modern casual shoes and ballerinas and excellent boots. As well as all of this there are handbags, belts and sunglasses. The website is well photographed and easy to use and provided you place your order before 10am you'll receive it the next day.

Site Usability:	★★★★	Based:	UK
Product Range:	★★★	Express Delivery Option? (UK)	Yes
Price Range:	Medium/Very Good Value	Gift Wrapping Option?	No
Delivery Area:	UK	Returns Procedure:	Down to you

www.duoboots.com

If you've ever (like me) gone into a shoe shop, discovered the perfect pair of boots and found that the zip won't do up to the top, you'll welcome this website. Duo Boots offers 21 calf sizes, from 30cm to 50cm. You just select your style and colour from the wide range, check out the pictures, which are excellent, then input your normal shoe size and calf measurement.

Site Usability:	★★★★★	Based:	UK
Product Range:	★★★★	Express Delivery Option? (UK)	Yes
Price Range:	Medium	Gift Wrapping Option?	No
Delivery Area:	Worldwide	Returns Procedure:	Down to you

www.faith.co.uk

In 1964 Samuel Faith established Faith shoes with the aim of combining style and affordability and he seems to have succeeded. You'll discover some extremely modern styles here plus some that are far more classic, and they're all at very reasonable prices. Faith Solo is the most avant-garde part of the collection and there are also some well-priced fun leather handbags.

Site Usability:	★★★★	Based:	UK
Product Range:	★★★	Express Delivery Option? (UK)	No
Price Range:	Very Good Value	Gift Wrapping Option?	No
Delivery Area:	UK	Returns Procedure:	Down to you

www.floydshoes.co.uk

You won't find this collection of well-priced shoes in any retail outlets (at least not at the time of writing) as they're currently offered only on this website and at regional fairs. All the shoes here are designed by Janice Floyd, who created her company in 2002 with the idea of producing distinctive, fashionable and elegant but fun shoes at an affordable price. There's also a small range of handbags in a selection of great colours.

Site Usability:	★★★★	Based:	UK
Product Range:	★★★	Express Delivery Option? (UK)	No
Price Range:	Medium	Gift Wrapping Option?	No
Delivery Area:	Worldwide	Returns Procedure:	Down to you

www.frenchsole.com

If you've been looking for the perfect ballet flat to update your spring/summer or autumn/winter wardrobe, you need search no more. French Sole is well known for offering a wide range of styles, from the classic two-tone pump to this season's must-have animal print and metallic versions and each season it brings out new styles. It also offers high-quality driving shoes and travel slippers.

Site Usability:	★★★★	Based:	UK
Product Range:	★★★	Express Delivery Option? (UK)	No
Price Range:	Medium	Gift Wrapping Option?	No
Delivery Area:	Worldwide	Returns Procedure:	Down to you

www.helenbateman.com

Winner at the 2002 Footwear Awards for Customer Service, this Edinburgh-based shoe designer offers a pretty and unusual selection of shoes for all occasions. There's a great deal of choice, from beaded Shantung silk evening shoes and stylish sandals to funky espadrilles in a range of colours. One of the great advantages of ordering shoes here is the amount of information on each style, from fit to fabric and heel height, plus different views.

Site Usability:	★★★★★	Express Delivery Option? (UK)	Yes
Product Range:	★★★★	Gift Wrapping Option?	No
Price Range:	Medium	Returns Procedure:	Down to you
Delivery Area:	Worldwide		

www.kurtgeiger.com

Browse the Kurt Geiger online store for shoes and accessories from many of your favourite designers, including Kurt Geiger, Marc Jacobs, KG, Gina and Carvela. With new arrivals daily, you can find styles ranging from young contemporary to modern classic, with the site also featuring a sale area. It currently delivers to the British Isles and ROI and offers a next-day service.

Site Usability:	★★★★★	Express Delivery Option? (UK)	Yes
Product Range:	★★★★	Gift Wrapping Option?	No
Price Range:	Luxury/Medium/Very Good Value	Returns Procedure:	Down to you
Delivery Area:	UK		

www.modainpelle.com

Moda in Pelle offers an excellent range of fashionable and well-priced shoes, boots and bags, including trendy daytime bags and shoes and a very good evening selection (check out the diamante sandals). They aim themselves at a young, high street audience (think River Island, Jane Norman and Morgan), but with their up-to-the-minute styling have a much wider appeal. Their new website allows you to see every detail of the shoes on offer and is well worth a look round.

Site Usability:	★★★★	Express Delivery Option? (UK)	No
Product Range:	★★★★	Gift Wrapping Option?	No
Price Range:	Very Good Value	Returns Procedure:	Down to you
Delivery Area:	UK		

www.plusinboots.co.uk

Here you'll find boots at price levels from £50 to about £200, plus calf measurements from 35cm to 46cm. You need to take a look at the measuring guide as the site offers both its own boots and those made by other manufacturers. There are some modern and some classic styles to choose from, plus a small range of shoes.

Site Usability:	★★★	Express Delivery Option? (UK)	Yes, worldwide
Product Range:	★★★	Gift Wrapping Option?	Yes
Price Range:	Medium/Very Good Value	Returns Procedure:	Down to you
Delivery Area:	Worldwide		

www.prettyballerinas.com

Established in 1918 to make ballet shoes, Pretty Ballerinas offers a wide selection of colours and prints, including animal prints (zebra, leopard or tiger), metallics, sequins, prints (such as purple butterflies) and fuchsia, green or blue satin. When you look at the site you need to be aware that all the prices are in euros, so you'll need to do the conversion to pounds, dollars or whatever currency you want to buy in.

Site Usability:	★★★★	Based:	UK
Product Range:	★★★	Express Delivery Option? (UK)	No
Price Range:	Medium	Gift Wrapping Option?	No
Delivery Area:	Worldwide	Returns Procedure:	Down to you.

www.schuhstore.co.uk

At schuhstore.co.uk there are lots of shoes from a wide choice of labels at very good prices. There are always some very modern styles and some may be overly colourful for you, but there's such a large range you'll surely discover something to suit. You can select from each range (boots, for example) whether you want high heel, mid heel, low heel or flat and the zoom feature allows you to get really close up to each product. You can also search by brand, style, price and what's new. The site offers a 365-day returns policy for shoes sent back in perfect condition.

Site Usability:	★★★★	Based:	UK
Product Range:	★★★★★	Express Delivery Option? (UK)	No
Price Range:	Medium/Very Good Value	Gift Wrapping Option?	No
Delivery Area:	UK	Returns Procedure:	Down to you

www.scorahpattullo.com

If your taste is for the very (I mean very) high heeled and extremely modern, then come and take a look round Scorah Pattullo where the latest collections are just waiting to be delivered to you by high-speed courier anywhere in the world. The emphasis is on sexy, modern styling, from flats and sandals to dressy heels, so if you're looking for something new this season you may well find it here.

Site Usability:	★★★★	Based:	UK
Product Range:	★★★	Express Delivery Option? (UK)	No
Price Range:	Luxury	Gift Wrapping Option?	No
Delivery Area:	Worldwide	Returns Procedure:	Down to you

www.shellys.co.uk

Here are the modern (think extremely, in some cases), well-priced shoes to go with your next buy from Miss Selfridge, Top Shop or River Island. It's a clear website and they tell you straight away what's leather and what's not and what's available right now. If you're into the latest 'Babe' platform slingback sandal with mega heels, you'll love it here.

Site Usability:	★★★★	Based:	UK
Product Range:	★★★★	Express Delivery Option? (UK)	No
Price Range:	Medium/Very Good Value	Gift Wrapping Option?	No
Delivery Area:	UK	Returns Procedure:	Down to you

www.ugsandkisses.co.uk

If you're a fan of the extraordinarily comfortable and popular Ugg boot from Australia, you'll love this website, which offers the full range of Ugg Australia boots including the Classic short and tall versions and a choice of colours. It also sells baby Uggs, Snow Joggers, Love from Australia, My Sweet Feet, Simple footwear and its own Ugs & Kisses brand. There's lots of information on how to care for your Uggs, including Ugg Shampoo which you can order. Delivery is free in the UK on orders over £45.

Site Usability:	★★★★★	Based:	UK
Product Range:	★★★	Express Delivery Option? (UK)	No
Price Range:	Medium	Gift Wrapping Option?	No
Delivery Area:	Worldwide	Returns Procedure:	Down to you

www.vivaladiva.com

This is an online store that's growing like topsy, with more and more styles and designers being added each season. You'll find couture shoes and boots by Beatrix Ong, Cavalli, Sergio Rossi and Lulu Guinness, the Boutique collection with names such as Amira and Carvela, plus much less expensive ranges like Schuh, Moda in Pelle and Converse. It's a fun website with a lot of attitude. The shoes are displayed very clearly and range from £25 to £300. Watch out for new designers being included.

Site Usability:	★★★★★	Express Delivery Option? (UK)	Yes
Product Range:	★★★★★	Gift Wrapping Option?	Yes/Automatic
Price Range:	Luxury/Medium/Very Good Value	Returns Procedure:	Free of charge by courier or Royal Mail
Delivery Area:	UK		

Chapter 9

Lingerie

D o you want lacy, sexy, sporty, strapless, full cup, underwired or not, balconette, plunge or backless (yes, really)? Thongs, French knickers, 'boy shorts', briefs, minis or shapewear? Hot pink, lime green, orange, chocolate, mocha, purple or printed with hearts, not to mention basics such as black, white, nude or ivory?

You've probably guessed – I must spend a great deal of time on lingerie websites to be able to come out with a list like this. Yes, I do, but the ranges online are so mindblowing it's not difficult. Take Figleaves, for example, which surely offers the widest selection online of just about everything lingerie related and combines this with a truly excellent service. Search by style, colour, size and type of bra and you'll still have lots of options.

If you want a more intimate, boutique-style shopping experience, go to some of the smaller retailers where you won't be bombarded by quite so much choice but where the brands and service are still very good.

Needless to say, one of the best things about being able to buy lingerie online is that you don't have to strip off in a draughty, maybe badly curtained changing room when you're not feeling your most elegant. Not only can you try on everything at home, the service is so good at most of the websites below that you can probably have your order tomorrow. Now what could be better than that?

Sites to Visit

www.agentprovocateur.com

Joseph Corre and Serena Rees opened the first Agent Provocateur shop in December 1994 and have never looked back. The look is overt and sexy and you'll find just that on their extremely unusual website, where their gorgeous lingerie is displayed with attitude on the most perfect bodies. Don't come here if you're looking for something in a size larger than a 36E or if you want a website where ordering is easy – it's not, until you've got used to it. Do come here if you love their products and don't want to have to go out to find them.

Site Usability:	★★★	Based:	UK
Product Range:	★★★★	Express Delivery Option? (UK)	Yes
Price Range:	Luxury/Medium	Gift Wrapping Option?	No, but packaging is very attractive
Delivery Area:	Worldwide	Returns Procedure:	Down to you

www.barenecessities.co.uk

An excellent site offering a range of lingerie and swimwear from brands such as Prima Donna, Marie Jo, Aubade, Lejaby, Felina, Gottex, Maryan, Fantasie/Freya, Seaspray and Anita. It stocks all items where possible with a size range from A to H. It also stocks mastectomy lingerie and swimwear. The company is excellent on service so give them a call if you want to ask them any questions.

Site Usability:	★★★★	Based:	UK
Product Range:	★★★★	Express Delivery Option? (UK)	Yes
Price Range:	Medium	Gift Wrapping Option?	Yes
Delivery Area:	Worldwide	Returns Procedure:	Down to you

www.belladinotte.com

This is a smiley website, with smiley models showing pretty nightwear, lingerie and tops. Italian silk and wool (washable) blend tops come in modern colours such as chocolate, aubergine and (of course) black. Lingerie is by Chantelle and Lejaby and their range of wool and silk thermals, sleeveless, short sleeved and long sleeved, frequently trimmed in lace and in white, ivory, black and, on occasion, garnet, could certainly be worn as tops.

Site Usability: ★★★★	Based:	UK
Product Range: ★★★★	Express Delivery Option? (UK)	Yes
Price Range: Medium	Gift Wrapping Option?	Yes
Delivery Area: Worldwide	Returns Procedure:	Down to you

www.bodas.co.uk

Much loved by glossy magazine fashion editors for its modern, minimal style, at Bodas you won't find loads of lace or extra details but just chic, seam-free and form-fitting lingerie in a choice of colours. Beautifully photographed, the range includes briefs, camisoles, vests, crop tops and a small choice of swimwear in season. Just a word of warning – you won't find much beyond a 36D, so if you're looking for a larger size this is not the place for you.

Site Usability: ★★★★★	Based:	UK
Product Range: ★★★	Express Delivery Option? (UK)	Yes
Price Range: Medium	Gift Wrapping Option?	No
Delivery Area: Worldwide	Returns Procedure:	Down to you

www.bonsoirbypost.com

Here's pretty nightwear from Bonsoir by Post, ranging from soft, dreamy cotton to Italian lace and pure silk in a range of colours. Be warned though – if your taste is for black or neutral you won't find much of it here. Colours tend to be more ash, heather, pale blue and white. There's also a small range of loungewear, including yoga pants, fluffy towels and bath robes, plus scented candles, mules, beaded slippers and bedsocks.

Site Usability: ★★★★	Based:	UK
Product Range: ★★★★	Express Delivery Option? (UK)	Yes
Price Range: Medium/Very Good Value	Gift Wrapping Option?	Yes
Delivery Area: Worldwide	Returns Procedure:	Down to you

www.bravissimo.com

Bravissimo was started to fill the niche in the market created by those who aren't looking for lingerie or swimwear in minute sizes. It offers a wide selection of lingerie in D to JJ cup, plus bra-sized swimwear in D to J cup, making it the essential site for the fuller figure. You'll find strappy tops and sports bras and fitting advice as well. The service is excellent and if you have any queries you can email them and they'll come back to you immediately. They'll ship to you speedily anywhere.

Site Usability:	★★★★★	Based:	UK
Product Range:	★★★★	Express Delivery Option? (UK)	Yes, but you need to call them
Price Range:	Medium	Gift Wrapping Option?	No
Delivery Area:	Worldwide	Returns Procedure:	Free

www.cku.com

This is the website for Calvin Klein's modern, minimal range of underwear and I should tell you right now that if you're anything larger than a D (or in a very few styles a DD) cup you should move on fast. If you're within the size range you'll probably find the collection of beautiful, sexy and not over-priced lingerie and basics quite irresistible. There are separate websites for overseas orders so you need to check whether they deliver to you.

Site Usability:	★★★★★	Based:	UK
Product Range:	★★★	Express Delivery Option? (UK)	No
Price Range:	Medium	Gift Wrapping Option?	No
Delivery Area:	Worldwide using their country-specific sites	Returns Procedure:	Free

www.contessa.org.uk

Contessa has a superb selection of bras and briefs in every colourway and style you can think of. You can choose by brand, style, size or colour, or to make matters even easier just click on your size on the home page and everything in stock can be viewed straight away. The emphasis here is very much on price and you will frequently find some excellent offers. They'll ship worldwide and gift wrap your order as well.

Site Usability:	★★★★★	Based:	UK
Product Range:	★★★★	Express Delivery Option? (UK)	Yes
Price Range:	Medium/Very Good Value	Gift Wrapping Option?	Yes
Delivery Area:	Worldwide	Returns Procedure:	Down to you

www.elingerie.uk.net

This is a calm, well-photographed and easy-to-navigate website, offering brands such as Rigby and Peller, Chantelle, Janet Reger, Huit, Freya, Splendour, Panache and lots more. The products are all easy to see, although I suggest you search for your size rather than pick on a range and find it's not available for you. There's also lots of help for men buying lingerie as gifts, plus a gift wrap service.

Site Usability:	★★★★	Based:	UK
Product Range:	★★★★	Express Delivery Option? (UK)	No
Price Range:	Luxury/Medium	Gift Wrapping Option?	Yes
Delivery Area:	Worldwide	Returns Procedure:	Down to you

www.elishalauren.co.uk

Sizing here is from AA to J and you'll find a full range, including everyday bras, smooth styles, shapewear, bridal lingerie, basques and corsets, plus maternity and sports bras. Ranges stocked are Ballet, Charnos, Panache, Naturana, Braza, Nubra and Ultimo. So if you want to take a look around on a website that is calm and easy to navigate and order from, try this one. They also offer some very good discounts from time to time.

Site Usability:	★★★★	Based:	UK
Product Range:	★★★	Express Delivery Option? (UK)	No
Price Range:	Luxury/Medium	Gift Wrapping Option?	No
Delivery Area:	Worldwide	Returns Procedure:	Down to you

www.figleaves.com

If you can't find it here, you may well not be able to find it anywhere else as this is definitely one of the best collections of lingerie, swimwear and sportswear available online. Almost every lingerie brand name is offered, from DKNY, Dolce & Gabbana and Janet Reger to Sloggi, Gossard and Wonderbra. And delivery is free throughout the world. All sizes are covered, from the very small to the very large, and there's a huge choice in just about every category.

Site Usability:	★★★★★	Based:	UK
Product Range:	★★★★★	Express Delivery Option? (UK)	Yes
Price Range:	Luxury/Medium/Very Good Value	Gift Wrapping Option?	Yes
Delivery Area:	Worldwide	Returns Procedure:	Free in the UK

www.glamonweb.co.uk

This is quite an unusual website with some slightly strange translations from the Italian (probably due to the fact that they're electronic, rather than done by real people), offering lingerie, hosiery and nightwear by La Perla, Marvel and Malizia. Here's beautiful and luxurious lingerie as you would expect with prices to match and I would suggest that you make sure that you know your La Perla size before you order as the sizing is not standard. If in doubt you can email or call the customer service team.

Site Usability:	★★★★	Based:	UK
Product Range:	★★★★	Express Delivery Option? (UK)	Yes
Price Range:	Luxury/Medium	Gift Wrapping Option?	No
Delivery Area:	Europe	Returns Procedure:	Down to you

www.glamorousamorous.com

You'll find some quite different lingerie here – think animal print and scarlet trim from Fifi Chachnil, sequin and silk camisoles from Guia La Bruna and a lace bustier and thong from Bacirubati and you'll get the idea. Extremely glam in other words. There's a Lingerie and Gift Guide with help for men buying presents and everything arrives in a silk organza bag, wrapped in tissue paper scented with Provençal lavender. UK mainland delivery is free.

Site Usability:	★★★★★	Based:	UK
Product Range:	★★★★	Express Delivery Option? (UK)	Yes
Price Range:	Luxury/Medium	Gift Wrapping Option?	Yes
Delivery Area:	Worldwide	Returns Procedure:	Down to you

www.heavenlybodice.com

This lingerie website is particularly good for gifts and particularly from him to her. You can choose from a wide range of designers, from Charnos and Warners to Naughty Janet and Shirley of Hollywood. There's an excellent selection of bridal lingerie, a separate section for larger sizes, swimwear by Fantasie, Panache and Freya, and gifts by price band or in the 'Naughty' category. There's also a gift guide specifically for men.

Site Usability:	★★★★	Based:	UK
Product Range:	★★★★	Express Delivery Option? (UK)	No
Price Range:	Luxury/Medium	Gift Wrapping Option?	Yes
Delivery Area:	Worldwide	Returns Procedure:	Down to you

www.hush-uk.com

Hush has a well-designed and beautifully photographed website where there are lots of clothes for going to sleep in or just for lounging around – nightdresses, pyjamas and gowns, vest tops, T-shirts and sloppy joes, sheepskin slippers and also kaftans and sarongs for the beach. In the gift ideas section you can combine various items to be wrapped up together and there are gift vouchers as well.

Site Usability: ★★★★	Based:	UK
Product Range: ★★★★	Express Delivery Option? (UK)	Yes
Price Range: Medium	Gift Wrapping Option?	Yes
Delivery Area: Worldwide	Returns Procedure:	Down to you

www.janetreger.co.uk

On Janet Reger's beautiful, dark website, there's the most gorgeous selection of lingerie, where the prices are definitely not for the faint-hearted. Once you've picked the style you like you can immediately see all the other items in the range, plus colourways and size options (don't expect large sizes here). This brand is about luxe and glamour, so be prepared to spend a small fortune – but on absolutely wonderful quality and style.

Site Usability: ★★★★★	Based:	UK
Product Range: ★★★★	Express Delivery Option? (UK)	Yes
Price Range: Luxury	Gift Wrapping Option?	Yes
Delivery Area: Worldwide	Returns Procedure:	Down to you

www.ladybarbarella.com

Specialising in exclusive vintage pieces, decadent silks and burlesque styles, plus designs aimed at the many of us who can't fit into a 32B, at Lady Barbarella you can browse through a delightful selection of less available designers including Damaris Evans, Emma Benham, Frankly Darling, FleurT, Spoylt and Yes Master, plus many more. This is a prettily and cleverly designed website, well worth a look if you like something a bit different.

Site Usability: ★★★★	Based:	UK
Product Range: ★★★	Express Delivery Option? (UK)	Yes
Price Range: Medium	Gift Wrapping Option?	Yes
Delivery Area: Worldwide	Returns Procedure:	Down to you

www.lasenza.co.uk

La Senza is an own-brand lingerie retailer originally based in Canada and also well established in the United Kingdom. You'll find a large choice of lingerie and nightwear ranging from beautiful basics to seriously sexy styles, as well as bra accessories. The site is clear and easy to use. It's great to know that retailers are actually catering for those who want something larger than a C cup as sizes go from 30A to 38F. Yes, you can buy colours, plunge bras and diamante-trimmed bras even if you're a DD or above and you'll also find cleavage enhancers, extra bra straps and strap extenders here.

Site Usability:	★★★★★	Based:	UK
Product Range:	★★★★★	Express Delivery Option? (UK)	Yes
Price Range:	Very Good Value	Gift Wrapping Option?	Yes
Delivery Area:	Worldwide	Returns Procedure:	Down to you

www.lingerie-company.co.uk

Based in Hinckley, Leicestershire, this retailer offers lingerie by a multitude of designers, including Aubade, Lejaby, Chantelle, Charnos, Fantasie, Passionata, Panache and Triumph. There is also swimwear by Aubade, Freya and Fantasie. A discount of 10% is automatically taken off the retail price on all orders. It is a simply designed website with an excellent search facility, so you can pick exactly what you are looking for. Expect a high level of personal service and quick delivery.

Site Usability:	★★★★	Based:	UK
Product Range:	★★★★	Express Delivery Option? (UK)	Yes – call
Price Range:	Medium	Gift Wrapping Option?	No
Delivery Area:	Worldwide	Returns Procedure:	Down to you

www.myla.com

Of course, chocolate body paint may be just what you're looking for, along with some of the more risque items offered on this sexy lingerie website (I'll say no more), but if what you're looking for is really beautiful feminine lingerie, just click into the lingerie section and ignore the rest. It also offers suspenders, thongs, feather boas, silk mules, camis and baby dolls. Sizing goes up to a 36E in some parts of the range.

Site Usability: ★★★★	Based:	UK
Product Range: ★★★	Express Delivery Option? (UK)	Yes
Price Range: Luxury/Medium	Gift Wrapping Option?	No
Delivery Area: Worldwide	Returns Procedure:	Down to you

www.mytights.co.uk

My Tights has a modern and easy-to-use website, offering the hosiery brands of Aristoc, Charnos, Elbeo, Gerbe, La Perla, Levante and Pretty Polly, to name but a few, plus maternity tights by Spanx and Trasparenze. So whether you want footless or fishnet tights and stockings, support tights, shapewear, knee highs or suspenders, you'll find it all here. Provided you order before 3pm you'll probably get it the next day.

Site Usability: ★★★★★	Based:	UK
Product Range: ★★★★	Express Delivery Option? (UK)	Yes
Price Range: Luxury/Medium	Gift Wrapping Option?	No
Delivery Area: Worldwide	Returns Procedure:	Down to you

www.rigbyandpeller.com

You may know the shop just round the side of Harrods where you can be properly fitted for your next bra and choose from a chic selection of lingerie. If you can't get to Knightsbridge, however, you can now see the range on the website, which offers a wide range of brands such as Aubade, Lejaby, La Perla, plus Rigby & Peller's own. Service is superb and they endeavour to despatch all orders within 48 hours, to anywhere in the world.

Site Usability: ★★★★	Based:	UK
Product Range: ★★★★	Express Delivery Option? (UK)	Yes
Price Range: Luxury/Medium	Gift Wrapping Option?	Yes
Delivery Area: Worldwide	Returns Procedure:	Down to you

www.sassyandrose.co.uk

If you're a collector of gorgeous nightwear (and definitely one of those who likes to look glam when she goes to bed rather than the novelty T-shirt kind), you should have a browse here. There is a colourful range of camisoles, chemises, nightdresses, kaftans and pjs in high-quality but well-priced silk and embroidered cotton. If you want delivery outside the

UK you need to call them and they aim to ship everything within two days.

Site Usability:	★★★	Based:	UK
Product Range:	★★★	Express Delivery Option? (UK)	No
Price Range:	Medium	Gift Wrapping Option?	No
Delivery Area:	Worldwide	Returns Procedure:	Down to you

www.silkstorm.com

The next time you're looking for something out of the ordinary, take a look around Silk Storm, an online lingerie boutique offering luxury French and Italian brands with collections including Aubade, Valery, Argentovivo, Cotton Club and Barbara. Everything is beautifully photographed and the sizing help is excellent, although don't expect anything to go much above a 36D. The site is aimed very much at men buying lingerie for their ladies, with sexy pictures and gorgeous gift wrapping.

Site Usability:	★★★★	Based:	UK
Product Range:	★★★	Express Delivery Option? (UK)	Yes
Price Range:	Medium	Gift Wrapping Option?	Yes
Delivery Area:	Worldwide	Returns Procedure:	Down to you

www.sophieandgrace.co.uk

Sophie and Grace offers top-quality lingerie, nightwear and swimwear, including the bridal ranges of Honeymoon Pearls and Verde Veronica where you'll find garters, bras and briefs, basques and nightgowns with touches such as embroidered lace and pearl straps. This is a very different and luxurious range of lingerie and you'll no doubt want some to take away on honeymoon as well. Delivery is free and everything is automatically tissue wrapped and gift boxed.

Site Usability:	★★★★	Based:	UK
Product Range:	★★★	Express Delivery Option? (UK)	Yes
Price Range:	Luxury/Medium	Gift Wrapping Option?	Yes
Delivery Area:	UK; call them for overseas	Returns Procedure:	Down to you

www.tightsplease.co.uk

Whether you want fishnets and crochet tights, bright colours, knee highs, stay-ups, stockings or footsies, you'll find them all here, plus leg warmers, socks and flight socks, maternity and bridal hosiery. This website really caters for all your hosiery needs and with names such as Aristoc, Pretty Polly and Charnos on offer, you should never run out again. As an extra benefit delivery is free in the UK and takes only 1 to 2 days.

Site Usability:	★★★★★	Based:	UK
Product Range:	★★★★★	Express Delivery Option? (UK)	Automatic
Price Range:	Luxury/Medium	Gift Wrapping Option?	No
Delivery Area:	Worldwide	Returns Procedure:	Free

www.vollers-corsets.com

This is quite simply an amazing collection of corsets, both for underwear and outerwear. The sexy and feminine designs include ruched velvet, satin, lace, leather, beaded brocade, gold and silver fabric, moire and tartan, with flower, feather, lace and velvet trims. Sizes go from an 18 to 38 waist or you can have a corset specially made for you. There are corsets perfect for weddings and special occasions and most are available in a range of colours.

Site Usability:	★★★★★	Based:	UK
Product Range:	★★★★★	Express Delivery Option? (UK)	Yes
Price Range:	Luxury/Medium	Gift Wrapping Option?	No
Delivery Area:	Worldwide	Returns Procedure:	Down to you

www.wolfordboutiquelondon.com

Wolford is world famous for its top-quality hosiery, bodies, tops and lingerie and you can now purchase its collection online, through its London South Molton Street shop. The range includes sexy, seasonally inspired pieces, beautifully photographed, and is being updated all the time. Wolford is definitely not the cheapest for any part of the range, but everything is of the highest quality and well worth an investment.

Site Usability:	★★★★	Based:	UK
Product Range:	★★★★★	Express Delivery Option? (UK)	Yes
Price Range:	Luxury	Gift Wrapping Option?	No
Delivery Area:	Worldwide	Returns Procedure:	Down to you

Also check out these websites for lingerie and swimwear:

Website address	**You'll find it in:**
www.victoriassecret.com	Shop America

Chapter 10

Resortwear Store

I've called this 'resortwear' rather than 'swimwear' as there are so many products available which are perfect for taking away on holiday along with that teeny-weeny bikini. Wraps, tops and the essential cover-it-all kaftan, espadrilles and flip flops, beach bags, printed towels, plus just about everything you can think of other than the bucket and spade is available here.

As with lingerie, the great joy here is that you can try on everything at home. Personally, I can't think of anything much worse than trying on swimwear in a shop when you aren't totally happy with the way you look/haven't had time to get that fake tan on/haven't spent enough time at the gym, let alone after going out for lunch. Order it online and try it on at home so you can have your resortwear ready, accessorised and waiting to be packed.

My advice here also is to buy early. It always horrifies me that when I'm ready to invest, some of the best pieces have already gone, even if I'm ordering well before what I consider to be the main holiday season. Start taking a look in February and March when the new stock comes in and if you can, buy then: you won't regret it. Happy holidays.

Sites to Visit

www.anula.co.uk

Anula has done the hard work for you when you're looking for all-year-round resortwear by putting together a range of swimsuits and bikinis with matching and contrasting kaftans, flip flops, beach bags, baskets and jewellery. This isn't a huge selection, but there are some stylish pieces which work well together.

Site Usability:	★★★★	Based:	UK
Product Range:	★★★	Express Delivery Option? (UK)	Yes
Price Range:	Medium	Gift Wrapping Option?	No
Delivery Area:	Worldwide	Returns Procedure:	Down to you

www.elizabethhurley.com

You may well have read in the press about the Elizabeth Hurley Beach collection and here it is online. There's sexy, stylish swimwear, chic kaftans, dresses and tops and a choice of knitwear and T-shirts. Then there are the totes, sarongs and towels to help complete the look. It's an expensive range, but you'll almost certainly want something. There's adorable swimwear for kids as well.

Site Usability:	★★★★	Based:	UK
Product Range:	★★★	Express Delivery Option? (UK)	No
Price Range:	Luxury	Gift Wrapping Option?	No
Delivery Area:	Worldwide	Returns Procedure:	Down to you

www.espadrillesetc.com

Whether or not you're an espadrilles fan, if you're going on holiday you really should take a look at this summer shoe website, where there's every colour, fabric and style you can think of, including soft-coloured suede and brightly coloured fabric espadrilles, plus some pretty sandals, brightly coloured beach bags and totes and children's espadrilles. They'll be happy to ship to you anywhere in the world and all the espadrilles are despatched in bright, colourful and transparent shoe bags.

Site Usability:	★★★★	Based:	Spain
Product Range:	★★★	Express Delivery Option? (UK)	No
Price Range:	Medium/Very Good Value	Gift Wrapping Option?	No
Delivery Area:	Worldwide	Returns Procedure:	Down to you

www.heidiklein.com

Heidi Klein offers beautiful holidaywear all the year round. The range includes chic bikinis and one-piece swimsuits, pretty and flattering kaftans, dresses and sarongs, plus all the accessories you could need for your next trip away to the sun (flip flops, hats, bags and more). The site offers a same-day delivery service in London and express delivery throughout the UK.

Site Usability:	★★★★	Based:	UK
Product Range:	★★★	Express Delivery Option? (UK)	Yes
Price Range:	Luxury/Medium	Gift Wrapping Option?	Yes
Delivery Area:	Worldwide	Returns Procedure:	Down to you

www.kikoy.com

For holidays and trips abroad you'll definitely want to know about this colourful website, offering fine cotton and muslin shorts, kaftans, cover-ups, trousers, hats and bags, plus beach towels. There are some excellent summer/holiday gift ideas here, but if you see something you want in a hurry give them a call to make sure that they have it in stock. If they do, they'll ship it to you for next-day delivery.

Site Usability:	★★★★	Based:	UK
Product Range:	★★★	Express Delivery Option? (UK)	Yes
Price Range:	Medium/Very Good Value	Gift Wrapping Option?	No
Delivery Area:	Worldwide	Returns Procedure:	Down to you

www.sand-monkey.com

If you fancy a change from run-of-the-mill synthetic flip flops, you should take a look at this collection of Sandmonkeys – leather sandals with cute, stylish and funky finishes including beads and shells, originally designed on a luxury safari camp in Kenya's Masai Mara to be worn by the camp's clients. You can now have them sent to you anywhere in the world and by express delivery if you ask especially nicely.

Site Usability:	★★★★	Based:	UK
Product Range:	★★★	Express Delivery Option? (UK)	Yes, on request
Price Range:	Medium	Gift Wrapping Option?	No, but all items arrive in a pretty
Delivery Area:	Worldwide		Sand Bag

www.sexykaftans.com

There were so many kaftans around last summer that you're almost certainly aware by now that this is a must-have for summer holidays. Whether they're in fashion or not (and I'm sure they will be for a while), they're great for wearing over a swimsuit when you want something to give more cover than a sarong. Here's an excellent collection, long, short, colourful or neutral and beautifully embroidered. You'll definitely find yours here.

Site Usability:	★★★	Based:	UK
Product Range:	★★★	Express Delivery Option? (UK)	Yes
Price Range:	Medium	Gift Wrapping Option?	No
Delivery Area:	Worldwide	Returns Procedure:	Down to you

www.simplybeach.com

At last, a really great website devoted just to swimwear and including designer brands Melissa Obadash, Gideon Oberson and Wahine, with swimsuits and bikinis in all shapes and sizes. There's a wide range of accessories as well, including cover-ups, towels, beach bags and inflatables. Direct links through to the company's other website will take you to everything for scuba diving and snorkelling. Get ready for your next beach holiday here.

Site Usability:	★★★★★	Based:	UK
Product Range:	★★★★	Express Delivery Option? (UK)	Yes
Price Range:	Medium	Gift Wrapping Option?	No
Delivery Area:	Worldwide	Returns Procedure:	Down to you

www.splashhawaii.com

Not for the faint-hearted, this Hawaii-based site really only sells bikinis (and diddy ones at that), but there's a good choice, so if you fit into the bikini category it's well worth having a look. Billabong, Roxy and Tommy Hilfiger are just some of the brands available, plus US designers you may well not have heard of. They'll ship worldwide, but if you take my advice you'll make that special journey and go and collect yours.

Site Usability:	★★★★	Based:	Hawaii
Product Range:	★★★	Express Delivery Option? (UK)	No
Price Range:	Medium	Gift Wrapping Option?	No
Delivery Area:	Worldwide	Returns Procedure:	Down to you

Also check out these websites for resortwear:

Website address	**You'll find it in:**
www.barenecessities.co.uk	Lingerie
www.bravissimo.com	Lingerie
www.figleaves.com	Lingerie
www.heavenlybodice.com	Lingerie
www.sophieandgrace.co.uk	Lingerie
www.the-lingerie-company.co.uk	Lingerie
www.grahamkandiah.com	Shop America
www.swimwearboutique.com	Shop America
www.victoriassecret.com	Shop America

Chapter 11

Modern Maternity

Where do you go for great maternity clothes? Do you want to go searching around in the shops, where you'll find some horrifically expensive items you'll be wearing for only a few months? (Well ok, maybe a few times for a few months, but even so...) Or would you rather look at maternity retailers where you'll find something much less expensive that almost certainly won't make you feel good as you get larger and larger? (And I know about this.)

It very much depends of course on what sort of lifestyle you lead. If you work full time you'll probably need smart clothes to take you right up to just before you're due to produce. You may likewise do a lot of entertaining. Or you may live out in the country and need great jeans, tops and jackets and just a few smart things.

Now that there are so many maternity stores online you can find all the smart and casual clothes you could possibly need without any trouble, from the extremely glamorous to simple and comfortable, from the quite expensive to the very well priced.

A few years ago you had to search for great maternity shops and if you'd left it rather late (until you really couldn't make do with your current wardrobe), you'd have to go round the shops and exhaust yourself in the process. Now, of course, the beauty of the internet is that you can just sit back, click round and make all your choices online. With next-day delivery being an option at most of the sites, your new clothes will be with you almost immediately.

So enjoy these excellent websites, whose main aim in life is to make your life easy at a time when you certainly need it to be, and to help you look your best at the same time.

Sites to Visit

www.bjornandme.co.uk

For choice and value you'd find it hard to beat this website, where the clothes are divided up into sections such as Outdoor and Exercise wear, Formalwear, Petite, Tall and Plus Size. There's also swimwear and lingerie, so whether you're looking for a pair of soft white linen trousers or something for the Oscars, you'll almost certainly find it here – the evening and occasionwear is particularly good. This is international designer-styled maternity wear and a very good collection.

Site Usability:	★★★★	Based:	UK
Product Range:	★★★★	Express Delivery Option? (UK)	Yes
Price Range:	Medium/Very Good Value	Gift Wrapping Option?	No
Delivery Area:	Worldwide	Returns Procedure:	Down to you

www.bloomingmarvellous.co.uk

There's a wide choice of well-priced but good-quality clothes for expectant mothers and babies on this fun, colourful website. Whether you're looking for casual wear or city clothes you're sure to find something as it offers everything from sophisticated skirts and tops to lots of modern, casual options. You'll also find information on how to dress with a bump, plus a monthly newsletter to sign up to, so make this one of your first stops for browsing when you're expecting a baby.

Site Usability:	★★★★★	Based:	UK
Product Range:	★★★★★	Express Delivery Option? (UK)	No
Price Range:	Medium/Very Good Value	Gift Wrapping Option?	No
Delivery Area:	Worldwide	Returns Procedure:	Down to you

www.blossommotherandchild.com

Blossom caters for the fashion-conscious expectant mum, with a collection of glamorous dresses and separates which combine high-end fashion with comfort and functionality. You'll also find customised jeans by brands such as Rock and Republic and James. Blossom uses an assortment of luxurious fabrics such as silk-cashmere, voile and jersey and expands the collection continuously.

Site Usability:	★★★★	Based:	UK
Product Range:	★★★★	Express Delivery Option? (UK)	Yes
Price Range:	Luxury/Medium	Gift Wrapping Option?	No
Delivery Area:	Worldwide	Returns Procedure:	Down to you

www.bumpsmaternity.com

Bumps Maternity was established several years ago to offer stylish and out-of-the-ordinary maternity wear, from occasion dressing to casual and holiday. It's available online only and consists of a fun, well-photographed range. This is not a huge selection but definitely merits clicking through as most items are very good value and they'll ship all over the world. You can buy maternity lingerie and plus-size clothes as well and they've just launched a nursery product range.

Site Usability:	★★★★	Based:	UK
Product Range:	★★★	Express Delivery Option? (UK)	Yes
Price Range:	Medium	Gift Wrapping Option?	No
Delivery Area:	Worldwide	Returns Procedure:	Down to you

www.cravematernity.co.uk

This is a well-designed, friendly and clearly photographed website offering well-cut and versatile separates and dresses in good fabrics and at reasonable prices. You'll find tailoring, evening wear and casual separates all aimed at the busy woman who wants to carry on with her normal life and look smart throughout her pregnancy and afterwards. This is a website just for maternity clothes, so you're not going to be sidetracked by the children's clothes and accessories you'll find on so many other sites.

Site Usability:	★★★★	Based:	UK
Product Range:	★★★	Express Delivery Option? (UK)	No
Price Range:	Medium	Gift Wrapping Option?	No
Delivery Area:	Worldwide	Returns Procedure:	Down to you

www.formes.com

Formes is a French company offering beautifully styled 'designer' pregnancy wear and selling all over the world. You won't find the full collection here, just an edited range, but it's well worth looking through. Unlike a lot of maternity shops you'll find all the information you could possibly want, from complete product detailing to fabric content and full measurements, plus very clear pictures.

Site Usability:	★★★★★	Based:	UK
Product Range:	★★★★	Express Delivery Option? (UK)	No
Price Range:	Medium	Gift Wrapping Option?	No
Delivery Area:	Worldwide	Returns Procedure:	Down to you

www.hommemummy.co.uk

This is where to come if you're looking for simple, elegant maternity wear that will travel well and look great all the time. Everything is made from soft, comfortable, luxury jersey, stretch lace and cord, from tops to trousers and skirts. You can also buy the Essential Maternity Wardrobe, which includes a go-anywhere trouser, elegant wrap top and glamorous versatile dress. There are good line drawings of all the items to go with the photos so you can see the shapes more clearly.

Site Usability:	★★★★	Based:	UK
Product Range:	★★★	Express Delivery Option? (UK)	Yes
Price Range:	Medium	Gift Wrapping Option?	No
Delivery Area:	Worldwide	Returns Procedure:	Down to you

www.isabellaoliver.com

Isabella Oliver is a maternity-wear company for pregnant women who love clothes. The sexy designs in soft jersey fabrics have signature-style details such as ruching and wrapping to flatter new curves. Every item arrives gift wrapped and the brochure and website include style tips to pick up on the season's trends. Isabella Oliver also offers lingerie, loungewear, sophisticated sleepwear, chic outerwear and sun and swimwear, plus gift vouchers from £30. Call them if you want some expert advice.

Site Usability:	★★★★★	Based:	UK
Product Range:	★★★	Express Delivery Option? (UK)	Yes
Price Range:	Medium	Gift Wrapping Option?	Yes
Delivery Area:	Worldwide	Returns Procedure:	Free

www.jojomamanbebe.co.uk

This is a pretty website offering a good choice for expectant mothers, babies and young children. The drop-down menus on the home page take you quickly and clearly to everything you might be looking for, whether it's maternity occasionwear or safety gates for young children. There's a good range of maternity underwear and swimwear as well. They have some good gift ideas and offer gift vouchers and gift boxes as well to make your life easier.

Site Usability:	★★★★★	Based:	UK
Product Range:	★★★★	Express Delivery Option? (UK)	No
Price Range:	Medium	Gift Wrapping Option?	No
Delivery Area:	Worldwide	Returns Procedure:	Down to you

www.mamasandpapas.co.uk

This company combines great attention to detail, high-quality fabrics and pretty designs in its well-priced maternity section, covering everything from evening wear and separates to sleepwear and swimwear. There's lovely clothing as well for babies and toddlers, plus a wide range of equipment and lots of gift ideas. This is a beautifully photographed website offering loads of advice on what to buy. They only deliver to the UK but you can click through to the US-based site.

Site Usability:	★★★★★	Based:	UK
Product Range:	★★★	Express Delivery Option? (UK)	No
Price Range:	Medium	Gift Wrapping Option?	No
Delivery Area:	UK, but US site available	Returns Procedure:	Down to you

www.pushmaternity.com

The Push boutique in Islington specialises in designer maternity wear and a high level of customer service. Now you can buy the collection online from labels such as Earl Jean, Tashia, Alex Gore Brown, Cadeau, Citizens of Humanity, Leona Edmistion (gorgeous jersey dresses) and Juicy Couture. There's maternity hosiery and chic baby bags here as well. Select from next-day or standard delivery (UK, though they ship overseas as well) and if you have any queries don't hesitate to give them a call.

Site Usability:	★★★★	Based:	UK
Product Range:	★★★	Express Delivery Option? (UK)	Yes
Price Range:	Medium	Gift Wrapping Option?	No
Delivery Area:	Worldwide	Returns Procedure:	Down to you

www.seraphine.com

Find excellent maternity wear on this prettily photographed website where the collection is stylish and different and the prices reasonable. You can choose from the latest looks, maternity essentials and glamorous partywear as well as lingerie by Elle Mcpherson, Nougatine and Canelle, gorgeous lay-ettes for newborns and Tommy's Ts. Delivery takes up to five working days; you'll find postage costs for the UK and EU on the website, email them for elsewhere.

Site Usability:	★★★★	Based:	UK
Product Range:	★★★★	Express Delivery Option? (UK)	No
Price Range:	Medium	Gift Wrapping Option?	No
Delivery Area:	Worldwide	Returns Procedure:	Down to you

www.tiffanyrose.co.uk

Here you'll find smart and quite unusual maternity wear including dresses and chic separates. It's quite a small range but very stylish, so if you're looking for something for a special occasion you should have a click round. There are also beautiful maternity wedding dresses and a sale area where you can usually find some good discounts. They deliver worldwide and offer a next-day and Saturday-delivery service for the UK.

Site Usability:	★★★★	Based:	UK
Product Range:	★★★	Express Delivery Option? (UK)	Yes
Price Range:	Medium	Gift Wrapping Option?	No
Delivery Area:	Worldwide	Returns Procedure:	Down to you

Also check out these websites for maternity wear:

Website address　　　　　**You'll find it in:**

www.figleaves.com　　　　　Lingerie

Chapter 12

Sunglasses

There's no doubt that a great pair of shades makes a difference and that's a difference not just in terms of protecting your eyes and reducing the glare of the sun (when there is some). A modern pair of sunglasses is up there with your handbag and shoes as an essential accessory that's not only useful but stylish and flattering. They can make you feel better on a bad day and fab on a good one. Not only are they great camouflage if you're tired or stressed, but no matter how smart or casual you've dressed, they're always a real fashion statement (or otherwise, so if in doubt go buy some new ones now).

If you're not sure what shape to buy, first take a good look at the ads in the glossies to get an idea of the overall trends, then visit their section on 'Choosing the right sunglasses for your face' where there's lots of advice on which styles for which face shape. Bear in mind also the sunglasses which you've felt are the most flattering in the past and stick to that shape. I certainly do even if I change brand and nine times out of ten it's the right shape for me. When choosing the shape, don't get carried away and forget to make sure you're getting the best protection – it may not be sunny now but you don't want to have to buy another pair when that sun does come out.

You can spend a fortune on your sunglasses but provided you're not one of those people always leaving theirs somewhere, it's worth investing a reasonable sum for a decent pair that you'll feel totally happy wearing. Believe me, they do make a difference.

Sites to Visit

www.shadestation.co.uk

For the cooler end of the market have a look round here, where the emphasis is on young, modern styles from brands such as Prada, Police, D & G, Diesel, Gucci and Armani. (You'll find watches by some of these names as well.) The site stocks the complete Oakley brand, including glasses, accessories, goggles and watches, plus replacement lenses and sunglass cases.

Site Usability:	★★★	Based:	UK
Product Range:	★★★	Express Delivery Option? (UK)	Yes
Price Range:	Luxury/Medium	Gift Wrapping Option?	No
Delivery Area:	UK	Returns Procedure:	Down to you

www.sunglasses-shop.co.uk

The Sunglasses Shop is based in the UK and offers you free, express UK delivery. You can choose from designer brands such as Prada, Gucci, Chanel, Versace, Dolce & Gabbana, Dior and many more. There is a comprehensive and modern range and if you click on the pair you like you not only get a close-up but also detailed pictures showing you what the side hinges and nose piece look like. You can shop by brand and by colour or select from the best sellers.

Site Usability:	★★★★★	Based:	UK
Product Range:	★★★★★	Express Delivery Option? (UK)	Yes
Price Range:	Luxury/Medium	Returns Procedure:	Down to you
Delivery Area:	UK		

www.sunglassesuk.co.uk

Just about every brand of sunglasses is available from this UK site, including Gucci, Chloe, Dolce & Gabbana, Moschino, Bolle and Prada. You can check out the best sellers or buy the same pair of sunglasses your favourite celebrity is wearing this year. It's a fun site with lots to see. It doesn't carry every style in stock so it's best to call them if you find something you really like to make sure it's available.

Site Usability:	★★★★	Based:	UK
Product Range:	★★★★	Express Delivery Option? (UK)	No
Price Range:	Luxury/Medium	Gift Wrapping Option?	No
Delivery Area:	UK	Returns Procedure:	Down to you

www.technical-gear.com

For sports and technical sunglasses and goggles look no further than this excellent website, offering brands such as Oakley, Bolle, Gargoyle, Action Optics and Spy. There is a full range of goggles for all sports activities and specific advice on which shades you need for driving, skiing, sailing, golf, fishing and many more activities.

Site Usability:	★★★★★	Based:	US
Product Range:	★★★★★	Express Delivery Option? (UK)	No
Price Range:	Medium	Gift Wrapping Option?	No
Delivery Area:	Worldwide	Returns Procedure:	Down to you

www.ten-eighty.co.uk

By far the best thing about this site is the range of Oakley sunglasses and lenses. Whereas on most sites you'll be offered a style and that's it, here with their help you can create your own, particularly for sports use, and the service is excellent. Some of the stuff on the site is hard to read and you do have to scroll around a lot, but persevere – it will be worth it. If you want extra advice, don't hesitate to call them – their service is excellent.

Site Usability:	★★★	Based:	UK
Product Range:	★★★	Express Delivery Option? (UK)	Yes
Price Range:	Luxury/Medium	Gift Wrapping Option?	No
Delivery Area:	UK	Returns Procedure:	Down to you

www.the-eye-shop.com

This website is based in Chamonix in France (where you do need sunglasses a lot of the time, of course) and the list of brand names is fantastic, including Chanel, Dior, Diesel, Bolle, Oakley, Quiksilver and Valentino. The site claims to hold almost everything in stock and delivery is free by UPS. You can also choose from a good selection of sport goggles from brands such as Cebe, Oakley and Adidas, plus binoculars and GPS systems.

Site Usability:	★★★★★	Based:	France
Product Range:	★★★★★	Express Delivery Option? (UK)	No
Price Range:	Luxury/Medium	Gift Wrapping Option?	No
Delivery Area:	Worldwide	Returns Procedure:	Down to you

www.unitedshades.com

This US-based website (now with a European arm) has a comprehensive range of the latest sunglasses. Choose from Versace, Armani, Ferragamo, Givenchy, Gucci, Yves St Laurent and many more. With over 25 brands on offer you're sure to find something you like. Delivery is free for most countries – check the Shipping Tariff form to make sure that yours is on there. Whatever you're thinking of buying you absolutely should have a look at the 'Choose the right sunglasses for your face' area where they give a lot of advice. Everyone who sells sunglass online should be doing this but most of them aren't yet (or they're hiding it) and it's essential if you're going to buy online.

Site Usability:	★★★★★	Based:	EU/US
Product Range:	★★★★★	Express Delivery Option? (UK)	Yes
Price Range:	Luxury/Medium	Gift Wrapping Option?	No
Delivery Area:	Worldwide	Returns Procedure:	Down to you

Chapter 13

Jewellery and Watches

Luxury Jewels   Gorgeous and Accessible

Fashion Rocks   Watches

I've divided this area into four sections as the range of jewellery websites is growing all the time and I wanted to make it easier for you to look in the right place, although all of the websites are lovely to have a browse through.

Needless to say, jewellery (apart from that 15-carat diamond you have your eye on) is perfect for buying online, provided you know and trust the retailer. What you buy is usually small, eminently packable and despatchable and, if necessary, returnable.

It's also a marvellous area for gifts as most of the retailers listed below automatically box or pack their orders beautifully And if you want them to send something on for you they will, of course, be delighted to do so.

Be warned though, there is a major problem in buying jewellery online – once you start to browse, for yourself or for someone else, it becomes extremely tempting to buy something you hadn't intended to. I've had my eye on a pair of earrings at a certain luxury jewellery designer for so long now I've forgotten when I first saw them. I know I mustn't buy them – I have three children, dogs and a husband – but I'm sure that before the year is out I will – if they're still there, of course.

Luxury Jewels

Sites to Visit

www.astleyclarke.com

New online designer jewellery retailer Astley Clarke has an attractive website, where you'll find the collections of New York- and London-based designers such as Coleman Douglas, Talisman Unlimited, Vinnie Day, Flora Astor and Catherine Prevost, some of which are exclusive to Astley Clarke. Prices for the precious and semi-precious jewels here start at around £100 and then go skywards. For gorgeous gifts or treats this is the perfect place, as everything arrives beautifully gift boxed and can be gift wrapped as well. There's also a collection for brides and bridesmaids.

Site Usability:	★★★★★	Based:	UK
Product Range:	★★★★★	Express Delivery Option? (UK)	Yes
Price Range:	Luxury/Medium	Gift Wrapping Option?	Yes
Delivery Area:	UK	Returns Procedure:	Down to you

www.boodles.co.uk

Gorgeous modern jewellery: the real thing. Some items you might just imagine buying for yourself, others you'd probably rather have bought for you, like the divine Asscher cut-diamond earrings that they don't even tell you the price for. Have a look round anyway, you might just be tempted. I should warn you though, there's almost nothing here for under £1000. Everything is gift wrapped and they'll ship all over the world.

Site Usability:	★★★★	Based:	UK
Product Range:	★★★★	Express Delivery Option? (UK)	Yes
Price Range:	Luxury	Gift Wrapping Option?	Yes
Delivery Area:	Worldwide	Returns Procedure:	Down to you

www.mikimoto-store.co.uk

Mikimoto is a name synonymous with beautiful and luxurious pearls (they've been in business for over 100 years) and now you can buy a selection of their best-selling jewellery online. Prices start at around £120 for a pair of timeless pearl studs and go up to around £2000 for the Tahitian pearl and pink sapphire pendants and earrings. Everything is beautifully gift wrapped and you can have your order within 48 hours.

Site Usability:	★★★★★	Based:	UK
Product Range:	★★★★	Express Delivery Option? (UK)	Yes
Price Range:	Luxury/Medium	Gift Wrapping Option?	Yes
Delivery Area:	Worldwide	Returns Procedure:	Down to you

www.theofennell.com

Theo Fennell is famous as the jewellery designer for stars such as Elton John. His modern, diamond-studded crosses and keys are recognised the world over, as are his solid silver Marmite lids and Worcester sauce bottle holders. Nothing on this website is inexpensive, but you'll find some extremely beautiful and unique designs and if you buy anything you can be sure it will be exquisitely presented. Browse the site and see whether you're tempted.

Site Usability:	★★★	Based:	UK
Product Range:	★★★★	Express Delivery Option? (UK)	No
Price Range:	Luxury	Gift Wrapping Option?	Yes
Delivery Area:	Worldwide	Returns Procedure:	Down to you

www.tiffany.com

Exquisite and expensive: the two words that sum up one of the world's most luxurious jewellery emporiums. Anything in the signature Tiffany blue box is sure to make a perfect present, from the smallest piece of Elsa Peretti or Paloma Picasso jewellery to wonderful classic diamonds and pearls. Beautiful Tiffany glass candlesticks, bowls and stemware, the new Tiffany fragrance in its lovely glass bottle or christening gifts for a new baby; it's all available online.

Site Usability:	★★★★★	Based:	UK
Product Range:	★★★★★	Express Delivery Option? (UK)	Yes
Price Range:	Luxury	Gift Wrapping Option?	Yes/Automatic
Delivery Area:	UK and USA	Returns Procedure:	Down to you

Gorgeous and Accessible

There's a wide range of prices and styles here, from modern/traditional diamond jewellery at Blitz to chic, glamorous gems at Emma Chapman, so plan to spend a bit (or a lot) of time looking through these websites.

Just a few of my favourites: the aforesaid Emma Chapman for wonderful coloured necklaces; Harriet Whinney for the highest quality, handpicked pearls by someone who really knows about them; Kirsten Goss for beautiful (and beautifully photographed) wedding jewellery; and Green & Frederick for unbelievably sparkly and real-looking cubic zirconias, hand-cut and set in 14ct gold. Be warned again though, if you wear anything from them your friends will think you've won the lottery.

Sites to Visit

www.absolutepearls.co.uk

This website was established in China but has relocated to the UK to offer you quality cultured pearl necklaces, earrings and bracelets. There's a good selection, from simple, single-strand necklaces to black Tahitian pearl-and-diamond pendants. If you want information about how to choose pearls and what makes them so special, you'll find it in the comprehensive information centre, together with suggestions for gifts and the message card service.

Site Usability:	★★★★★	Based:	UK
Product Range:	★★★★	Express Delivery Option? (UK)	Yes
Price Range:	Luxury/Medium	Gift Wrapping Option?	No
Delivery Area:	UK	Returns Procedure:	Down to you

www.blitzjewellery.co.uk

The sister site to Blitz Watches, this is well worth having a look through if you're hunting for something new or for a gift. Prices range from the very reasonable up into the thousands, with discounts shown for everything (although it's hard to compare like with like). The watch discounts are very reliable, but it's not as easy to get a direct comparison with the jewellery. Find what you want and compare prices on other sites for similar items. You may well do better here.

Site Usability: ★★★★★	Based:	UK
Product Range: ★★★★	Express Delivery Option? (UK)	Yes
Price Range: Luxury/Medium	Gift Wrapping Option?	Yes
Delivery Area: UK	Returns Procedure:	Down to you

www.bobijou.com

BoBijou is a reasonably priced European designer jewellery brand, offering a collection of chic colourful pieces, designed in-house and handmade using natural cultured pearls and gemstones with silver and gold. Many designs carry the BoBijou signature design feature, MLMF (Multi Look Multi Function), so a long design can be a belt, a lariat-style necklace, a chunky choker or a bracelet, making them flexible and giving you more value for money. New styles are added each season.

Site Usability: ★★★★★	Based:	UK
Product Range: ★★★★	Express Delivery Option? (UK)	Yes
Price Range: Luxury/Medium	Gift Wrapping Option?	No
Delivery Area: EU	Returns Procedure:	Down to you

www.dinnyhall.com

Here you can see beautifully designed, well-priced modern jewellery from one of Britain's foremost jewellery designers. Every piece is handcrafted using traditional jewellery-making techniques with high-quality silver, gold and precious and semi-precious stones. If you haven't discovered Dinny Hall's work up until now, this is definitely the time to start collecting. She has a clear and modern website where you can see all the products in each category at once, which is extremely helpful.

Site Usability: ★★★★★	Based:	UK
Product Range: ★★★★	Express Delivery Option? (UK)	No
Price Range: Medium	Gift Wrapping Option?	Yes
Delivery Area: Worldwide	Returns Procedure:	Down to you

www.emmachapmanjewels.com

Emma Chapman is a new jewellery designer, based in London, who creates exotic designer gemstone jewellery with a contemporary edge. It's a covetable collection, grouped by descriptions such as Beach Babe, Baroque Goddess and Indian Princess. Everything is individually made and reasonably priced, so if you see something you like you need to contact them immediately.

Site Usability: ★★★★	Based:	UK
Product Range: ★★★	Express Delivery Option? (UK)	No
Price Range: Medium	Gift Wrapping Option?	No
Delivery Area: Worldwide	Returns Procedure:	Down to you

www.geraldonline.com

Here you can choose from a wide range of mostly diamond-set jewellery from very reasonably priced pieces to your next pair of 18ct gold 2 carat certified diamond studs. The emphasis here is on price and quality. Alongside some of the excellent gift ideas you can make a real investment (although going back to said diamonds you should always compare prices and quality elsewhere). In the 'Get the Look for Less' section you can be inspired by stars such as Mischa Barton and Rachel Hunter and buy into modern looks to keep you well ahead of the rest.

Site Usability: ★★★★★	Based:	UK
Product Range: ★★★★★	Express Delivery Option? (UK)	Yes
Price Range: Medium/Very Good Value	Gift Wrapping Option?	Yes
Delivery Area: UK	Returns Procedure:	Down to you

www.green-frederick.co.uk

If you love beautiful jewellery and the sparkle of diamonds but the real thing is slightly out of your range (like most of us), you'll need to spend some time on this wonderful but unsophisticated website. You'll find 18ct gold necklaces, bracelets and earrings set with glittering hand-cut cubic zirconias plus a wide range of real pearl jewellery. This is not cheap jewellery but superb quality at a very good price and it's very hard to tell the difference between the highest quality zirconias used here and the real thing.

Site Usability: ★★★★	Based:	UK
Product Range: ★★★★	Express Delivery Option? (UK)	Yes
Price Range: Medium	Gift Wrapping Option?	No
Delivery Area: Worldwide	Returns Procedure:	Down to you

www.harriet-whinney.co.uk

Harriet Whinney specialises in pearl jewellery made to order and beautiful timeless pearl earrings, necklaces and bracelets. You can select from her ready-made range or choose the quality of the pearl you want for your piece of jewellery and then select the type of clasp. There are some extremely special pieces here such as baroque and South Sea pearls.

Site Usability: ★★★★	Based:	UK
Product Range: ★★★★	Express Delivery Option? (UK)	No
Price Range: Luxury/Medium	Gift Wrapping Option?	No
Delivery Area: Worldwide	Returns Procedure:	Down to you

www.icecool.co.uk

At Ice Cool you can select from a range of modern and classic well-priced jewels, including diamond studs, tennis bracelets, pendants and rings, mostly set in 18ct gold and with sparkling diamonds. Prices start at around £100. Two of the best things here are the Trend section, where you can find out what you should be wearing jewellery-wise this year, and Discover Diamonds, where you can read all you could possibly want to know (and more) about what are definitely my favourite stones. The site offers a bespoke service as well.

Site Usability: ★★★★★	Based:	UK
Product Range: ★★★★	Express Delivery Option? (UK)	No
Price Range: Medium	Gift Wrapping Option?	No
Delivery Area: Worldwide	Returns Procedure:	Down to you

www.kirstengoss.com

After studying jewellery design in South Africa, Kirsten Goss moved to London and launched her own company where she creates exclusive, modern collections of jewellery using semi-precious stones and sterling silver. Having been featured by *Harpers*, *Elle*, *Glamour* and *In Style* and described as 'the next big thing' by the *Sunday Times Magazine*, this is definitely one to watch.

Site Usability: ★★★★	Based:	UK
Product Range: ★★★	Express Delivery Option? (UK)	Yes
Price Range: Medium	Gift Wrapping Option?	No
Delivery Area: Worldwide	Returns Procedure:	Down to you

www.linksoflondon.com

Links of London is well known for an eclectic mix of jewellery in sterling silver and 18ct gold, charms and charm bracelets, cufflinks, gorgeous gifts and leather and silver accessories for your home. Inevitably each season it designs a new collection of totally desirable pieces (in other words, I want them), such as the 'Sweetie Rolled Gold Bracelet', or 'Annoushka' gold and ruby charm. This website is perfect for gifts and if you need something sent in a hurry, it offers an express service worldwide.

Site Usability:	★★★★★	Based:	UK
Product Range:	★★★★★	Express Delivery Option? (UK)	Yes
Price Range:	Luxury/Medium	Gift Wrapping Option?	Yes
Delivery Area:	Worldwide	Returns Procedure:	Down to you

www.manjoh.com

On Manjoh's attractively designed contemporary jewellery website, you'll find designers such as Izabel Camille, Benedicte Mouret, Vinnie Day and Scott Wilson and the list is regularly being added to. Most recent additions include DAY Jewels, a luxury jewellery line from Day Birger et Mikkelsen, which Manjoh sells exclusively online, and ultra-fashionable R jewellery. The site includes monthly features on the latest trends and interviews with designers.

Site Usability:	★★★★★	Based:	UK
Product Range:	★★★	Express Delivery Option? (UK)	Yes
Price Range:	Medium	Gift Wrapping Option?	Yes
Delivery Area:	Worldwide	Returns Procedure:	Down to you

www.murrayforbes.co.uk

Based in Inverness in the Scottish Highlands, Murray Forbes has an unusual selection of not overpriced jewellery online, comprising earrings, bracelets and necklaces, some quite traditional and some modern, using semi-precious stones, pearls, black and white diamonds and 9ct or 18ct gold. The pictures are clear and the details and information excellent. The site offers free shipping and shipping insurance in the UK and will deliver worldwide.

Site Usability:	★★★★	Based:	UK
Product Range:	★★★	Express Delivery Option? (UK)	No
Price Range:	Medium	Gift Wrapping Option?	Yes
Delivery Area:	Worldwide	Returns Procedure:	Down to you

www.palenquejewellery.co.uk

Palenque is a young, contemporary jewellery company offering a unique collection of earrings, necklaces, bracelets and pendants quite different to what you'll find elsewhere. The range consists of brushed, frosted and polished finishes to both gold and silver, combined with vibrant glass, semi-precious stones, sparkling crystals and pearls. It's well worth a look.

Site Usability:	★★★★	Based:	UK
Product Range:	★★★	Express Delivery Option? (UK)	No
Price Range:	Medium	Gift Wrapping Option?	Yes
Delivery Area:	Worldwide	Returns Procedure:	Down to you

www.pascal-jewellery.com

Here's a collection of timeless, stylish jewellery from a retailer that was established in Liberty of London about 25 years ago and which you can now find in stores such as Harvey Nichols. As Pascal is a member of the National Association of Goldsmiths, you can be sure that you're buying real quality. The collection is updated at least four times a year so you can be tempted regularly. Prices start at around £50 (and average about £300).

Site Usability:	★★★★★	Based:	UK
Product Range:	★★★★	Express Delivery Option? (UK)	No
Price Range:	Luxury/Medium	Gift Wrapping Option?	Yes
Delivery Area:	UK	Returns Procedure:	Down to you

www.reglisse.co.uk

For those of you who are searching for something different and unusual, take a look round here. This collection of accessories and jewellery, created by an eclectic group of modern luxury designers, includes some beautiful pieces, such as the lizard embossed calfskin passport cover, assymetric glass wine carafe and crystal and hammered gold necklace. There's a good choice at a wide range of prices and a speedy delivery service within the UK.

Site Usability:	★★★★	Based: UK		
Product Range:	★★★★	Express Delivery Option? (UK)		Yes
Price Range:	Luxury/Medium	Gift Wrapping Option?	No	
Delivery Area:	Worldwide	Returns Procedure:	Down to you	

www.selectraders.co.uk

This is a company based in Germany, offering a superb range of pearls including Akoya, South Sea and freshwater, with a gorgeous choice of necklaces, earrings, rings, bracelets and pendants. Everything is beautifully and extremely clearly photographed, with many views of the same item, and you can choose pearls on their own or match them with diamonds and 18ct gold settings. They'll deliver all over the world.

Site Usability:	★★★★	Based:	Germany
Product Range:	★★★★★	Express Delivery Option? (UK)	No
Price Range:	Medium	Gift Wrapping Option?	No
Delivery Area:	Worldwide	Returns Procedure:	Down to you

www.stonedjewellery.co.uk

With its main boutique in Nottingham, Stoned stocks a unique mix of local designers, directional London studios and Far Eastern pearl specialists. Everything on offer is chic, stylish and beautifully photographed, of the highest quality and at a mid-price range, with necklaces starting at around £100 and earrings at £55 (and going up steeply). You'll find designers such as Claire Henry, Dower and Hall and Monica Vinader, plus others you probably won't have heard of.

Site Usability:	★★★★	Based:	UK
Product Range:	★★★	Express Delivery Option? (UK)	No
Price Range:	Medium	Gift Wrapping Option?	Yes
Delivery Area:	UK	Returns Procedure:	Down to you

www.swarovski.com

You've almost certainly heard of Swarovski (and seen those sparkling faceted crystal collectibles and objects). You may also have passed the glorious shops, with glittering and stylish jewellery and accessories inside (and I mean really glittering). You'll no doubt be delighted to know that you can buy a wide selection online, all set with the Swarovski signature crystals and extremely hard to resist.

Site Usability:	★★★★★	Based:	Germany
Product Range:	★★★★★	Express Delivery Option? (UK)	No
Price Range:	Medium	Gift Wrapping Option?	Yes
Delivery Area:	Worldwide	Returns Procedure:	Down to you

www.vanpeterson.com

This is a small collection of extremely modern and unusual jewellery designed by Eric van Peterson, who opened his Walton Street, London jewellery store in 1981 to offer easily distinguished, modern/ethnic designs. It's a highly edited selection of his range, but hopefully it will be increasing season on season.

Site Usability:	★★★	Based:	UK
Product Range:	★★★	Express Delivery Option? (UK)	No
Price Range:	Medium	Gift Wrapping Option?	No
Delivery Area:	Worldwide	Returns Procedure:	Down to you

Fashion Rocks

Sites to Visit

www.accessoriesonline.co.uk

This is the home of modern designer jewellery by Les Nereides, Butler and Wilson, Tarantino and Kleshna with a varied and attractive, well-priced range. Click here when you want your next fashion jewellery fix or when you're looking for a treat for a friend and you'll definitely not be disappointed. Les Nereides in particular is really unusual and pretty, not cheap but always in line with the season.

Site Usability:	★★★★★	Based:	UK
Product Range:	★★★★	Express Delivery Option? (UK)	No
Price Range:	Medium/Very Good Value	Gift Wrapping Option?	No
Delivery Area:	Worldwide	Returns Procedure:	Down to you

www.accessorize.co.uk

Accessorize is the essential destination if you're looking for up-to-the-minute and extremely well-priced accessories, including a wide range of jewellery. It's also an excellent place for a gift for an older child or if your early teen and upwards needs (as in *I need*) a new pair of earrings, flip flops, party slip-on shoes, a scarf or a bag. Not only do the prices make it a great place for gifts but all the products are fun and modern too.

Site Usability: ★★★★★	Based:	UK
Product Range: ★★★★	Express Delivery Option? (UK)	No
Price Range: Very Good Value	Gift Wrapping Option?	No
Delivery Area: UK	Returns Procedure:	Down to you

www.butlerandwilson.co.uk

Famous for its signature whimsical fashion jewellery, you can now choose from a glamorous and well-priced online range of necklaces, bracelets, earrings and brooches. Both costume jewellery and jewellery using semi-precious stones such as rose quartz, agate, amber and jade are available. You can also see the collection of pretty printed and beaded handbags, plus bridal jewellery and accessories.

Site Usability: ★★★★	Based:	UK
Product Range: ★★★★	Express Delivery Option? (UK)	No
Price Range: Medium	Gift Wrapping Option?	No, but everything is beautifully
Delivery Area: Worldwide		packaged

www.chezbec.com

For a pretty and well-priced jewellery fix from an attractive and helpful website you need look no further. Chez Bec has an unusual selection sourced from designers around the world, incorporating shells, semi-precious stones, pearls, silver and glass beads. Most pieces retail for less than £100 and everything is beautifully presented in Chez Bec's fuchsia-pink gift boxes.

Site Usability: ★★★★	Based:	UK
Product Range: ★★★	Express Delivery Option? (UK)	No
Price Range: Medium	Gift Wrapping Option?	No, but everything is beautifully
Delivery Area: Worldwide		packaged

www.jewel-garden.co.uk

Brand new online jewellery company Jewel Garden offers an attractive range of well-priced jewellery by modern designers that you won't find in the stores. It concentrates on silver and semi-precious stones such as smokey quartz, agate, turquoise and citrine, plus pearl, crystal and coloured glass. Combine this with the clear layout, fast worldwide delivery and gift wrapping services and this becomes a very attractive place to shop for gifts or treats.

Site Usability: ★★★★★	Based:	UK
Product Range: ★★★	Express Delivery Option? (UK)	Yes
Price Range: Medium/Very Good Value	Gift Wrapping Option?	Yes
Delivery Area: Worldwide	Returns Procedure:	Down to you

www.justdivine.co.uk

Just Divine is a collection of vintage-inspired jewellery and gifts designed by Shelley Cooper of the USA, a fashion and jewellery historian whose passion for the past is reflected in her work. If you love vintage-style jewellery you'll be spoilt for choice here. The website offers a limited edition of favourites from the huge range of designs in the main collection and highlights select pieces each month.

Site Usability: ★★★★★	Based:	UK
Product Range: ★★★	Express Delivery Option? (UK)	No
Price Range: Medium	Gift Wrapping Option?	No
Delivery Area: EU	Returns Procedure:	Down to you

www.lolarose.co.uk

This is an unusually designed website, where you see all the products as on the pages of a book. However, it's very clever as well, as you not only see everything very clearly but also view all the different colourways of the necklaces and bracelets made with rose quartz, white jade, green aventurine, mother of pearl and black agate. The prices for these beautifully designed pieces are very reasonable, so it's well worth having a look.

Site Usability: ★★★★	Based:	UK
Product Range: ★★★	Express Delivery Option? (UK)	No
Price Range: Medium	Gift Wrapping Option?	No
Delivery Area: Worldwide	Returns Procedure:	Down to you

www.piajewellery.com

Pia has a quick and clever website where you can choose from the creative jewellery by type or browse page by page through the catalogue. The pictures of this modern, well-priced jewellery range are extremely clear and definitely make you want to buy. There are natural stones such as carnelian, agate, labradorite and coral mixed with silver, all turned into very wearable necklaces, earrings and bracelets. The site also offers soft leather handbags, a small selection of leather and shearling clothing and pretty scarves and shawls.

Site Usability:	★★★★★	Based:	UK
Product Range:	★★★★	Express Delivery Option? (UK)	Yes
Price Range:	Medium	Gift Wrapping Option?	Yes
Delivery Area:	Worldwide	Returns Procedure:	Down to you

www.ros-mari.co.uk

With a passion for fashion and jewellery, the Ros Mari Jewellery Store was established in October 2000. Regularly updated to keep up with the latest fashion trends, it's well priced enough for you to order essential pieces to go with your new looks. All the jewellery is wrapped in tissue paper and delivered in pink or pastel-coloured boxes with ribbons. If you want them to provide a special message to go with the jewellery, you need to call or email.

Site Usability:	★★★★	Based:	UK
Product Range:	★★★	Express Delivery Option? (UK)	No
Price Range:	Very Good Value	Gift Wrapping Option?	Yes
Delivery Area:	Worldwide	Returns Procedure:	Down to you

www.temptationjewellery.com

This is a young and funky website aimed, they say, at the stylish desk-bound professional but, I say, perfect for the jewellery-collecting teen of almost any age. After all, there is a wide range of well-priced and modern earrings, necklaces and other accessories starting at around £10. The site offers free UK delivery, an express service and gift wrapping and voucher options, plus a 14-day money-back guarantee.

Site Usability:	★★★★	Based:	UK
Product Range:	★★★★	Express Delivery Option? (UK)	Yes
Price Range:	Very Good Value	Gift Wrapping Option?	Yes
Delivery Area:	UK	Returns Procedure:	Down to you

www.tictocsnrocks.co.uk

Tictocsnrocks is a collection of modern jewellery and designer watches at a range of prices from a retailer based in Devon. There are watches by Calvin Klein, D&G, Diesel, DKNY and Roberto Cavalli, jewellery by Angie Gooderham, Azuni, Philippe Ferrandis, Pilgrim and Taratata, and lots more. This would make a great place to find an accessory gift as the site offers a gift wrapping service and they'll also ship worldwide.

Site Usability:	★★★	Based:	UK
Product Range:	★★★	Express Delivery Option? (UK)	No
Price Range:	Medium	Gift Wrapping Option?	Yes
Delivery Area:	Worldwide	Returns Procedure:	Down to you

www.treasurebox.co.uk

Here you'll find a wealth of costume jewellery from Butler and Wilson, Tarina Tarantino, Angie Gooderham and Les Nereides to name just a few, with the emphasis on what's in fashion right now. You can select your jewellery to go with each new season's look and they're adding in new designers all the time. This is a really fun website where there's not only a lot of choice but also a great deal of information about the trends the pieces go with.

Site Usability:	★★★★	Based:	UK
Product Range:	★★★★	Express Delivery Option? (UK)	Yes
Price Range:	Medium	Gift Wrapping Option?	Yes
Delivery Area:	Worldwide	Returns Procedure:	Down to you

Watches

You can buy a marvellously wide range of watches online, from designer and premium-brand timpieces by Gucci, Dior, Cartier, Rolex, Tag Heuer and Baume and Mercier (plus more) to more accessibly priced watches by Tissot, Citizen and Seiko. Then there are places such as buyaswatch.co.uk where you can buy just about every colourful, different Swatch watch ever designed, and others for fashion brands such as DKNY, Versace and Burberry.

Don't be tempted by the replica watch websites that come up if you should decide to go on a search engine and look for a premium-brand watch – many of these websites photograph the real thing then sell you something totally different. It simply isn't worth the effort. Do, however, take advantage of the very good prices you can get at some of the websites below, having checked the main recommended price as well, of course. I say this not because I have any doubts about what you'll be offered here, but because this is something you should do in any case, particularly if you're thinking of a large spend.

For premium watches also look to the Luxury Jewellers above, as you will find beautiful examples at Theo Fennell, Boodles (Patek Philippe) and Tiffany.

Sites to Visit

www.blitzwatches.co.uk

Browse through the best brands such as Tag Heuer, Tissot, Baume and Mercier, Rolex and Cartier to name but a few. Place your order and you can have your delivery the next day. The pictures are beautifully clear and extremely tempting and on some watches there are substantial savings to be had which are clearly shown with each model. For some premium watches you receive the manufacturer's warranty, for others the warranty is provided by Blitz, so check before you buy.

Site Usability:	★★★★★	Based:	UK
Product Range:	★★★★★	Express Delivery Option? (UK)	Yes
Price Range:	Luxury/Medium	Gift Wrapping Option?	Yes
Delivery Area:	UK		

www.buyaswatch.co.uk

With names such as Colour the Sky, Chessboard and Black Injection, you can imagine the sort of watches you'll find here – fun, different, colourful (in many cases) and modern. You can choose from the range of watches in stock for express delivery or check out the themed or limited-edition selection. There's even a choice of watches you can load with your next ski pass data which you can use at more than 450 resorts worldwide.

Site Usability:	★★★★★	Based:	UK
Product Range:	★★★★★	Express Delivery Option? (UK)	Yes
Price Range:	Medium/Very Good Value	Gift Wrapping Option?	No
Delivery Area:	UK	Returns Procedure:	Down to you

www.ernestjones.co.uk

Ernest Jones has a beautifully designed website where you can buy watches by a wide range of premium designers such as Tag Heuer, Gucci, Longines and Rado. The advantage of buying here is that if you have any problems you can choose to visit one of the 190 UK-based stores or use the online address. The site has a good gift finder and offers gift packaging and express delivery services.

Site Usability: ★★★★★	Based:	UK
Product Range: ★★★★★	Express Delivery Option? (UK)	Yes
Price Range: Luxury/Medium	Gift Wrapping Option?	Yes
Delivery Area: UK	Returns Procedure:	Down to you

www.goldsmiths.co.uk

Here's another well-known offline chain of jewellery stores offering a wide range of its products online on a well-designed and easy-to-navigate website. Alongside the jewellery ranges where there's an excellent choice, there are watches by Seiko, Tissot, Longines and Citizen, plus fashion brands Gucci, DKNY, Armani, Versace and Burberry. Expect delivery within three days.

Site Usability: ★★★★★	Based:	UK
Product Range: ★★★★★	Express Delivery Option? (UK)	No
Price Range: Medium	Gift Wrapping Option?	No
Delivery Area: UK	Returns Procedure:	Down to you

www.thewatchhut.co.uk

Buy your next watch from thewatchhut.co.uk and you'll know that you're buying from an authorised dealer with the full manufacturer's guarantee. There are excellent discounts on some of the watches, so it's worth having a good look through the brands on offer such as Ebel, Accurist, Breil, Diesel and Fossil.

Site Usability: ★★★★★	Based:	UK
Product Range: ★★★★	Express Delivery Option? (UK)	Yes
Price Range: Medium	Gift Wrapping Option?	No
Delivery Area: UK	Returns Procedure:	Down to you

Chapter 14

Leather, Shearling and Faux Fur

There's nothing nicer when it's really cold (other than a mug of mulled wine, of course) than slipping into a beautifully soft shearling coat or jacket – at least that's my opinion and it hasn't changed over the years. And, of course, your glass of mulled wine may disappear fast but your shearling will last a long, long time.

Where leather and suede jackets and coats are concerned, again, a great one will last you for years. I'm not saying that you need to spend thousands of pounds, but if you buy something made of good-quality skin and in a style that suits you, rather than what's absolutely of the moment, you'll find it works for smart and casual wear and most of the year round.

Don't be fooled by some of the amazing prices you can find both on and offline. Here again you get what you pay for, although on some of the websites below you'll be buying skins that are also supplied to some of the superbrands, but of course at a much lower price as you're not paying the brand premium. If you're in any doubt call the retailer and ask them to send you a swatch of the skin they'll be using – if they mind, don't buy from them.

123

Sites to Visit

www.celtic-sheepskin.co.uk

There are some excellent clothes and accessories here, particularly for the winter months. They include chic Toscana shearling jackets and coats, gloves, scarves, sheepskin-lined boots and slippers, waistcoats and gilets and cute shearling duffles and boots for children. Prices are reasonable and everything's clearly pictured. If you want to order a coat or jacket you'll probably have to wait a couple of weeks, so take a look now.

Site Usability:	★★★★★	Based:	UK
Product Range:	★★★	Express Delivery Option? (UK)	No
Price Range:	Luxury/Medium	Gift Wrapping Option?	No
Delivery Area:	UK	Returns Procedure:	Down to you

www.dlux-ltd.co.uk

Dlux is a boutique mail-order company specialising in beautiful sheepskin and shearling collections. The selection is made of the highest quality soft and supple Merino and Toscana skins and there are two ranges, which they call Classic and Modern, although everything is chic and stylish here, whichever you choose. To order you need to download the order form, then email it to them. If you're in the mood for something luxuriously soft and warm this winter, take a good look here.

Site Usability:	★★★★	Based:	UK
Product Range:	★★★	Express Delivery Option? (UK)	No
Price Range:	Luxury/Medium	Gift Wrapping Option?	No
Delivery Area:	UK	Returns Procedure:	Down to you

www.ewenique.co.uk

This is an attractive and comprehensive range of leather, suede and shearling coats and jackets for men and women, plus flying jackets and accessories such as scarves and stoles, hats, hide bags, gloves and snuggly slippers. Everything is beautifully photographed, with close-ups of the sheepskins so that you can see exactly what you are buying, plus there's lots of information about each garment.

Site Usability:	★★★★	Based:	UK
Product Range:	★★★★	Express Delivery Option? (UK)	No
Price Range:	Medium	Gift Wrapping Option?	No
Delivery Area:	Worldwide	Returns Procedure:	Down to you

www.fabulousfurs.com

No, these are not the real thing. You'll almost certainly be fooled when you look at them on this US-based website, but everything here is made of the highest quality mod-acrylic fibre, which gives it the look and feel of real fur. You can choose from full-length coats to modern jackets, fake fur-trimmed knits, stoles and wraps and there are luxurious throws for the home as well. You will have to pay duty on anything you buy, but for the quality nothing is overpriced.

Site Usability:	★★★★	Based:	US
Product Range:	★★★★	Express Delivery Option? (UK)	No
Price Range:	Luxury/Medium	Gift Wrapping Option?	No
Delivery Area:	Worldwide	Returns Procedure:	Down to you

www.faux.uk.com

If you like to wrap yourself in something soft and furry but you don't want to wear the real thing, then here's a collection of the softest faux-fur coats, jackets and shrugs, plus gorgeous accessories, cushions and throws. These are perfect additions to winter evenings, whether you choose a jacket to go over your evening dress or an unbelievably soft throw to snuggle up in at home.

Site Usability:	★★★	Based:	UK
Product Range:	★★★	Express Delivery Option? (UK)	Yes, but you need to call them
Price Range:	Medium	Gift Wrapping Option?	No
Delivery Area:	Worldwide	Returns Procedure:	Down to you

www.higgs-leathers.co.uk

This is an unsophisticatedly designed website (although improving all the time) with a marvellous collection of leather, suede and shearling clothing. They obviously know what they're doing and offer very high-quality items at reasonable (though not cheap) prices. Expect to pay around £900 for the best Toscana shearling full-length coat. You need to call them to order to ensure that you take the right size.

Site Usability: ★★★★	Based:	UK
Product Range: ★★★★	Express Delivery Option? (UK)	No
Price Range: Luxury/Medium	Gift Wrapping Option?	No
Delivery Area: Worldwide	Returns Procedure:	Down to you

www.hyde-online.net

Here's real designer-quality, beautifully made leather, suede and shearling from a company that makes products for for some world-famous designers. Nothing here is cheap, but you definitely get what you pay for. You may not know the difference between the various types of suede and shearling, but they certainly do and use only the highest-quality skins. The focus is on modern styling, but you'll also find some great classics that'll last you for years.

Site Usability: ★★★★	Based:	UK
Product Range: ★★★★	Express Delivery Option? (UK)	No
Price Range: Luxury	Gift Wrapping Option?	No
Delivery Area: Worldwide	Returns Procedure:	Down to you

Chapter 15

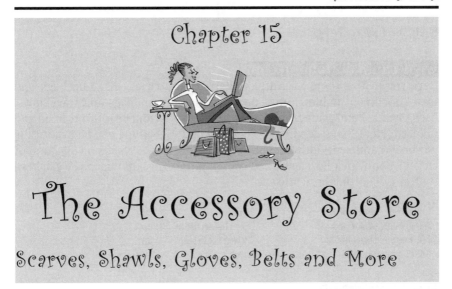

The Accessory Store

Scarves, Shawls, Gloves, Belts and More

I nvest in a designer handbag, buy that perfect pair of the new season's heels and the most stylish shades you've ever owned and you think you're done? Well sorry, but not quite. You still need to finish off your look with those little extras which can make an enormous difference between looking good but missing something and looking really great.

Take belts, for example. Even I, though vertically challenged (as my children kindly tell me) and not nearly as slim as I'd like to be, wear the kind of belt that's shaped at the front and it does make a big difference to smart but simple clothes. I'd love to be able to wear the kind of glitzy jeans belt my size 8 daughter wears, but somehow I don't think that's going to happen, so before I bore on any more, get a great belt and one that suits your shape.

Then take a look at the rest of the accessories here which work depending on the time of year, where you're going and how smart you want to be – are you or aren't you a glove person (unless it's really cold, of course) and how many scarves and shawls and pashminas do you want/need to own? Personally, I don't think you can ever have enough. Do you?

Sites to Visit

www.aspinaloflondon.com

Here you'll find some beautiful wallets, vanity cases, make-up bags and travel document holders, plus the new range of handbags and travel bags. Each piece is handmade from high-quality leathers and beautifully lined and finished. Most items can be personalised and everything can be beautifully gift boxed and sent out with your personal message. This is a collection of elegant, sophisticated, classic and contemporary designs which you can have sent anywhere in the world.

Site Usability:	★★★★★	Based:	UK
Product Range:	★★★★★	Express Delivery Option? (UK)	Yes
Price Range:	Luxury/Medium	Gift Wrapping Option?	Yes
Delivery Area:	Worldwide	Returns Procedure:	Down to you

www.black.co.uk

If you're not a black and neutral person you won't like this website. However, if, like me, you're known for being a black addict, you should have a browse through this website offering beautiful – and beautifully photographed – accessories such as shawls and scarves, gloves, bags, jewellery and belts in (you guessed it) black, grey, cream and beige. Look out for the new swimwear and homeware ranges.

Site Usability:	★★★★	Based:	UK
Product Range:	★★★	Express Delivery Option? (UK)	Yes
Price Range:	Luxury/Medium	Gift Wrapping Option?	Yes
Delivery Area:	Worldwide	Returns Procedure:	Down to you

www.caxtonlondon.com

Browse round here for a wide choice of high-quality gifts, including leather travel accessories, photograph albums, address books and organisers in colours such as cerise, white, sky blue, lilac and lime. You'll also find games such as backgammon and solitaire, silver pens by Lalex and the Mont Blanc Meisterstuck range and delightful baby and christening gifts. Postage within the UK is free and the site offers a free gift wrapping service.

Site Usability:	★★★★	Based:	UK
Product Range:	★★★★	Express Delivery Option? (UK)	No
Price Range:	Medium/Very Good Value	Gift Wrapping Option?	Yes
Delivery Area:	Worldwide	Returns Proce dure:	Down to you

www.cityorg.co.uk

You may well not have heard of this excellent website, offering Filofax organisers and accessories, Cocinelle handbags, wallets and keyrings, Lo Scritto leather-bound notebooks in lots of colours, Quo Vadis diaries, Paul Smith handbags and accessories, pens by Cross, Azuni jewellery, Paul Smith and Mont Blanc cufflinks, Leatherman tools and gadgets by Oregon Scientific. The website is easy to navigate and the pictures are large and clear. This is an excellent place for accessories.

Site Usability:	★★★★	Based:	UK
Product Range:	★★★★	Express Delivery Option? (UK)	No
Price Range:	Luxury/Medium	Gift Wrapping Option?	Yes
Delivery Area:	Worldwide	Returns Procedure:	Down to you

www.corneliajames.com

Long-standing glove maker Cornelia James has expanded its range to include fashion accessories such as faux-fur wraps and gilets, stoles and silk scarves. There's a small but special selection of gloves to buy online, including leather, snaffle trimmed gloves, sexy lace mittens, opera-length satin gloves trimmed with boa feathers and long and short velvet, leopard-print gloves perfect for Christmas.

Site Usability:	★★★★	Based:	UK
Product Range:	★★★	Express Delivery Option? (UK)	No
Price Range:	Luxury/Medium	Gift Wrapping Option?	No
Delivery Area:	Worldwide	Returns Procedure:	Down to you

www.davidhampton.com

Here you'll find wallets and purses in Oak Grain leather, in colours such as aubergine, fuchsia and straw, plus photo albums and frames and travel accessories, wash bags, luggage tags and even mouse mats in Oxford Hide. This is quite a small collection, but beautifully photographed (often with three or four views to each product) and with lots of detail. Many of the items can be personalised with the recipient's initials.

Site Usability: ★★★★	Based:	UK
Product Range: ★★★	Express Delivery Option? (UK)	No
Price Range: Medium/Very Good Value	Gift Wrapping Option?	No
Delivery Area: Worldwide	Returns Procedure:	Down to you

www.heroshop.co.uk

There are lots of places you can buy leather goods online, but very few that offer the quality and service you'll find here. It's not a huge range, but a selection of classic luggage and weekenders, photo albums, home accessories, document wallets, jewellery boxes and cosmetic bags for her, wet packs for him, plus shooting accessories and luxury dog leads, collars and baskets.

Site Usability: ★★★★	Based:	UK
Product Range: ★★★	Express Delivery Option? (UK)	No
Price Range: Medium	Gift Wrapping Option?	No
Delivery Area: Worldwide	Returns Procedure:	Down to you

www.julieslaterandson.co.uk

Everything on this website is beautifully pictured, so you'll know exactly what you're ordering. There's a wonderful selection of leather purses, gifts and travel accessories and you'd have to search long and hard elsewhere to find the colour range offered, which includes pistachio, pale blue, meadow green, hot pink, carnation and royal blue. Delivery is worldwide, with an express delivery option for the UK, and they'll gift wrap for you as well.

Site Usability: ★★★★	Based:	UK
Product Range: ★★★	Express Delivery Option? (UK)	Yes
Price Range: Medium	Gift Wrapping Option?	Yes
Delivery Area: Worldwide	Returns Procedure:	Down to you

www.leatherglovesonline.com

This is a marvellous glove (surprise) retailer where the prices are excellent and the delivery service is speedy. You should have a good look round before it gets really cold out there. There are plain leather gloves with silk or cashmere linings, contrast stitched and extra long cuffs, fur and faux-fur trims and linings and the warmest of all, gloves lined in shearling.

Site Usability: ★★★★	Based:	US
Product Range: ★★★★	Express Delivery Option? (UK)	No
Price Range: Medium	Gift Wrapping Option?	No
Delivery Area: Worldwide	Returns Procedure:	Down to you

www.perilla.co.uk

At Perilla you'll find 'the ultimate treat for feet', a range of high-quality, British-made alpaca socks in a choice of colours and styles, from the delux, lightweight City Sock to the sturdier, ribbed Country Sock. You can choose from a selection of gift boxes containing up to five pairs and select the colours and sizes you want to be included. You can also buy luxurious alpaca scarves and wraps, which will be automatically gift wrapped for you, so if you're looking for a special gift this could be the perfect place.

Site Usability: ★★★	Based:	UK
Product Range: ★★★	Express Delivery Option? (UK)	Yes
Price Range: Luxury/Medium	Gift Wrapping Option?	Yes
Delivery Area: Worldwide	Returns Procedure:	Down to you

www.pickett.co.uk

Gloves, wallets and purses, embroidered cashmere scarves and shawls, umbrellas, belts, briefcases and stud boxes are just some of the high-quality, beautifully made accessories you'll find on Pickett's website. If you've ever visited one of its shops you'll know that everything is the best you can find and most items would make lovely gifts. Couple this with the distinctive dark green and orange packaging and excellent service and you can't go wrong, whatever you buy. Luxury packaging is standard, delivery speedy and they'll ship worldwide.

Site Usability: ★★★★★	Based:	UK
Product Range: ★★★★★	Express Delivery Option? (UK)	Yes
Price Range: Luxury/Medium	Gift Wrapping Option?	Yes
Delivery Area: Worldwide	Returns Procedure:	Down to you

www.safigloves.com

I don't know if you're anything like me but the minute it gets cold I have to search through any and all of my winter coats and jackets for the gloves I left behind as, I'm sure you'll agree with me, cold hands are the worst. Anyway, here's a website that'll solve that problem for you with an excellent range, including gloves with fur cuffs and cashmere lining, silk-lined gloves, fingerless gloves, driving gloves and gloves for kids of all ages.

Site Usability:	★★★★	Based:	UK
Product Range:	★★★	Express Delivery Option? (UK)	No
Price Range:	Medium	Gift Wrapping Option?	No
Delivery Area:	UK	Returns Procedure:	Down to you

www.trehearneandbrar.com

This must surely be the most beautiful collection of pashminas and shawls available. Don't expect cheap prices here and don't expect to be able to see them all online either. You need to email them or call for a brochure. (Hopefully they'll be online soon, although it would be very difficult to show the constantly changing range.) The collection includes plain, dyed-to-order, lined and reversible shawls, plus blankets and exquisite beaded shawls, all of the best quality you can find.

Site Usability:	★★★	Based:	UK
Product Range:	★★★	Express Delivery Option? (UK)	No
Price Range:	Luxury	Gift Wrapping Option?	No
Delivery Area:	Worldwide	Returns Procedure:	Down to you

www.wonderfulwraps.com

Established for over ten years, Wonderful Wraps has featured in major UK retail outlets such as Harrods, Selfridges and Harvey Nichols in London and Saks Fifth Avenue and Neiman Marcus in the US. The website offers a collection of sumptuous velvets, silk organzas, chiffons and tulles, satins, faux furs, marabous and other luxury wraps, stoles and capes, with styles ranging from luxurious embroidered organzas to classic angora throws. To place your order you need to call them.

Site Usability:	★★★	Based:	UK
Product Range:	★★★	Express Delivery Option? (UK)	No
Price Range:	Luxury/Medium	Gift Wrapping Option?	No
Delivery Area:	Worldwide	Returns Procedure:	Down to you

www.zocaloalpaca.com

This is a small, fairly new online retailer, specialising in (yes, you guessed it) South American alpaca products from soft and light baby alpaca scarves to brightly coloured striped shawls and chunky wraps. The advantage here is that the products look lovely, with a wide choice of colourways, the prices are very reasonable and the site offers an express service plus gift wrapping. So if you want to give a pretty scarf or shawl that isn't cheap pashmina, you can shop here instead.

Site Usability:	★★★★	Based:	UK
Product Range:	★★★	Express Delivery Option? (UK)	Yes
Price Range:	Medium/Very Good Value	Gift Wrapping Option?	Yes
Delivery Area:	Worldwide	Returns Procedure:	Down to you

Section 2
Fashion for Men

*A*s you've probably realised, this book is for you, girls, and I forgive you if at this point you're wondering why I've included menswear. The fact is that having three men in my family, I simply felt that it would be wrong to leave them out entirely – after all, when you're buying that essential new cashmere shrug for yourself and a fragranced candle for a friend, you might want to have a browse through some of the stylish men's websites to find something for your husband/partner/best male friend's next birthday, mightn't you?

Having said that, this range is too good to be just for gifts, as it covers everything from socks and shoes to his next kilt. And because of the online competition for products such as shirts, you'll often find really good deals online that you won't find in the shops, from premium menswear brands such as Hilditch and Key and Harvie and Hudson and sales that seem to start practically at the beginning of the season.

Where suits are concerned, obviously that's over to him (with a bit of input from you, maybe, regarding cloth and cut), but for those who really do have little time, to be able to order an extremely high-quality suit online, cut to fit, must be a huge benefit. Or the kilt, of course (and yes, I am being serious, sort of).

Chapter 16

Shirts, Ties, Cufflinks and Belts

This is the easiest range of men's products to buy online as fit tends to be standard (although always check the size charts), the competition, as I've said before, is driving prices downwards all the time for premium products and the amount of choice is breathtaking. So whether he's a stripe, check or Oxford cloth man and likes cutaway, standard or button-down collars, double or single cuffs and shirts with or without pockets, he or you will find every choice here.

The same goes for the accessories: ties, cufflinks and belts – take a look round and you'll see what I mean.

Sites to Visit

www.coles-shirtmakers.com

Here you'll find high-quality shirts with an excellent choice of fabrics and styles and an emphasis on finish. You can order from the standard selection or alternatively have your new shirt made exactly to your measurements (be careful here as, of course, you won't be able to return a bespoke shirt unless it's faulty). There's a discount system if you spend over a certain amount and a lot of information on how to order the perfect shirt. The site also offers ties and cufflinks.

Site Usability: ★★★★	Based:	UK
Product Range: ★★★★	Express Delivery Option? (UK)	Yes
Price Range: Medium	Gift Wrapping Option?	No
Delivery Area: Worldwide	Returns Procedure:	Down to you

www.ctshirts.co.uk

Well known for its colourful and well laid out catalogue, now you can order all the shirts, handmade shoes, ties and other accessories online. The website is attractive and easy to navigate and the service is excellent. A range of shirt qualities and styles is available and there are frequently special offers. There's a good selection of casual shirts and knitwear, tailoring, ladies' shirts, cashmere knits and accessories and 'Tiny Tyrwhitt' clothing too.

Site Usability: ★★★★★	Based:	UK
Product Range: ★★★★★	Express Delivery Option? (UK)	Yes
Price Range: Medium	Gift Wrapping Option?	Yes
Delivery Area: Worldwide	Returns Procedure:	Down to you

www.curtisanddyer.co.uk

Curtis and Dyer does not have retail outlets, so you may well find that the shirts sell online for quite a lot less than you would expect to pay for the quality. You will also be given the opportunity of supplying them with your exact specification. The shirt selector is excellent. First you choose your fabric, then collar type, cuff type and neck measurement, then input your exact measurements if you want to or use the standard sizing.

Site Usability: ★★★★★	Based:	UK
Product Range: ★★★★	Express Delivery Option? (UK)	No
Price Range: Medium	Gift Wrapping Option?	No
Delivery Area: UK	Returns Procedure:	Down to you

www.gievesandhawkes.com

Situated at Number 1 Savile Row, London and established in 1785, Gieves and Hawkes has always stood for the very best in men's tailoring, whether for formal evening wear, suiting or casual wear. On its website you can now not only find out a great deal about the brand, but also choose from the high-quality range of shirts, belts and braces, cufflinks, shoes and ties.

Site Usability:	★★★★	Based:	UK
Product Range:	★★★	Express Delivery Option? (UK)	No
Price Range:	Luxury/Medium	Gift Wrapping Option?	Yes
Delivery Area:	EU	Returns Procedure:	Down to you

www.harvieandhudson.com

Harvie and Hudson is a family-owned London shirtmaker and gentlemen's outfitter based in Jermyn Street, St James's and Knightsbridge. It offers a wide range of shirts online, from deep button-down to classic striped, plain and check shirts, unusual colour combinations and excellent country shirts. You can have your shirt custom-made by selecting from the fabrics, then choosing your cuff and collar style. You can also order from the selection of ties, links, socks and evening-wear shirts and accessories.

Site Usability:	★★★★	Based:	UK
Product Range:	★★★★★	Express Delivery Option? (UK)	No
Price Range:	Medium	Gift Wrapping Option?	No
Delivery Area:	Worldwide	Returns Procedure:	Down to you

www.hilditchandkey.co.uk

Recognised as one of the longest established Jermyn Street retailers of men's shirts and accessories (as well as some women's shirts), Hilditch manages to give you a top-of-the-range shopping experience without you having to leave home. The shirts are not the cheapest, definitely, but if you order from them you'll be absolutely certain that you'll get the high quality you're paying for. The site also offers silk ties and some clothing.

Site Usability:	★★★★★	Based:	UK
Product Range:	★★★★	Express Delivery Option? (UK)	No
Price Range:	Luxury	Gift Wrapping Option?	No
Delivery Area:	Worldwide	Returns Procedure:	Down to you

www.josephturner.co.uk

Joseph Turner offers men's shirts, ties, cufflinks, sweaters, shoes and accessories with a wide choice in all areas and regular special offers. The shoes are made for the company by Loake. There's much more information than usual on sizing, together with an alterations service. As with all the men's clothing websites they're extremely keen to offer something extra, so you'll find cashmere sweaters, socks and belts here as well.

Site Usability:	★★★★★	Based:	UK
Product Range:	★★★★★	Express Delivery Option? (UK)	No
Price Range:	Medium	Gift Wrapping Option?	No
Delivery Area:	UK	Returns Procedure:	Down to you

www.manning-and-manning.com

This is not one of the modern, beautifully photographed websites, but what you will find here are not only classic Jermyn Street-style shirts but also the 'Stateside' fit which the company recommends for more casual shirts. Here you choose your shirt measurements by going for the standard fit or inputting your own, then you select from a wide range of fabrics and finally the fit you want. Prices are high, but bearing in mind you'll end up with a unique shirt, if you're looking for the very best that's what you'll get.

Site Usability:	★★★	Based:	UK
Product Range:	★★★★★	Express Delivery Option? (UK)	No
Price Range:	Luxury/Medium	Gift Wrapping Option?	No
Delivery Area:	Worldwide	Returns Procedure:	Down to you

www.thomaspink.co.uk

Thomas Pink has a slick and beautifully designed site offering shirts, clothing and accessories for men and women. There's an enormous amount of detail available for every product, plus clear pictures and a speedy search facility by pattern, style and finish. You can also buy scarves, knitwear, accessories and nightwear. What's more, you can always be sure that what you'll receive will be a high-quality product, beautifully packaged and extremely well made.

Site Usability:	★★★★	Based:	UK
Product Range:	★★★★	Express Delivery Option? (UK)	Yes
Price Range:	Luxury	Gift Wrapping Option?	Yes
Delivery Area:	Worldwide	Returns Procedure:	Down to you

www.woodsofshropshire.co.uk

This is a shirt retailer with a difference, offering you high-quality shirts, not cheap and not overpriced, free and easy returns, worldwide delivery, extra collar stiffeners with every shirt, plus complimentary silk knots with double-cuff shirts. Roll your mouse over the shirt and tie pics and you can home in on the fabrics. You can buy large-size shirts here too, up to a collar size 20. A great deal of thought has gone into this website and it shows. Couple that with a well-made shirt for £30 (at time of writing) and you have a website well worth a try.

Site Usability:	★★★★	Based:	UK
Product Range:	★★★★	Express Delivery Option? (UK)	No
Price Range:	Medium	Gift Wrapping Option?	No
Delivery Area:	Worldwide	Returns Procedure:	Down to you

Chapter 17

Tailoring and Formal Wear

This is an excellent place to take a look at a wide variety of suiting, whether or not you want to buy online (and by 'you' I'm talking to him now – just for the next few chapters, I promise). I'm sure that if you're a suit man you've worked out whether wide or narrow stripes suit you, or whether you prefer single- or double-breasted jackets, but if you're thinking of a change or would like to see a range first without having to go to the shops, then this is the place.

If you're thinking of ordering an expensive suit online, and particularly if any aspect of it is bespoke, I suggest you call the tailor and ask for some swatches of cloth as there would be nothing worse than having something expensive made for you and then finding you don't like the feel of the fabric. I think this applies particularly to men's formal wear as many of the cloths look the same but feel different – most of the difference, of course, showing in the price.

Once you've decided what you want, many of the tailors below will give you a very good deal on a second pair of trousers which is well worth taking up – after all, most of the investment is made on the jacket and most of the wear on the trouser. You would never be able to match that exact fabric again, so consider it now.

Sites to Visit

www.austinreed.co.uk

The choice on this website is growing every season and now you can buy men's tailoring, shirts and ties, casual jackets, trousers and knitwear. The photography is very simple compared with most of the other men's websites and some of the products are quite hard to see. Balance this against the fact that you almost certainly know the name and the quality that it represents and you'll want to have a look round.

Site Usability:	★★★	Based:	UK
Product Range:	★★★	Express Delivery Option? (UK)	No
Price Range:	Medium	Gift Wrapping Option?	No
Delivery Area:	UK	Returns Procedure:	Down to you

www.blackstonelewis.co.uk

Blackstone Lewis offers you the facility of designing a bespoke suit online. This may sound daft, but as soon as you visit the website you can tell that they really know what they're talking about. It's a cleverly laid-out site, but you'll need quite a lot of time to work through the whole process of choosing your cloth, style of jacket and trouser and all the details such as buttons and pockets. I suggest you ask them for a sample of your chosen cloth(s) before you start.

Site Usability:	★★★★★	Based:	UK
Product Range:	★★★★	Express Delivery Option? (UK)	No
Price Range:	Luxury/Medium	Gift Wrapping Option?	No
Delivery Area:	Worldwide	Returns Procedure:	Down to you

www.crombie.co.uk

The Crombie name has been synonymous for over 200 years with high-quality, hard-wearing cloth and while that continues, the Crombie brand has been developed into an excellent collection of clothing for men and women, some of which you can find online. There's an extensive range for men, including the famous Crombie coat, blazers and jackets, shirts, ties and other accessories, as well as some good gift ideas. There's a much smaller range for women, including some leather and suede.

Site Usability: ★★★★	Based:	UK
Product Range: ★★★★	Express Delivery Option? (UK)	No
Price Range: Luxury/Medium	Gift Wrapping Option?	No
Delivery Area: Worldwide	Returns Procedure:	Down to you

www.cromwellandsmith.co.uk

Cromwell & Smith is a Shrewsbury-based, high-quality men's outfitter offering a range of carefully selected suppliers for tailoring, shirts, shoes and casual wear, with labels such as Henry Cotton, Hilditch and Key, Bladen, Feraud, Crockett and Jones and Eton Shirts. This is a well-edited collection with simple, clear pictures and several views of each item. Expect quite high prices but excellent quality and service.

Site Usability: ★★★★★	Based:	UK
Product Range: ★★★	Express Delivery Option? (UK)	No
Price Range: Luxury/Medium	Gift Wrapping Option?	No
Delivery Area: Worldwide	Returns Procedure:	Down to you

www.haggarts.com

Haggarts of Aberfeldy is one of the most famous Scottish tweed producers, having been in business since 1801. Now it has put its excellent country clothing catalogue online, so if you're one for the great outdoors (think shooting, hunting, fishing), this website is a must. Traditional coats, sports jackets and shooting waistcoats, plus moleskins, plus twos, cords and cavalry twills, hunter boots, caps and hats, are just some of the items you can buy here. (You can even buy your Sherlock Holmes hat.)

Site Usability: ★★★	Based:	UK
Product Range: ★★★	Express Delivery Option? (UK)	No
Price Range: Medium	Gift Wrapping Option?	No
Delivery Area: Worldwide	Returns Procedure:	Down to you

www.hawesandcurtis.com

Hawes and Curtis was established in 1913 and is famous for being the creator of the backless waistcoat, which was worn under a tailcoat and was renowned for its comfort. Now on the excellently designed website you can choose from the range of classic and fashion shirts, ties, cufflinks, silk knots and boxer shorts. The site also offers a range of women's classic, high-quality shirts in three different styles.

Site Usability:	★★★★	Based:	UK
Product Range:	★★★	Express Delivery Option? (UK)	No
Price Range:	Medium	Gift Wrapping Option?	No
Delivery Area:	Worldwide	Returns Procedure:	Down to you

www.kinlochanderson.co.uk

The only place to buy a Scottish tartan kilt is, of course, Scotland, but if you can't make it up there then you can order it online from Kinloch Anderson. (Don't mock, my husband's a Scot and looks great in his kilt and now my eldest son has his as well.) You need to know which tartan you want to order from the site's extensive selection. You can also buy all the necessary accessories, including jackets and sporrans, skien dubhs (decorative knives), kilt pins, belts and footwear. There are kilts, jackets, sashes and accessories for ladies and children as well.

Site Usability:	★★★★	Based:	UK
Product Range:	★★★	Express Delivery Option? (UK)	No
Price Range:	Luxury/Medium	Gift Wrapping Option?	No
Delivery Area:	UK	Returns Procedure:	Down to you

www.milanclothing.com

At Milan Clothing you'll find casual clothing from brands such as Fake London, Paul Smith, Pringle and Paul and Shark. There's a wide selection, so you'll no doubt want to take advantage of the speedy search facility where you can search by brand, or type of clothing, or both. The pictures are very simple indeed because the range is changing all the time. However, this is a clear and easy-to-navigate site and one of the best for casual wear.

Site Usability:	★★★★★	Based:	UK
Product Range:	★★★★★	Express Delivery Option? (UK)	Yes
Price Range:	Medium	Gift Wrapping Option?	No
Delivery Area:	Worldwide	Returns Procedure:	Down to you

www.mossdirect.co.uk

No, this is not the place you can hire your dinner jacket, but an offshoot of the famous brand (and men's hire shop) retailing Moss Bros's own brand, plus Savoy Tailors Guild, De Havilland, Pierre Cardin and Baumler. You won't find an enormous range but a well-designed website with some good special offers and particularly good dress shirts (which is one of the things they're famous for, after all). Delivery is UK only and you need to allow ten days.

Site Usability:	★★★★	Based:	UK
Product Range:	★★★	Express Delivery Option? (UK)	No
Price Range:	Medium	Gift Wrapping Option?	No
Delivery Area:	UK	Returns Procedure:	Down to you

www.newandlingwood.com

In 1865 a Miss New and a Mr Lingwood founded the business which still bears their names. Now based in Jermyn Street, London, this is almost certainly the most traditional of the gentlemen's outfitters, supported by its own workrooms where they make bespoke and ready-made shirts, the finest quality piped pyjamas and bespoke shoes and boots. The website offers a selection of classic, casual and fashion shirts, footwear from luxury boots to casual shoes, and everything from velvet-collared coats to evening-wear accessories. Expect high prices and the very best quality here.

Site Usability:	★★★★	Based:	UK
Product Range:	★★★★	Express Delivery Option? (UK)	No
Price Range:	Luxury	Gift Wrapping Option?	No
Delivery Area:	Worldwide	Returns Procedure:	Down to you

www.pakeman.co.uk

Here's an extensive range of good-quality, sensibly priced classic clothing from this Cotswold-based retailer. For men you can choose from black-tie tailoring, suits, flannels, cords, jeans, shirts and ties, belts, shoes, cufflinks and underwear. The site offers a next-day delivery service for items in stock and the emphasis is on service and quality. This is not a complicated website but one where there is high standards in every area, so don't be put off by the simplicity of the pictures.

Site Usability: ★★★★		Based:	UK
Product Range: ★★★★		Express Delivery Option? (UK)	No
Price Range:	Medium	Gift Wrapping Option?	No
Delivery Area:	Worldwide	Returns Procedure:	Down to you

www.perlui.co.uk

This is an excellent designer menswear store offering ranges by Lacoste, Ralph Lauren, Tommy Hilfiger, Ted Baker and many more. You'll find good discounts in the end-of-season sales, but otherwise the site offers full-price new season's stock. The collection is mainly casual and sportswear. You can also order from the Hackett range, but you have to call them to do so.

Site Usability: ★★★★		Based:	UK
Product Range: ★★★★		Express Delivery Option? (UK)	No
Price Range:	Luxury/Medium	Gift Wrapping Option?	No
Delivery Area:	Worldwide	Returns Procedure:	Down to you

www.racinggreen.co.uk

Famous for its well-priced men's and ladies' wear for several years, Racing Green has relaunched its website with a good range of menswear only, including shirts, tailoring, dinner jackets, dress shirts, shoes and accessories. It's an easy site to navigate and much more classic than it used to be, with smart pictures of a wide range of products. The prices are reasonable and the branding is classy, so definitely give it a try.

Site Usability: ★★★★★		Based:	UK
Product Range: ★★★★		Express Delivery Option? (UK)	Yes
Price Range:	Medium/Very Good Value	Gift Wrapping Option?	No
Delivery Area:	UK	Returns Procedure:	Down to you

www.savilerowco.com

This is a fast-developing range of menswear with everything you could possibly need, including tailoring (and dinner jackets), a wide range of formal shirts, casual shirts, trousers and sweaters, plus a full collection of accessories. The site is clearly photographed and the order system is really easy. There are also some men's gift ideas here, such as cashmere scarves and cufflinks.

Site Usability:	★★★★★	Based:	UK
Product Range:	★★★★★	Express Delivery Option? (UK)	Yes
Price Range:	Medium	Gift Wrapping Option?	No
Delivery Area:	Worldwide	Returns Procedure:	Free

www.tmlewin.co.uk

T M Lewin has one of the easiest sites to navigate, with simple drop-down menus and clear pictures. It also frequently has some very good special offers. You can buy almost everything here, from formal tailoring to casual trousers and a good selection of accessories. There is also a wide range of striped, check and solid-coloured shirts, with simple size and length options.

Site Usability:	★★★★	Based:	UK
Product Range:	★★★★	Express Delivery Option? (UK)	Yes
Price Range:	Medium	Gift Wrapping Option?	No
Delivery Area:	Worldwide	Returns Procedure:	Down to you

Chapter 18

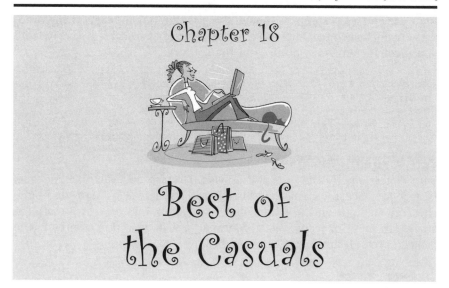

Best of the Casuals

From the essential country Barbour jacket to the best of the new season's hoodies from Quiksilver, O'Neill or Billabong, there are clothes for all lifestyles and ages here, so no matter how traditional or modern you like to dress take a look through and forget about trekking to the shops at the weekend.

If you want something really different and modern, take a look at www. oki-ni.co.uk, where special editions are created for brands such as Adidas and Evisu. For great jeans go straight to www.stone-island.co.uk (although they're quite expensive) and for great modern casuals to www.hackett.co.uk – expensive again, but it's a great brand.

A number of the other websites in this section also offer great casual wear, such as www.ctshirts.co.uk and www.racinggreen.co.uk, so don't forget to look through those as well.

Sites to Visit

www.countryattire.co.uk

Country Attire offers the best of the range of Barbour outerwear and clothing online, from the traditional wax jackets to quilted and tweed jackets, gilets, footwear and accessories. Although the photographs of some of the products are not as good as they could be, the selection is excellent. This website is a must for anyone who lives in the country.

Site Usability: ★★★★	Based:	UK
Product Range: ★★★★	Express Delivery Option? (UK)	Yes
Price Range: Medium	Gift Wrapping Option?	No
Delivery Area: Worldwide	Returns Procedure:	Down to you

www.d2-clothing.co.uk

With collections by Diesel, Adidas, Evisu, Firetrap and Fake London, this is a good place for casual clothing. You can choose by item or brand, click on an item and see immediately whether they have your size in stock. Try here for jeans, casual footwear, a wide selection of urban-style jackets, great T-shirts and essential beanies.

Site Usability: ★★★★	Based:	UK
Product Range: ★★★★	Express Delivery Option? (UK)	No
Price Range: Medium	Gift Wrapping Option?	No
Delivery Area: UK	Returns Procedure:	Down to you

www.extremepie.com

There are enough sportswear brands here to sink a ship, from famous brands such as O'Neill, Quiksilver, Animal, Vans, Billabong, RipCurl, Addict, Extreme and Reef, to loads more that you may not have heard of. This is definitely a good site for anyone who's addicted to sport, or who just wants the sporty, casual look. It also sells snowboards, skateboards, wetsuits, accessories and sunglasses by Animal and Roxy.

Site Usability: ★★★★	Based:	UK
Product Range: ★★★★	Express Delivery Option? (UK)	Yes
Price Range: Medium	Gift Wrapping Option?	No
Delivery Area: Worldwide	Returns Procedure:	Down to you

www.fatface.com

When you first take a look at the fatface.com website you may be a little disconcerted. It's certainly not like most others, with pictures and type used to reinforce Fatface's idiosyncratic, 'cool', active style. But it works.

You'll find a wide selection of tops and T-shirts, jackets and fleece, denim and sweats, all in unique fabrics and style and the company's more-often-than-not muted colour palette.

Site Usability:	★★★★	Based:	UK
Product Range:	★★★★	Express Delivery Option? (UK)	Yes
Price Range:	Medium	Gift Wrapping Option?	No
Delivery Area:	Worldwide	Returns Procedure:	Down to you

www.hackett.co.uk

Famous for using Jonny Wilkinson as its model as well as for great-quality clothing, Hackett now offers a selection of sportswear, tailoring, shirts and ties, knitwear and outerwear online. In the Rugby Shop you can choose from a good selection of striped rugby shirts, while in the Aston Martin Shop you'll find 'Aston Martin Racing by Hackett' socks, hats and brollies.

Site Usability:	★★★★	Based:	UK
Product Range:	★★★	Express Delivery Option? (UK)	No
Price Range:	Medium	Gift Wrapping Option?	No
Delivery Area:	UK	Returns Procedure:	Down to you/complicated

www.oki-ni.com

Oki-ni is an independent, London-based design group, working in collaboration with a range of globally renowned brands and designers such as Aquascutum, Adidas, Evisu and Tanner Krolle to create products unique to Oki-ni and available only online from its website. You can choose from footwear, jeans, jackets and accessories, all with an unusual designer twist. All items are available in limited numbers, so if you see something you like, order it fast.

Site Usability:	★★★★	Based:	UK
Product Range:	★★★	Express Delivery Option? (UK)	2 working days
Price Range:	Luxury/Medium	Gift Wrapping Option?	No
Delivery Area:	UK	Returns Procedure:	Down to you

www.orvis.co.uk

Originally a company specialising in fishing equipment, Orvis has developed its brand to offer a full clothing and accessories range for men and women. You'll find high-quality classic outerwear here, from Donegal tweed jackets to quilted, microfibre coats, plus knitwear, shirts, polos, T-shirts and accessories, all in a wide choice of colours. There is also hardwearing footwear and the Barbour Collection.

Site Usability:	★★★★★	Based:	UK
Product Range:	★★★★★	Express Delivery Option? (UK)	Yes
Price Range:	Medium	Gift Wrapping Option?	Yes
Delivery Area:	Worldwide	Returns Procedure:	Down to you

www.rohan.co.uk

Specialist in easy-care (easy-wear, easy-wash-and-dry) travel and casual clothing, Rohan offers trousers, shirts, underwear and accessories for men and women. You select depending on the type of activity, clothing or climate and there's a good selection, lots of information and fast service. If you're planning a visit to the jungle, this is an excellent website as you can buy not only your clothing but also clever washbags, microfibre towels, dry wash, travel bottles and lots of other accessories.

Site Usability:	★★★★	Based:	UK
Product Range:	★★★★	Express Delivery Option? (UK)	Yes
Price Range:	Medium	Gift Wrapping Option?	No
Delivery Area:	Worldwide	Returns Procedure:	Down to you

www.routeone.co.uk

Route One is a young, committed, independent store aimed at inline skaters and skateboarders. But with such a large selection of shoes, clothing and accessories by brands such as Converse, Atticus, Fenchurch, Billabong and Carhatt (and, I have to confess, loads of others I hadn't heard of), it's bound to appeal to anyone who likes a contemporary, sporty look. The service is speedy and reliable.

Site Usability:	★★★★	Based:	UK
Product Range:	★★★★	Express Delivery Option? (UK)	Yes
Price Range:	Medium	Gift Wrapping Option?	No
Delivery Area:	Worldwide	Returns Procedure:	Down to you

www.stoneisland.co.uk

Trendy, relaxed and well-photographed, this website offers Stone Island and C.P. casual wear (and some more formal jackets), plus outerwear, jeans, shirts, knitwear and accessories. This is an extremely fast and attractive website. Be warned though, the products are high-quality designer gear and not inexpensive, so if you're looking for a cheap pair of casual jeans you'll be disappointed.

Site Usability:	★★★★★	Based:	UK
Product Range:	★★★	Express Delivery Option? (UK)	No
Price Range:	Luxury/Medium	Gift Wrapping Option?	No
Delivery Area:	UK	Returns Procedure:	No

www.theclothesstore.com

Click on the cute icons here to choose the type of clothing you're looking for and select from the excellent collections by Burberry London, Nigel Hall, Lacoste, Puma and One True Saxon and 'Urban Menswear' by Fred Perry, Ben Sherman, Wrangler and Edge. The designer ranges are changing all the time so check back to see who's listed each season. They also offer a funky collection from Converse and Kickers.

Site Usability:	★★★★	Based:	Channel Islands
Product Range:	★★★★	Express Delivery Option? (UK)	No
Price Range:	Medium	Gift Wrapping Option?	No
Delivery Area:	Worldwide	Returns Procedure:	Down to you

www.w1style.co.uk

This is an excellent website offering new and current brands such as Quiksilver, Roxy, O'Neill, Bench, Billabong, Diesel and FCUK in an easy-to-view format. Although most of the items offered are brand-new current season's stock (and new stock is regularly being added to the site), there are also some good reductions. They will ship to North America as well as Europe and all items are shipped from Gibraltar.

Site Usability:	★★★★	Based:	Gibraltar
Product Range:	★★★★★	Express Delivery Option? (UK)	Yes
Price Range:	Medium	Gift Wrapping Option?	Yes
Delivery Area:	EU and North America	Returns Procedure:	Down to you

Chapter 19

Shoes and Accessories

For some reason people have the idea that buying shoes online is difficult when actually it's even easier than buying clothes – after all, put weight on or take it off, your shoe size doesn't normally change (within reason). Particularly with men's shoes, if you have a favourite brand, the sizing is even more likely to stay constant, so do take a look here. There are so many high-quality brands available, you can see all the styles in one place and many of these retailers offer extremely quick shipping.

You'll also find accessories here that weren't included in the Shirts and Ties chapter, although separating out the ranges becomes quite complicated when some of the retailers offering shirts and ties start to include shoes, wallets and cufflinks as well, so don't take this as the final list – look there as well.

International Shoe Size Conversion Table

UK	7	7.5	8	8.5	9	9.5	10	10.5	11	11.5	12
EU	40.5	41	42	42.5	43	44	44.5	45	46	46.5	47
US	7.5	8	8.5	9	9.5	10	10.5	11	11.5	12	12.5

Sites to Visit

www.aspinal.co.uk

Aspinal specialises in leather gifts and accessories and there's a wide choice of styles and colours in each section. In the 'Executive Folios and Cases' there are zipped document cases in a choice of eight colours, conference portfolios, leather ring binders, jotters and memos and leather document envelopes. There are other gift ideas here, including stud boxes, leather journals and handmade books using age-old traditional leather and bookbinding skills.

Site Usability:	★★★★★	Based:	UK
Product Range:	★★★★★	Express Delivery Option? (UK)	Yes
Price Range:	Medium	Gift Wrapping Option?	Yes
Delivery Area:	Worldwide	Returns Procedure:	Down to you

www.bexley.com

This is a French-based website (although you'll probably be glad to know that there's an English translation) offering excellent shoes and accessories for men. Clearly and attractively photographed and easy to navigate, you can buy socks, formal and casual shoes, ties, shoe trees, polishing kits, belts and gloves at reasonable prices. Average shipping time for Europe is roughly one week and up to two weeks for the rest of the world.

Site Usability:	★★★★	Based:	France
Product Range:	★★★★	Express Delivery Option? (UK)	No
Price Range:	Medium	Gift Wrapping Option?	No
Delivery Area:	Worldwide	Returns Procedure:	Down to you

www.dunhill.com

In 1893 Alfred Dunhill inherited his father's saddlery business on London's Euston Road and developed a luxurious line of accessories. The first collection included car horns and lamps, leather overcoats, goggles, picnic sets and timepieces. Over 100 years later Dunhill is one of the leading makers of English luxury accessories for men. Here you can choose from the range, which includes luggage, briefcases, washbags, wallets, diaries and belts, ties and cufflinks.

Site Usability:	★★★★	Based:	UK
Product Range:	★★★	Express Delivery Option? (UK)	No
Price Range:	Luxury	Gift Wrapping Option?	No
Delivery Area:	UK	Returns Procedure:	Down to you

www.forzieri.com

Italian company Forzieri offers ties by Dolce & Gabbana, Kenzo and Versace (among others), belts by Gianfranco Ferre, wallets, briefcases, leather travel bags and other small accessories, plus high-quality shoes by Packerson, Mariano Campanile, Brunori and Forzieri's own brand, where you'll expect to pay around £240. Very good descriptions are given about the products and their manufacturers and the pictures are exceptionally clear.

Site Usability:	★★★★★	Based:	Italy
Product Range:	★★★★★	Express Delivery Option? (UK)	Yes
Price Range:	Luxury/Medium	Gift Wrapping Option?	Yes
Delivery Area:	Worldwide	Returns Procedure:	Down to you

www.kjbeckett.com

K J Beckett has a good selection of accessories for men, including Regent Belt Company belts, cufflinks by Simon Carter, Ian Flaherty and Veritas, silk ties, cummerbunds, wallets and handkerchiefs – and that's just a few of the many items on offer. They'll deliver almost anywhere in the world using the site's priority service and UK delivery is free of charge.

Site Usability:	★★★★★	Based:	UK
Product Range:	★★★★★	Express Delivery Option? (UK)	Yes
Price Range:	Luxury/Medium	Gift Wrapping Option?	Yes
Delivery Area:	Worldwide	Returns Procedure:	Down to you

www.pickett.co.uk

Gloves, wallets, umbrellas, belts, briefcases and stud boxes are just some of the high-quality, beautifully made men's accessories available on Pickett's website. If you've ever visited one of the company's shops you'll know that everything is the best you can buy and most items would make lovely gifts. Couple this with the distinctive dark green and orange packaging and excellent service and you can't go wrong, whatever you choose.

Site Usability:	★★★★	Based:	UK
Product Range:	★★★★	Express Delivery Option? (UK)	No
Price Range:	Luxury/Medium	Gift Wrapping Option?	No, but luxury packaging is standard
Delivery Area:	Worldwide	Returns Procedure:	Down to you

www.pierotucci.com

There's a good range of briefcases and bags on this Florence-based website, from hard-sided briefcases to slim portfolios, soft travel and duffle bags, wallets and belts. Everything is made in Italy (as you'd expect) and because it's an Italian brand (rather than a 'designer' brand), some of the prices are quite reasonable, although you are looking at top Italian quality. The site offers UPS express shipping to anywhere in the world.

Site Usability:	★★★★	Based:	Italy
Product Range:	★★★★	Express Delivery Option? (UK)	Yes
Price Range:	Medium	Gift Wrapping Option?	No
Delivery Area:	Worldwide	Returns Procedure:	Down to you

www.sandstormbags.com

If you're a luxury consumer on the lookout for products that not only work well but have a high degree of authenticity, Sandstorm fits the bill. Sandstorm is the only range of authentic premium, safari-style bags out of Africa. These beautiful bags are handcrafted in Kenya and are perfect for your next safari, walking in the Cotswolds or weekend city breaks in five-star hotels. They look good anywhere, delivering a striking combination of luxury, style and durability.

Site Usability:	★★★★	Based:	UK
Product Range:	★★★★	Express Delivery Option? (UK)	Yes
Price Range:	Luxury/Medium	Gift Wrapping Option?	No
Delivery Area:	Worldwide	Returns Procedure:	Down to you

www.shiptonandheneage.co.uk

Shipton and Heneage has been trading for more than 12 years and offers a good, high-quality collection of over 120 styles of shoe. You choose first from different types of shoes, such as brogues, country shoes, town shoes,

Oxfords, extra wide and loafers. Then you make your choice from the selection of each that rapidly appears. There is also a range of sailing shoes, plus slippers, socks and accessories.

Site Usability: ★★★★★	Based:	UK
Product Range: ★★★★	Express Delivery Option? (UK)	Yes
Price Range: Medium	Gift Wrapping Option?	No
Delivery Area: Worldwide	Returns Procedure:	Down to you

www.shoesdirect.co.uk

For reasonably priced smart and casual shoes, stop here, where you'll find Loake, Rockport, Gregson, Ecco, Clarks and Barker. Everything is clearly shown and the order process couldn't be easier. Some of the shoes go up to a UK size 16, which is really large. If you're in doubt about which size to use, the shoe size conversion chart is always available. The site will also tell you which shoes have extra width. Mainland UK deliveries are free for orders over £30.

Site Usability: ★★★★★	Based:	UK
Product Range: ★★★★★	Express Delivery Option? (UK)	No
Price Range: Medium	Gift Wrapping Option?	No
Delivery Area: UK	Returns Procedure:	Down to you

www.wellie-web.co.uk

Here's a website with a name that you won't forget quickly, but if you're someone who spends a lot of time outdoors, particularly in wet weather, you'll find it indispensable. You can find a cheap pair of wellies here with prices starting at £22 and you'll also find some with flowers all over them (er, maybe not). However, this website specialises in the quality end of the market where a top-notch pair of boots can set you back up to £200.

Site Usability: ★★★★	Based:	UK
Product Range: ★★★★	Express Delivery Option? (UK)	No
Price Range: Luxury/Medium	Gift Wrapping Option?	No
Delivery Area: UK	Returns Procedure:	Down to you

Also visit the following websites for men's shoes and accessories:

Website address	You'll find them in:
www.ctshirts.co.uk	Shirts and Ties
www.josephturner.co.uk	Shirts and Ties
www.gucci.com	Handbag Temptation/The A List

Chapter 20

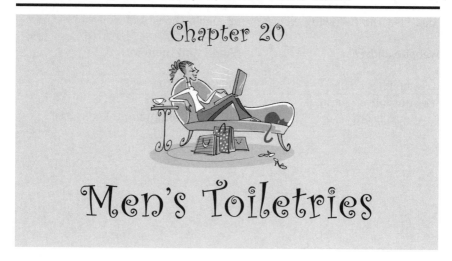

Men's Toiletries

There probably isn't a brand of fragrance or grooming product that you can't find online. There are some excellent websites where you can get discounts and/or free delivery, such as www.beautybay.com and www.strawberrynet.com. Be aware that if you're ordering from overseas (Strawberrynet, for example, is based in Hong Kong) you may well have to pay duty. So it's probably worthwhile doing this only if you're getting a good discount, or if you're buying something very different which you can't buy here.

Of course, the real problem for shopaholics is that when you're browsing the fragrance websites (for men) you'll no doubt find something you like as well, as most of the websites, other than the ones dedicated to men's shaving and grooming, sell women's fragrances too, so if necessary grit your teeth and click on the 'men's fragrance' button.

Some of the websites I've included below carry the full range of well-known products from makes such as Dior, Chanel, Lacoste, etc. - everything for everyone, as it were. What I've also included are those specialised websites which offer something a bit different - www.carterandbond.co.uk for modern and traditional men's grooming products and accessories, www.jasonshankey.co.uk, which has an amazing range for both men and women, including some products you probably won't have heard of (well I hadn't, anyway), and www.theenglishshavingcompany.co.uk, which offers exactly what you'd expect.

Sites to Visit

www.1001beautysecrets.com/beauty/caswell

I've included this website because here you can buy products from Caswell Massey, one of America's oldest perfumers. If you'd like to try something different, check out the excellent men's range, including the Newport, Lime and Verbena fragrances. There's a full range of products, from cologne to soap to shower gel, and with everything so smartly packaged they'd make great gifts as well.

Site Usability:	★★★★	Based:	US
Product Range:	★★★	Express Delivery Option? (UK)	No
Price Range:	Medium	Gift Wrapping Option?	No
Delivery Area:	Worldwide	Returns Procedure:	Down to you

www.aehobbs.com

This is a simple website from a retailer which has been based in Tunbridge Wells for over 100 years. It offers traditional grooming and toiletry products from the barbershop from brands such as Truefitt and Hill, Woods of Windsor, Mason and Pearson and Kent and from the beauty department from Klorane, Perlier and Olverum. The site stocks Zambesia Botanica as well, which is a special range for people with sensitive skin.

Site Usability:	★★★★	Based:	UK
Product Range:	★★★	Express Delivery Option? (UK)	No
Price Range:	Medium	Gift Wrapping Option?	No
Delivery Area:	Worldwide	Returns Procedure:	Down to you

www.carterandbond.com

Carter and Bond was established in 2002 to bring together the very finest male grooming products around. The simple-to-use, secure website is home to over 600 products from more than 40 brands, including Molton Brown, American Crew, Baxter of California, Geo F Trumper and Proraso. Whether you're looking for skincare, hair care, fragrance, shaving products or gift ideas, you'll find it all here. Orders received by 2.30pm are despatched the same day (to anywhere in the world) and gift wrapping is available for just 95p per item.

Site Usability:	★★★★★	Based:	UK
Product Range:	★★★★★	Express Delivery Option? (UK)	Yes
Price Range:	Medium	Gift Wrapping Option?	Yes
Delivery Area:	Worldwide	Returns Procedure:	Down to you

www.jasonshankey.co.uk

If you're a fan of Tigi, Fudge, NV Perricone, Skin Doctors or Dermatologica products, this could well be the place for you, and there are lots of other brands as well. The range includes everything from hair and nail care to hair appliances, men's grooming and slimming products. The easiest way to use this website is definitely to know the brand you're looking for, then just click on the list to your left and you'll be away.

Site Usability:	★★★★	Based:	UK
Product Range:	★★★★	Express Delivery Option? (UK)	Yes
Price Range:	Medium	Gift Wrapping Option?	Yes
Delivery Area:	Worldwide	Returns Procedure:	Down to you

www.mankind.co.uk

This is definitely one of the best men's websites. It's modern, easy to use and has a great range of products, showcasing the very best and most innovative shaving, skin and hair-care brands made for men such as Lab Series, Nickel and K2 and offering them in a way that makes buying simple, fast and fun. There are shaving products, skin basics and problem-skin solutions as well as gift ideas here.

Site Usability:	★★★★★	Based:	UK
Product Range:	★★★★★	Express Delivery Option? (UK)	Yes
Price Range:	Medium	Gift Wrapping Option?	Yes
Delivery Area:	Worldwide	Returns Procedure:	Down to you

www.theenglishshavingcompany.co.uk

Here you'll find the highest quality handcrafted razors and shaving sets, plus travel sets, soaps, brushes and aftershaves from Geo Trumper, Edwin Jagger, D R Harris and Molton Brown. You can read the 'shaving tutorial' in Useful Information, plus razor shaving tips. So if you're tired of using your electric razor and want to turn traditional you'll definitely need this site.

Site Usability:	★★★★	Based:	UK
Product Range:	★★★★	Express Delivery Option? (UK)	No
Price Range:	Luxury/Medium	Gift Wrapping Option?	Yes
Delivery Area:	Worldwide	Returns Procedure:	Down to you

www.trumpers.com

Established in 1875 in Curzon Street, Mayfair, this famous traditional London barber is well known for superb exclusive men's fragrances and grooming products. Think of fragrances such as Sandalwood, Bay Rum and Spanish Leather, which all have matching soaps and body washes. Now you can buy the full range online, plus an exclusive collection of ties and cufflinks, and they'll be delighted to ship to you anywhere in the world.

Site Usability:	★★★★	Based:	UK
Product Range:	★★★★	Express Delivery Option? (UK)	Yes
Price Range:	Luxury/Medium	Gift Wrapping Option?	Yes
Delivery Area:	Worldwide	Returns Procedure:	Free

Other websites to visit for men's toiletries:

Website address	You'll find them in:
www.escentual.co.uk	Fragrance, Bath and Body
www.penhaligons.co.uk	Fragrance, Bath and Body
www.woodruffs.co.uk	Fragrance, Bath and Body
www.boots.com	Modern Cosmetics and Skincare
www.garden.co.uk	Modern Cosmetics and Skincare

Section 3
Pamper Yourself

This is an extremely dangerous area in which to go shopping online, so be warned. (I think I said that before somewhere, but anyway, here again.) Whatever your current pampering requirements you'll find them here, plus there is lots to explore, to discover for the first time and to be dreadfully tempted by.

So whether you're looking for your favourite skincare and cosmetic brand or a new, special treatment that you can normally find only in salons, essential aromatherapy oils, luxurious fragranced candles or organic skincare lines, you'll find them all here.

I know only too well that some of you will want to point out to me that you can't yet find the full range of modern US brands such as Bobbi Brown and Trish McEvoy online, but as you can find Laura Mercier and Nars (Space NK), Benefit, Pout, Bloom and Philosophy, and the others will surely be available very soon, you shouldn't complain too much.

Chapter 21

Fragrance, Bath and Body

S ome of the websites you'll find here just produce bath and body products and not fragrance, but the majority of premium brands offer the full range, from perfume and eau de toilette to bath and shower gels, body lotion, soaps and scented candles.

Alongside this choice there are lots of different price levels, so frankly you can spend a fortune if you want to or just invest in one product (and spend a fortune there). If you're trying something for the first time, I would – particularly for an expensive brand – call and ask them for a sample before leaping into a new range. Personally I find that no matter how good the description, I have to smell something before I can be sure that I'll like it. Alternatively, start off by trying the soap or shower gel and go from there – it's much less risky.

Sites to Visit

www.arranaromatics.com

If you want to find something a little unusual, beautifully presented and well priced, look no further than Arran Aromatics, where you can discover bath and body products, candles and much more with names such as After the

Rain, Angelica, Bay Citrus and Parfumeur. The packaging is very pretty and you can select from individual items such as living fragrances, shower gels and bath soak grains or the excellent gift boxes.

Site Usability:	★★★★★	Based:	UK
Product Range:	★★★★	Express Delivery Option? (UK)	Yes
Price Range:	Medium/Very Good Value	Gift Wrapping Option?	No
Delivery Area:	Worldwide	Returns Procedure:	Down to you

www.bathandunwind.com

Bath & Unwind specialises in luxury products that help you to relax (and unwind) after a hard day's work. It aims to provide the highest quality bath and spa products from around the world, including brands such as Aromatherapy Associates, Korres, Nougat, Burt's Bees and Jane Packer. Delivery is free (UK) provided you spend over a certain amount and they'll ship to you anywhere in the world. There is also a gift selector and an express service for the next time you forget that special present.

Site Usability:	★★★★	Based:	UK
Product Range:	★★★★	Express Delivery Option? (UK)	Yes
Price Range:	Medium	Gift Wrapping Option?	No
Delivery Area:	Worldwide	Returns Procedure:	Down to you

www.beautybay.com

This is a beautifully laid out website offering just about every fragrance, with bath and body products to match, and a small range of cosmetics and skincare, plus jewellery and fragrance giftsets (excellent for presents). Delivery is free on orders over £30, they'll ship to just about anywhere in the world and offer a next-day service. What's particularly good here is that on many of the products you'll find yourself spending less than you expected. What more could you want?

Site Usability:	★★★★★	Based:	UK
Product Range:	★★★★	Express Delivery Option? (UK)	Yes
Price Range:	Luxury/Medium/Very Good Value	Gift Wrapping Option?	No
Delivery Area:	Worldwide	Returns Procedure:	Down to you

www.crabtree-evelyn.co.uk

Well-known and sold throughout the world, Crabtree & Evelyn offers a wide range of bath, body and spa products, from classic fragrances such as Lily of the Valley to the ultra modern La Source. Everything is cleverly and attractively packaged and offered here on the well-designed and easy-to-use website. Particularly good as gifts are the pretty boxes containing miniatures of the company's most popular products.

Site Usability:	★★★★★	Based:	UK
Product Range:	★★★★★	Express Delivery Option? (UK)	No
Price Range:	Medium	Gift Wrapping Option?	No
Delivery Area:	Worldwide	Returns Procedure:	Down to you

www.cologneandcotton.com

This is a very special website offering some unusual and hard-to-find bath and body products and fragrance by Diptyque (if you haven't already tried their candles you really should: they're gorgeous), Cath Collins, La Compagnie de Provence and Cote Bastide. There are also fragrances by Annik Goutal, Coudray and Rosine and for the bathroom there are lovely fluffy towels and bathrobes.

Site Usability:	★★★★★	Based:	UK
Product Range:	★★★★	Express Delivery Option? (UK)	Yes
Price Range:	Luxury/Medium	Gift Wrapping Option?	Yes
Delivery Area:	Worldwide	Returns Procedure:	Down to you

www.escentual.co.uk

Escentual carries what is probably the widest range of fragrance for men and women in the UK. Choose a fragrance or fragrance-linked bath and body product, then search for it on this site – you're almost certain to find it. Bath and body products include Burberry, Bvlgari, Calvin Klein, Gucci, Guerlain, Rochas and Versace, plus Crabtree & Evelyn, Tisserand and I Coloniali. Delivery is free on orders over £30 and they also offer free gift wrapping.

Site Usability:	★★★★★	Based:	UK
Product Range:	★★★★★	Express Delivery Option? (UK)	Yes
Price Range:	Luxury/Medium/Very Good Value	Gift Wrapping Option?	Yes
Delivery Area:	Worldwide	Returns Procedure:	Down to you

www.florislondon.com

Floris is one of the oldest and most traditional perfumers, established in 1730. You'll find favourites such as Lavender, China Rose, Gardenia and Stephanotis and more modern fragrances including Night Scented Jasmin, Bouquet de la Reine and No 89. The updated packaging is lovely and for each fragrance there's a full range of bath and body products, plus special wrapped sets for Christmas.

Site Usability:	★★★★★	Based:	UK
Product Range:	★★★★★	Express Delivery Option? (UK)	Yes
Price Range:	Luxury/Medium	Gift Wrapping Option?	Yes
Delivery Area:	Worldwide	Returns Procedure:	Down to you

www.harrods.com

Personally I think that Harrods deserves a prize for taking the plunge and going online where other major department stores fear to tread – I'm sure you can guess who I mean. The range available is growing all the time and is very well presented. The strongest area is definitely beauty currently, where the bath and body ranges include REN, Floris, Korres, Acqua di Parma and Vie Lux. Buy from the site and encourage them to put more of the shop online.

Site Usability:	★★★★★	Based:	UK
Product Range:	★★★★	Express Delivery Option? (UK)	No
Price Range:	Luxury/Medium	Gift Wrapping Option?	No
Delivery Area:	Worldwide	Returns Procedure:	Down to you

www.jomalone.co.uk

When they think of Jo Malone, most people think of her gorgeous and luxurious fragrance and bath and body products. Take a good look again at her attractively designed website and you'll also find beautifully scented cleansers, serums and moisturisers and her facial finishers: finishing fluid and powder, lip gloss, blush and mascara. But beware: once you're on her site it's extremely hard to escape without buying. The service is excellent and everything is exquisitely packaged in her signature cream and black.

Site Usability:	★★★★★	Based:	UK
Product Range:	★★★★★	Express Delivery Option? (UK)	Yes
Price Range:	Luxury	Gift Wrapping Option?	Yes
Delivery Area:	Worldwide	Returns Procedure:	Down to you

www.kennethturner.co.uk

White Flowers, Wild Garden, Magnolia Grandiflora and Rose (plus his Original fragrance) are some of the fragrances you'll find on this pretty website, presented as candles, tea lights, shower gel and body lotions, room colognes and pot pourri. His packaging, in flower-printed blue and white boxes, turns his products into perfect gifts and you'll find travel sets and prepared gift boxes here as well.

Site Usability:	★★★★	Based:	UK
Product Range:	★★★	Express Delivery Option? (UK)	Yes
Price Range:	Luxury/Medium	Gift Wrapping Option?	Yes
Delivery Area:	Worldwide	Returns Procedure:	Down to you

www.laboutiquedelartisanparfumeur.com

If you're not already aware of this gorgeous collection of French fragrance and bath and body products by L'Artisan Parfumeur, with names such as Mure et Musc (blackberry and musk), Figuier (fig tree) and Orchidee Blanche (white orchid), then now's the time to discover this beautifully presented range and order it online. You'll also find unusual ideas such as the blackberry-shaped glass bottle, scented silk peonies and terracotta amber balls, all of which make exceptional gifts.

Site Usability:	★★★★	Based:	UK
Product Range:	★★★	Express Delivery Option? (UK)	Yes
Price Range:	Luxury	Gift Wrapping Option?	Automatic
Delivery Area:	Worldwide	Returns Procedure:	Down to you

www.lessenteurs.com

Les Senteurs is a famous parfumerie based in London, offering unusual fragrance and bath and body products and excellent service. Brands on offer are Creed, Annick Goutal, Diptyque, E Coudray, Serge Lutens, Carons and Parfums Historique, to name but a few. The ranges are split into categories, such as fragrance, bath and body, or fragrance notes, such as citrus, oriental and fruity.

Site Usability: ★★★	Based:	UK
Product Range: ★★★★	Express Delivery Option? (UK)	No
Price Range: Luxury/Medium	Gift Wrapping Option?	Yes
Delivery Area: UK	Returns Procedure:	Down to you

www.miam-miam.co.uk

I had to find this one out. Dorothy Day of miam-miam tells me that the name is the French equivalent of our 'yummy' – 'because everything in my shop is yummy'. Take note: if you're passing through Edinburgh visit her shop, it certainly looks lovely. Anyway, you can buy your L'Occitane products from here wherever you are in the world, along with gorgeous hand-stitched quilts from Une Histoire Simple and Blanc d'Ivoire and decorative wall clocks by Roger Lascelles.

Site Usability: ★★★★	Express Delivery Option? (UK)	Yes
Product Range: ★★★	Gift Wrapping Option?	Yes
Price Range: Medium	Returns Procedure:	Down to you
Delivery Area: Worldwide		

www.millerharris.com

If you'd like to give someone a gorgeous fragrance or bath and body product which is not so well known, then Miller Harris may have the answer. This is a small, independent company which specialises in blending its own fragrances, with enticing names such as Tangerine Vert, Fleur Oriental and Terre de Bois. In each one you'll find not only the eau de parfum, but bath and body products and candles as well.

Site Usability: ★★★★	Based:	UK
Product Range: ★★★	Express Delivery Option? (UK)	Yes
Price Range: Luxury/Medium	Gift Wrapping Option?	Yes
Delivery Area: Worldwide	Returns Procedure:	Down to you

www.moltonbrown.co.uk

The range of Molton Brown's bath, skincare, make-up and spa products seems to increase daily and you will want to try every single one. The packaging is lovely and the products not only look and smell wonderful but they are not overpriced. Delivery is quick and you quite often get sent delicious trial-sized products with your order. A great site for gifts, travel-size products and that extra body lotion and bath gel you simply won't be able to resist.

Site Usability:	★★★★★	Based:	UK
Product Range:	★★★★★	Express Delivery Option? (UK)	No
Price Range:	Medium	Gift Wrapping Option?	Yes
Delivery Area:	Worldwide	Returns Procedure:	Down to you

www.ormondejayne.co.uk

Sometimes you feel that you'd really like to find a new range of fragrance and candles, one that most people haven't heard of but that's still luxurious and beautifully presented. That's exactly what you'll find here, with a unique range of fragrances such as the citrussy Osmanthus and floral Champaca. There are bath and body products to complement the fragrances, plus the most beautiful candles, and everything is gorgeously packaged.

Site Usability:	★★★★	Based:	UK
Product Range:	★★★	Express Delivery Option? (UK)	Yes – call them
Price Range:	Luxury	Gift Wrapping Option?	Yes
Delivery Area:	Worldwide	Returns Proce dure:	Down to you

www.parfumsdorsay.co.uk

Here you'll find a small, beautifully photographed range of fragrance, soaps and scented candles from long-established fragrance house Parfums d'Orsay of France. If you already know the fragrances you'll be delighted that they're now available here. If you haven't tried them before, email and ask for the sample of your choice – you'll find they're very special. Gift wrapping was not available at time of writing but may be now.

Site Usability:	★★★★★	Based:	UK
Product Range:	★★★	Express Delivery Option? (UK)	Yes – call them
Price Range:	Luxury/Medium	Gift Wrapping Option?	No
Delivery Area:	UK	Returns Procedure:	Down to you

www.penhaligons.co.uk

Penhaligons offers fragrance, candles and bath and body products for perfect and luxurious gifts for men and women. Choose from classics Lily of the

Valley, Elizabethan Rose or Bluebell, or the more modern and spicy Malabah, Artemesia or LP No 9. Each fragrance is matched up to its own shower gel, soap, body lotion and candle. Gift wrapping is gorgeous and free and they deliver worldwide.

Site Usability:	★★★★★	Based:	UK
Product Range:	★★★★★	Express Delivery Option? (UK)	Yes
Price Range:	Luxury	Gift Wrapping Option?	Automatic
Delivery Area:	Worldwide	Returns Procedure:	Down to you

www.scentstore.co.uk

This website is well worth checking out if you know exactly which fragrance you want to buy as you can find some excellent discounts. So although you won't find every product in each range, it's a good idea to have a look here in case your favourite is on offer. Brands for men include Lacoste, Hugo Boss, Burberry and Tommy Hilfiger and for women, Gucci, Ralph Lauren and Issey Miyake.

Site Usability:	★★★★★	Based:	UK
Product Range:	★★★★	Express Delivery Option? (UK)	Yes
Price Range:	Medium/Very Good Value	Gift Wrapping Option?	No
Delivery Area:	Worldwide	Returns Procedure:	Down to you

www.skye-soap.co.uk

Here's a beautifully designed website offering natural aromatherapy soaps produced on the Isle of Skye. There isn't a huge range of products, but if you like lovely, natural soaps and oils you'll want to buy from here, not only for yourself but also for your friends from the selection of attractively packaged gift boxes. You'll discover fragrances such as Lavender, Lemon and Lime, Geranium, Patchouli, Sandalwood, Tea Tree and Orange for the soaps and essential oils, plus gifts of bath bombs and soaks.

Site Usability:	★★★★	Based:	UK
Product Range:	★★★	Express Delivery Option? (UK)	No
Price Range:	Medium/Very Good Value	Gift Wrapping Option?	No
Delivery Area:	Worldwide	Returns Procedure:	Down to you

www.strawberrynet.com

Check to see whether your favourite product is available on this Hong Kong-based website where shipping is free and most products are discounted. There's a huge range of designers, so big it's not worth trying to list. To be clear, as this site is based overseas you may well get charged duty. However, delivery to anywhere in the world is free of charge and the discounts can be very good.

Site Usability:	★★★	Based:	Hong Kong
Product Range:	★★★★★	Express Delivery Option? (UK)	No
Price Range:	Medium/Very Good Value	Gift Wrapping Option?	Yes
Delivery Area:	Worldwide	Returns Procedure:	Down to you

www.thesanctuary.co.uk

Just looking at this spa website makes you feel more relaxed, with the shades of blue in its background and the attractive, simple packaging of pampering products such as Sanctuary Salt Soak, Body Polisher and Eastern Massage and Body Oil. You can buy the full range of Sanctuary products here, plus gift vouchers and information on treatments at the Covent Garden spa. You need to give them a call for international orders.

Site Usability:	★★★★	Based:	UK
Product Range:	★★★★	Express Delivery Option? (UK)	Yes
Price Range:	Medium/Very Good Value	Gift Wrapping Option?	Automatic
Delivery Area:	Worldwide	Returns Procedure:	Down to you

www.woodruffs.co.uk

This fragrance and gift retailer offers an excellent range of bath, body and fragrance products by Roger et Gallet, Diptyque, Kenneth Turner, Crabtree & Evelyn, Floris, Cath Collins and Jane Packer, to name but a few. They'll deliver anywhere in the world, offer an express delivery service for the UK and are happy to gift wrap for you. You'll find unusual accessory ideas as well.

Site Usability:	★★★★★	Based:	UK
Product Range:	★★★★	Express Delivery Option? (UK)	Yes
Price Range:	Medium	Gift Wrapping Option?	Yes
Delivery Area:	Worldwide	Returns Procedure:	Down to you

Chapter 22

Beauty Accessories

By accessories I mean cosmetic brushes, hairdryers and hairbrushes and small items such as tweezers and eyelash curlers, plus attractive and useful toiletry bags. When searching for all of these you need to take a look at www.hqhair.com, which stocks all of the above and more. If you haven't already visited this website, take a look round soon – you've definitely been missing something.

Also pay a visit to www.spacenk.co.uk for Frederick Fekkai hairbrushes, Chantecaille cosmetic brushes and the site's own-brand tweezers and curlers.

You can, if you want, buy the premium-brand accessories (particularly brushes) you'll find at Chanel, Lancôme, Clarins and the rest and they are usually fabulous quality, but you will also pay a fabulous price if you want the whole set. Take a look here and you can find a good selection at reasonable prices. If you want quite a few, visit www.screenface.com, where they are good quality and very well priced. For the best hairdryers try www.saloneasy.co.uk, whose Parlux range is, in my opinion, unbeatable.

Sites to Visit

www.beautysleuth.co.uk

Beauty Sleuth offers a wide range of beauty products on its attractively designed website. It also has Air Stocking (spray it on and your legs look as if you're wearing stockings), Tweezerman products, Mister Mascara's mascaras and eyelash curlers, ID Essentials make-up brushes and GHD straighteners and accessories. This is a well-edited range, so it shouldn't take you long to find what you're looking for.

Site Usability:	★★★★★	Based:	UK
Product Range:	★★★	Express Delivery Option? (UK)	Yes
Price Range:	Medium	Gift Wrapping Option?	No
Delivery Area:	UK	Returns Procedure:	Down to you

www.corioliss.co.uk

For high-tech hair straighteners and dryers that you may well not have come across before, take a look here. There are wide-plate, wet and dry and cordless irons, plus the new C2 range which, they claim, kills the bacteria in your hair, the Infralite high-speed hairdryer, plus folding travel dryers in purple, silver, gold and white. The irons are definitely the best part of the range and I'm definitely not showing this website to my daughter – they're expensive (but marvellous, I'm sure).

Site Usability:	★★★★	Based:	UK
Product Range:	★★★	Express Delivery Option? (UK)	No
Price Range:	Luxury/Medium	Gift Wrapping Option?	No
Delivery Area:	Worldwide	Returns Procedure:	Down to you

www.ferobeauty.com

Buying high-quality make-up brushes can be an expensive business. On this unsophisticated but not overpriced website there's a professional range of brushes, wallets and holders, manicure and pedicure tools, beauty kits, waxing systems and Mavala nail enamels. Be slightly careful what you buy here as some of the items are strictly for professionals. Delivery is to the UK only and free when you spend over £50.

Site Usability:	★★★	Based:	UK
Product Range:	★★★	Express Delivery Option? (UK)	No
Price Range:	Medium	Gift Wrapping Option?	No
Delivery Area:	UK	Returns Procedure:	Down to you

www.saloneasy.com

This is the place to find your professional-standard hairdryer by Parlux (they're really excellent and not overpriced), hair straighteners and stylers and a wide range of hairbrushes. This site is aimed at the professional, so there is a wide range of salon products that you almost certainly won't be interested in, but the prices for the dryers and brushes are some of the best you'll find and the service is speedy.

Site Usability:	★★★	Based:	UK
Product Range:	★★★★	Express Delivery Option? (UK)	No
Price Range:	Medium	Gift Wrapping Option?	No
Delivery Area:	UK	Returns Procedure:	Down to you

www.screenface.com

The next time you want to buy a new set of make-up brushes, have a good look here before you rush off and spend hundreds of pounds on some of the major brands. The selection is huge and well priced and you can also buy make-up bags and cases, professional make-up and Tweezerman products. Some of the pictures are not very clear (if they're there at all), but you can send off for the catalogue.

Site Usability:	★★★	Based:	UK
Product Range:	★★★★	Express Delivery Option? (UK)	No
Price Range:	Very Good Value	Gift Wrapping Option?	No
Delivery Area:	UK	Returns Procedure:	Down to you

www.smoothgroove.co.uk

Star hairdresser Daniel Hersheson has salons in Conduit Street, London and Harvey Nichols. You can now find his high-quality range of styling tools online at www.smoothgroove.co.uk. There are Ceramic Ion brushes in five sizes, a smoothing iron and waving tongs and his professional hairdryer which he states is the most powerful tool of its kind available (and so it should be at around £90).

Site Usability:	★★★★	Based:	US
Product Range:	★★★	Express Delivery Option? (UK)	No
Price Range:	Luxury	Gift Wrapping Option?	No
Delivery Area:	Worldwide	Returns Procedure:	Down to you

www.themakeupbrushcompany.co.uk

Make-up artist to the stars Christine Allsopp has created this website not just to offer a small but excellent range of brushes and brush sets, but also to give you lots of information on how to use your brushes to get the best effect. You can watch online video clips of actresses and models applying their make-up (expertly, of course). In order to get the best out of this website you need to buy something, which gives you the pass through to all the information.

Site Usability:	★★★	Based:	UK
Product Range:	★★★	Express Delivery Option? (UK)	Yes
Price Range:	Medium	Gift Wrapping Option?	No
Delivery Area:	Worldwide	Returns Procedure:	Down to you

www.zpm.com

If you know someone who does a lot of travelling, you'll find a perfect gift here, as ZPM specialises in pretty and useful make-up bags – everything from small cosmetic purses to hanging weekenders, all in a range of patterns. In addition you'll find ideas for kids and babies and some attractive laundry and kitchen accessories. There's also a gift finder by occasion or personality to make life even easier.

Site Usability:	★★★★	Based:	UK
Product Range:	★★★	Express Delivery Option? (UK)	Yes
Price Range:	Medium	Gift Wrapping Option?	No
Delivery Area:	Worldwide	Returns Procedure:	Down to you

Chapter 23

Healthcare and Contact Lenses

C ontact lenses are a growing area of online retailing and the competition to get you away from your local provider is excellent from your point of view. You will find good savings here for most lenses – up to a third off what you're paying outside – so consider ordering your replacement lenses online provided they're a standard prescription.

If (or when) you start ordering your lenses online you will probably be asked to pay a fee for a sight check and new prescription from the ophthalmologist who was charging you the original inflated prices. Provided your prescriptions are lasting a while and your eyes aren't changing too much, it's worth your while to go down this route.

Prescriptions are another area you can consider getting filled online, particularly for items such as the malaria drug Malarone which you cannot get on the NHS (unless in an exceptional case). Here again you can make huge savings against what you'd pay in your local chemist. Just make sure before you order that the online pharmacy you're buying from is a member of the Royal Pharmaceutical Society of Great Britain. Check its membership if you want to. Then order from it.

Sites to Visit

www.auravita.com

Claiming to stock over 20,000 products (phew), you'll find everything here from Nurofen to eyelash curlers, homeopathy remedies, health foods and drinks and sport supplements and vitamins. There's also a wide choice of cosmetics, including Elizabeth Arden, Kanebo, Clarins, Lancôme, Christian Dior lipstick and nail polish and Max Factor. It's a confusing website to go round, so make use of the Brand Search and Store Guide facilities near the top of the Home Page.

Site Usability:	★★★	Express Delivery Option? (UK)	No
Product Range:	★★★★★	Gift Wrapping Option?	No
Price Range:	Medium/Very Good Value	Returns Procedure:	Down to you
Delivery Area:	Worldwide		

www.bs4health.com

The B & S House of Health takes itself extremely seriously, with a mission statement that sets out exactly what it is trying to do – offer you high-quality vitamins and supplements from sources that it has found to be totally reliable. Click on each area and you get a full list of subsections describing exactly what you'll find and what the products are for, which then links through to each individual product and the buying facility. This is an excellent, clear and informative website.

Site Usability:	★★★★	Express Delivery Option? (UK)	No
Product Range:	★★★★	Gift Wrapping Option?	No
Price Range:	Medium	Returns Procedure:	Down to you
Delivery Area:	Worldwide		

www.chemistdirect.co.uk

Chemist Direct operates out of London and is a member of the National Pharmaceutical Association. There's a wide range of products here, from vitamins and health supplements, baby products, toiletries, holiday and sun care. They're also happy to fulfil your prescriptions for you, either private or NHS, and the prices are excellent (always check against an offline chemist if you're not sure about the price). You send payment to the site online and your prescription by post, after which they'll immediately despatch your order to you.

Site Usability:	★★★★	Express Delivery Option? (UK)	Yes
Product Range:	★★★★	Gift Wrapping Option?	No
Price Range:	Medium	Returns Procedure:	Down to you
Delivery Area:	UK		

www.contactsdirect.co.uk

Here's another contact lens retailer trying to get your business away from your local supplier and it should certainly be considered. Remember that when you do order your contacts online and you need a check-up or a new prescription, you'll probably have to pay a fee. Even so, you'll save lots of money by buying online. The prices are keen here and you can expect a speedy service.

Site Usability:	★★★★★	Express Delivery Option? (UK)	No
Product Range:	★★★★	Gift Wrapping Option?	No
Price Range:	Medium	Returns Procedure:	Free
Delivery Area:	UK		

www.goldshield.co.uk

As well as all the vitamins and supplements you would expect from a health food store, here you can buy food and snacks. There are assortments of fruit and nuts, crystallised ginger, dried fruit, pistachios and pumpkin seeds and everything for making your own yoghurt, plus not quite so 'healthy' (but very tempting) snacks, including chocolate-coated ginger and brazils. There's lots of information on all the different sections, plus health books.

Site Usability:	★★★★	Express Delivery Option? (UK)	No
Product Range:	★★★★	Gift Wrapping Option?	No
Price Range:	Medium	Returns Procedure:	Free
Delivery Area:	Worldwide		

www.goodnessdirect.co.uk

There's a vast range here with 3000-plus health foods, vitamins and items selected for those with special dietary needs. You can search for foods that are dairy free, gluten free, wheat free, yeast free and low fat, plus organic fruit, vegetables (in a selection of boxed choices), fish and meat. You'll also find frozen and chilled foods, so you can do your complete shopping here. Don't be worried by the amount of choice, the website is very easy to navigate and order from.

Site Usability:	★★★★	Based:	UK
Product Range:	★★★★★	Express Delivery Option? (UK)	No
Price Range:	Medium	Gift Wrapping Option?	No
Delivery Area:	UK	Returns Procedure:	Down to you

www.hollandandbarrett.com

This famous health supplement and information retailer has a simple and easy-to-use website, offering products within sections such as Sports Nutrition, Digestive Aids, Weight Management and Women's Products. You do really need to know what you're looking for, as you'll find the details on each individual product only when you click on it. However, the order system is very simple, so if you want something specific, have a look here.

Site Usability:	★★★	Based:	UK
Product Range:	★★★★	Express Delivery Option? (UK)	No
Price Range:	Medium	Gift Wrapping Option?	No
Delivery Area:	Worldwide	Returns Procedure:	Down to you

www.lensway.com

Lensway is one of the best online places to buy contact lenses (and I've tested them many times). The prices are just about the best you'll find online, the website is very easy to use and your lenses arrive incredibly fast. You can buy most types, from daily to monthly lenses by Johnson & Johnson, Acuvue, Bausch and Lomb and others.

Site Usability:	★★★★	Express Delivery Option? (UK)	No, but fast delivery is automatic
Product Range:	★★★★★	Gift Wrapping Option?	No
Price Range:	Medium/Very Good Value	Returns Procedure:	Down to you
Delivery Area:	Worldwide		

www.marnys.com

On this website you can find organic products such as muesli, toasted sesame seeds, brown lentils, texturised soya, flax seeds, pumpkin and sunflower seeds as well as salt crystal lamps. There's a wide range of supplements, vitamins and minerals, divided into sections such as Royal Jelly, Korean Ginseng and Bee Pollen as specific products and Weight Control, Cardiovascular System and Hormonal System as separate areas.

Site Usability:	★★★★	Based:	Spain
Product Range:	★★★★★	Express Delivery Option? (UK)	No, but fast delivery is automatic
Price Range:	Medium	Gift Wrapping Option?	No
Delivery Area:	Worldwide	Returns Procedure:	Down to you

www.pharmacy2u.co.uk

All your regular medicines and healthcare essentials are available on this site, plus plenty of advice and suggestions. If you can't be bothered or don't have the time to go out to the chemist, this is definitely the site for you. It's clear and well laid out and I doubt whether there would be anything you couldn't find. You can also arrange for your prescriptions to be filled. The site is a member of the Royal Pharmaceutical Society of Great Britain and the National Pharmaceutical Association.

Site Usability:	★★★★★	Express Delivery Option? (UK)	No
Product Range:	★★★★★	Gift Wrapping Option?	No
Price Range:	Medium	Returns Procedure:	Down to you
Delivery Area:	Worldwide for most products		

www.thefitmap.co.uk

Do you really want to know how fit you are (and do something about it)? Thefitmap.co.uk gives you loads of information on where to find a personal trainer, diet and fitness news and health club reviews. If you really want to get going, click to subscribe on the Fitness Training Planner and get your own schedule against which you can then plot your success (or not). This may not be quite the same as having your personal trainer banging on the door to take you through your paces, but it's certainly an incentive worth trying out.

Site Usability:	★★★★★	Delivery Area:	UK
Product Range:	★★★★★	Based:	UK
Price Range:	Luxury/Medium		

www.travelpharm.com

TravelPharm is an independent private pharmacy and a member of the National Pharmaceutical Association. You can buy first aid and medical kits, total sun block, travel sickness tablets, water purification tablets and flight socks on this well-designed website. As a registered pharmacy it can also provide you with pharmacy-only medication such as malaria tablets and it offers up-to-the-minute details of vaccinations and anti-malarial requirements for your destination as a free-of-charge service.

Site Usability:	★★★★★	Express Delivery Option? (UK)	No
Product Range:	★★★★★	Gift Wrapping Option?	No
Price Range:	Medium	Returns Procedure:	Down to you
Delivery Area:	UK		

You'll also find healthcare products at the following websites:

Website address

You'll find them in:

www.boots.com Skincare and Cosmetics

www.garden.co.uk Skincare and Cosmetics

Chapter 24

Hair and Nails

There are lots of websites springing up offering ranges of hair care products, plus the very latest in brushes, straighteners, dryers and every other possible accessory you can think of. (I know, I've dealt with them in Chapter 22, but they also have to be mentioned here as most of these websites sell them as well.)

These websites are excellent if you have a particular range that you like and it's hard to get hold of where you live and also for learning about the latest equipment 'must-haves'. All those listed offer an excellent service, but do compare prices before you buy just to ensure that you're getting the best deal.

Regarding nail polishes and treatments, the philosophy is much the same as hair products, although there are far fewer ranges. It's best to know which colours you like in advance of buying online as the colour charts are not usually terribly accurate, but if you use Jessica, Opi, Essie or Darielle, which are quite difficult to buy in the shops, you'll probably want to start ordering here. They can often be less expensive as well.

Sites to Visit

www.beverlybeaute.com

Once you've taken a good look here you may well decide to order your nail products from this US-based retailer. The site stocks the full range of Jessica, Opi, Essie, Seche and Creative, plus less well-known brands Star Nail, Qtica and Gena and everything is at a very good discount. You can also order from the Thalgo range of marine algae and plant-based products here. Delivery is fast and there's a standard charge of £3, but don't forget you may have to pay duty.

Site Usability:	★★★★★	Based:	US
Product Range:	★★★★★	Express Delivery Option? (UK)	No
Price Range:	Very Good Value	Gift Wrapping Option?	No
Delivery Area:	Worldwide	Returns Procedure:	Down to you

www.hqhair.com

If you haven't used it already you should try this fun and incredibly useful website. Along with funky beauty products and jewellery (and absolutely everything you could need for your hair, including Blax, Nexxus and Paul Mitchell products), you'll discover Anya Hindmarch, Kate Spade and Lulu Guinness exquisite cosmetic bags (perfect for presents and also for treats). There are also lots of beauty accessories, including high-quality make-up and hairbrushes.

Site Usability:	★★★★★	Based:	UK
Product Range:	★★★★★	Express Delivery Option? (UK)	No
Price Range:	Luxury/Medium	Gift Wrapping Option?	No
Delivery Area:	Worldwide	Returns Procedure:	Down to you

www.johnmasters.co.uk

Here you'll find an excellent range of organic hair care (and skincare) from Lavender and Rosemary or Honey and Hibiscus shampoo to Rosemary and Peppermint Detangler and Bourbon, Vanilla and Tangerine Hair Texturizer. The packaging is simple and chic and delivery is free within the UK (at time of writing).

Site Usability:	★★★★	Based:	UK
Product Range:	★★★	Express Delivery Option? (UK)	No
Price Range:	Medium	Gift Wrapping Option?	No
Delivery Area:	Worldwide	Returns Procedure:	Down to you

www.johnnylovesrosie.co.uk

Famous for its chic, modern collection of hair accessories, Johnny Loves Rosie has now branched out into a collection of small, beautifully detailed bags, flip flops and pretty beaded jewellery. There's a small selection online, but how can you resist the carved marigold bobby pins, crystal hair clips and flower clips and elastics, featuring orchids, buttercups, hyacinths and carnations, in a variety of colours? They're simply a must for any hair-conscious girl.

Site Usability:	★★★★	Based:	UK
Product Range:	★★★★	Express Delivery Option? (UK)	No
Price Range:	Medium	Gift Wrapping Option?	No
Delivery Area:	Worldwide	Returns Procedure:	Down to you

www.kaven.co.uk

This site offers skincare from Guerlain, Decleor and Guinot, plus St Tropez self-tanning products and the full range of Jessica nail care, although the colours are hard to see if you're not sure exactly which one you want. It's a quick and easy site to order from, with details and pictures of each and every item. Guerlain make-up is also available. If you have any queries you can call them and they're always delighted to help.

Site Usability:	★★★★	Based:	UK
Product Range:	★★★★	Express Delivery Option? (UK)	No
Price Range:	Medium	Gift Wrapping Option?	No
Delivery Area:	Worldwide	Returns Procedure:	Down to you

www.lookfantastic.com

Here's a marvelous selection of hair care products from well-known brands such as Kerastase, Paul Mitchell, Tigi and Redken, plus nailcare by Essie, Opi,

Jessica and Nailtiques. In the Beauty Accessories section there are straighteners, dryers, brushes and clippers by GHD, Babyliss, T3 and Icon and if you haven't discovered GHD ceramic brushes yet you can order them here. Try them – they're excellent. Provided you join the site's club, you can take advantage of the very good discounts on offer.

Site Usability:	★★★★	Based:	UK
Product Range:	★★★★★	Express Delivery Option? (UK)	Yes
Price Range:	Medium/Very Good Value	Gift Wrapping Option?	No
Delivery Area:	Worldwide	Returns Procedure:	Down to you

www.martynmaxey.co.uk

There are lots of hair care websites springing up but this is definitely one of the most well designed. It offers products by J F Lazartigue, GHD, Babyliss, Kerastase, Philip Kingsley and Sebastian, plus skincare by MD Formulations, Murad and Prevage (plus more). Sign up to become a member and take advantage of the discounts.

Site Usability:	★★★★★	Based:	UK
Product Range:	★★★★★	Express Delivery Option? (UK)	No
Price Range:	Medium/Very Good Value	Gift Wrapping Option?	No
Delivery Area:	UK	Returns Procedure:	Down to you

www.nailsbymail.co.uk

Calling itself 'the UK's leading nail boutique', Nails by Mail offers products by Essie and Seche (and if you haven't yet tried the truly marvellous Seche Vite quick dry, you should) together with colours, treatments, files and buffers, making this is an excellent, well-priced site for all the elements necessary for keeping your nails in top shape. If you need any advice you can give them a call and the nail technicians will be happy to help.

Site Usability:	★★★★	Based:	UK
Product Range:	★★★★★	Express Delivery Option? (UK)	No
Price Range:	Medium	Gift Wrapping Option?	No
Delivery Area:	UK	Returns Procedure:	Down to you

www.nailsinc.com

If you've visited the US you'll know that there are several nail bars in each and every shopping mall, no matter how big or small, and much of the time you don't even have to book, you can just walk in on a whim. The UK has taken a long time to catch up, but now with Nails Inc you can visit one of its 35 locations in the UK for an excellent, speedy manicure. You can also buy the products online, from high-quality treatments and gift sets to the outlet store offering goodies for less.

Site Usability:	★★★	Based:	UK
Product Range:	★★★	Express Delivery Option? (UK)	No
Price Range:	Medium	Gift Wrapping Option	No
Delivery Area:	UK	Returns Procedure:	Down to you

www.salonlines.co.uk

Here's another hair product website offering a good range of Schwarzkopf hair care products, plus Tigi and Joico, GHD straighteners and ceramic brushes. There are loads of other beauty products, including specialist hair treatments and some grooming products. You can go to the advice section and find out about how to deal with specific problems or you can email the site's expert and ask for help. They're happy to ship all over the world, offer an express delivery option and bulk shipping discount.

Site Usability:	★★★★	Based:	UK
Product Range:	★★★★	Express Delivery Option? (UK)	Yes
Price Range:	Medium	Gift Wrapping Option?	No
Delivery Area:	Worldwide	Returns Procedure:	Down to you

Chapter 25

Scented Candles

Here you'll find fragranced candles from manufacturers which specialise just in candles, so don't expect to find all the other bath and body products to go with. Most of these are beautifully packaged and so make excellent gifts and there's a choice of prices. If you're looking for a wide range of different but well-known brands, go straight to Kiarie, whose ever-expanding selection is quite incredible. For gorgeous aromatherapy candles head to Natural Magic, where you just have to look at the candles, their glass holders and the packaging to want to order one straight away.

Sites to Visit

www.ancienneambiance.com

The Ancienne Ambiance concept of antiquity-inspired luxury goods has been designed and developed by Adriana Carlucci, a graduate of the London College of Fashion with a degree in product development. She began by creating a unique collection of six glass-encased candles, each featuring fragrances evocative of an ancient culture, together with elegant handcrafted packaging. You'll also discover small inserts of authentic handmade

Egyptian papyrus which carry the description and the ancient associations of each scent used.

Site Usability:	★★★★	Based:	UK
Product Range:	★★★	Express Delivery Option? (UK)	Yes
Price Range:	Medium	Gift Wrapping Option?	Yes
Delivery Area:	Worldwide	Returns Procedure:	Down to you

www.kiarie.co.uk

Kiarie has one of the best ranges of scented candles, by brands such as Geodosis, Kenneth Turner, Manuel Canovas, Creation Mathias, Rigaud and Millefiori. There are literally hundreds to choose from at all price levels (this site is very fast, so don't panic) and you can also choose your range by price, maker, fragrance, colour and season. Once you've made your selection you can ask them to gift wrap it for you and include a handwritten message.

Site Usability:	★★★★★	Based:	UK
Product Range:	★★★★★	Express Delivery Option? (UK)	Yes
Price Range:	Medium	Gift Wrapping Option?	Yes
Delivery Area:	Worldwide	Returns Procedure:	Down to you

www.naturalmagicuk.com

Unlike almost all conventional candles (which contain paraffin wax and synthetic oils), Natural Magic candles are made from clean, pure vegetable wax, scented with the best-quality organic aromatherapy oils. They're also twice the size of the average candle (1kg), with 3 wicks and up to 75 hours of burn time. Each candle has a specific therapeutic task, such as uplifting, inspiring, soothing and de-stressing and all are beautifully packaged and perfect for treats and gifts.

Site Usability:	★★★★★	Based:	UK
Product Range:	★★★	Express Delivery Option? (UK)	Yes
Price Range:	Medium	Gift Wrapping Option?	No
Delivery Area:	Worldwide	Returns Procedure:	Down to you

www.parkscandles.com

Parks Candles has an easy-to-navigate website offering a beautiful range of scented candles in decorative containers. Three wick candles in silver bowls, perfumed candles in glass containers with silver lids and scented dinner candles in green, burgundy or cream are just some of the selection. Delivery is excellent and the prices are lower than you'd find in most shops.

Site Usability:	★★★★★	Based:	UK
Product Range:	★★★	Express Delivery Option? (UK)	Automatic
Price Range:	Medium	Gift Wrapping Option?	No
Delivery Area:	Worldwide	Returns Procedure:	Down to you

www.timothyhan.com

If you haven't already come across these luxurious candles, then take a look now. Timothy Han has a small but gorgeous range, including aromatherapy candles, with names such as Orange, Grapefruit and Clove or Lavender and Scent of Fig and his unfragranced candles which are perfect for entertaining. You can also buy his candles in Bill Amberg's specially created leather travel case. Call for urgent deliveries.

Site Usability:	★★★★★	Based:	UK
Product Range:	★★★	Express Delivery Option? (UK)	Yes, but call them
Price Range:	Luxury/Medium	Gift Wrapping Option?	Yes
Delivery Area:	Worldwide	Returns Procedure:	Down to you

www.truegrace.co.uk

If you want to pamper someone with something small and beautiful and you don't want to spend a fortune, you should choose from the gorgeous candles here. All beautifully wrapped and in glass containers, you'll find the 'Never a Dull Day' range in pretty printed boxes with fragrances such as Vine Tomato, Stem Ginger and Hyacinth. Then there is 'As it Should Be', the more simply (but equally attractively) boxed candle in 37 fragrances, including Citrus, Cappuccino and Raspberry. Try them.

Site Usability:	★★★★	Based:	UK
Product Range:	★★★★	Express Delivery Option? (UK)	No
Price Range:	Medium	Gift Wrapping Option?	No
Delivery Area:	Worldwide	Returns Procedure:	Down to you

www.waxandwane.co.uk

This is an unsophisticated website offering a large choice of well-priced candles where the selection is almost too much. However, persevere because if you don't want to pay the earth and you know someone (don't we all) who loves prettily packaged, good-quality (and hand-poured) scented candles, you will definitely find something here. Fragrances range from Cinnamon and Cashmere to Bergamot and Bay leaf to Vanilla.

Site Usability:	★★★	Based:	UK
Product Range:	★★★★	Express Delivery Option? (UK)	No
Price Range:	Medium/Very Good Value	Gift Wrapping Option?	No
Delivery Area:	Worldwide	Returns Procedure:	Down to you

Chapter 26

Modern Skincare and Cosmetics

As I've said before, most of the premium-brand cosmetic companies are now online, so whether your choice is Chanel, Elizabeth Arden, YSL or Lancôme, there probably isn't a product you can't buy, either from Boots (www.boots.com) or The Garden Pharmacy (www.garden.co.uk).

Here is where you'll find the modern ranges of skincare and cosmetics from brands such as Dr Hauschka, Bumble and Bumble, Benefit, Aveda, Bliss and Dermalogica, brands that are very well known to those who use them but which have not had as much advertising exposure (nor been around as long) as the others.

Yes, if you've walked through the beauty department of somewhere like Selfridges, Harrods or Harvey Nichols you'll probably have seen them, but have you had the time to look properly? If so, you're most likely already buying. If not, take the time now.

Sites to Visit

www.beautique.com

Beautique is a new beauty and hair website, divided into three sections: Learn, where you can find tips and advice written by industry experts in all areas of beauty and hair; Buy, where you can order all the products offered; and Experience, showcasing treatments, spas and salons in the UK and around the world, with personal recommendations and reviews. Brands include Aveda, Bumble and Bumble, Carole Franck, Dr Hauschka, Guerlain and J C Brosseau. It's beautifully designed and well worth having a look round.

Site Usability:	★★★★★	Based:	UK
Product Range:	★★★★★	Express Delivery Option? (UK)	Yes
Price Range:	Luxury/Medium	Gift Wrapping Option?	No
Delivery Area:	UK	Returns Procedure:	Down to you

www.benefitcosmetics.co.uk

You can find Benefit cosmetics in the major stores, but you'll be hard put to see this complete range anywhere else online. With tempting products such as Benetint, Lip Plump, Super Strength Blemish Blaster and Ooh La Lift, how can you resist buying from this veritable candy store for the face? There's the cleverly packaged make-up, foundations, concealers and glitters, body care, skincare, accessories and a great gift selection.

Site Usability:	★★★★★	Based:	UK
Product Range:	★★★★	Express Delivery Option? (UK)	Yes
Price Range:	Medium	Gift Wrapping Option?	Yes
Delivery Area:	Worldwide	Returns Procedure:	Down to you

www.blisslondon.co.uk

Sign up for Bliss Beut emails and stay in the 'Glow'. Does that give you some idea of the tone from New York and London's hottest spa? If you don't have the time to visit the spas themselves, you can at least now buy the products online and relax at home amid your own treatments, shower gels and shampoos with simple names like Body Butter, Rosy Toes and Glamour Glove Gel. Some of the products are reasonably priced, but you'll also find some of the marvellous anti-ageing products will set you back a bit. It'll be worth it though.

Site Usability:	★★★★	Based:	UK
Product Range:	★★★	Express Delivery Option? (UK)	Yes
Price Range:	Medium	Gift Wrapping Option?	No
Delivery Area:	Worldwide	Returns Procedure:	Down to you

www.bnevertoobusytobebeautiful.com

I find this website quite confusing. However, stick to the product list on the left and you'll be ok. There's an excellent range of cosmetics (in 'makeup'), from blushers, concealers and cream foundation to glitter eye shadows and metallic loose powder. What makes everything really special is the packaging, which is unique. Think foundation bottles decorated with Moroccan metal and blushers in jewelled pots and you'll get the idea.

Site Usability:	★★★	Based:	UK
Product Range:	★★★★	Express Delivery Option? (UK)	Yes
Price Range:	Medium	Gift Wrapping Option?	No
Delivery Area:	Worldwide	Returns Procedure:	Down to you

www.bobbibrown.co.uk

Just occasionally a website appears that I know I'm going to be using a lot as it's one I've been waiting for. This is definitely one of those because, quite frankly, I'm a Bobbi Brown addict. They have some of the best colours and tools you can find and they seem to manage to create something I really can't resist each season. If you haven't yet tried this excellent all-American cosmetics and skincare company then click here now.

Site Usability:	★★★★★	Based:	UK
Product Range:	★★★★★	Express Delivery Option? (UK)	Yes
Price Range:	Luxury/Medium/Very Good Value	Gift Wrapping Option?	No
Delivery Area:	UK	Returns Procedure:	Down to you

www.boots.com

Not only can you stock up on your basic bathroom cupboard items here, plus fragrance from most of the major brands, but from the Brand Boutique you can also buy the full ranges from Chanel, Clarins, Clinique, Dior, Estée Lauder, Elizabeth Arden and Lancôme, plus ultra-modern brands Ruby and Millie, Urban Decay and Benefit. Delivery is free when you spend £40 and returns are free too. The excellent service is simply not publicised enough.

Site Usability:	★★★★★	Express Delivery Option? (UK)	Yes
Product Range:	★★★★★	Gift Wrapping Option?	Yes
Price Range:	Luxury/Medium/Very Good Value	Returns Procedure:	Free
Delivery Area:	UK		

www.clinique.co.uk

If you're a dedicated Clinique follower, this is the site for you. Not only can you purchase replacements for all your favourite products, but you can also read all about what's new, visit the Gift Centre for special sets and accessory kits and join Club Clinique, where you can register for fast checkout, free samples with your orders, 'Beauty Scoops' and expert advice. Delivery is to the UK only, but there's an express service and gift wrap option.

Site Usability:	★★★★★	Based:	UK
Product Range:	★★★★★	Express Delivery Option? (UK)	Yes
Price Range:	Medium	Gift Wrapping Option?	Yes
Delivery Area:	UK	Returns Procedure:	Down to you

www.cosmeticsalacarte.com

Christina Stewart and Lynne Sanders, both creative cosmetic chemists, founded Cosmetics à la carte 30 years ago – the first made-to-measure make-up range. If you can't get to the Knightsbridge store, you can order this range of 'make-up to fit' online with easy-to-see choices of colours for face, cheek, lip and eye products (including the wonderful lip gloss), plus 'Skin Basics' skin treats and a great selection of brushes and other beauty accessories.

Site Usability:	★★★★★	Express Delivery Option? (UK)	No
Product Range:	★★★★	Gift Wrapping Option?	No
Price Range:	Medium	Returns Procedure:	Down to you
Delivery Area:	Worldwide		

www.esteelauder.co.uk

As you'd expect, Estée Lauder has a beautiful website and although you can buy the products from other online retailers, here there are lots of extra goodies, such as information on the latest products and best sellers and where you can find (offline, of course) the company's free gifts and brow bars around the country. The site offers express and Saturday delivery services, plus gift wrapping.

Site Usability:	★★★★★	Express Delivery Option? (UK)	No
Product Range:	★★★★	Gift Wrapping Option?	No
Price Range:	Luxury/Medium	Returns Procedure:	Down to you
Delivery Area:	Worldwide		

www.garden.co.uk

The Garden Pharmacy's list of top brands seems to be growing by the day. Here you'll find Chanel, Elizabeth Arden, Lancôme, Revlon, Clinique and Clarins online together with Vichy, Avene, Caudalie and Roc. There are spa products by I Coloniali, L'Occitane, Roger et Gallet and Segreti Mediterranei (and no doubt a few more will have appeared by the time you read this). The list of fragrances on offer is huge. The site also offers free gift wrapping and 24-hour delivery.

Site Usability:	★★★★	Based:	UK
Product Range:	★★★★★	Express Delivery Option? (UK)	Yes
Price Range:	Luxury/Medium/Very Good Value	Gift Wrapping Option?	Yes
Delivery Area:	Worldwide	Returns Procedure:	Down to you

www.maccosmetics.co.uk

You've seen the cosmetics in all the best beauty stores and now you can buy them online, direct from this ultra chic website. Shop by category – lips, eyes, nails, skincare, etc. – or from one of the collections, with names such as Viva Glam, Barbie Loves Mac, Untamed, Rockocco or Technacolour – these change each season. Click on 'What's New' to discover the latest treats and tips or go through to 'Looks' to discover how they're created (and buy the products, of course). Be warned, it's extremely hard to leave without buying.

Site Usability:	★★★★★	Based:	UK
Product Range:	★★★★★	Express Delivery Option? (UK)	Yes
Price Range:	Medium	Gift Wrapping Option?	No
Delivery Area:	UK	Returns Procedure:	Down to you

www.pixibeauty.com

Pixi is an independent British beauty company consisting of cosmetics and skincare ranges and beauty accessories. It was started by three sisters, Sara, Sophia and Petra, two of whom are make-up artists while the third is a skin therapist, so you're definitely in the hands of experts. In their words, the range is 'magical, individual, feminine, small, cute, playful, free-spirited, mischievous, friendly, colourful, cheeky, unique, illusive and tempting'. Irresistible (my word).

Site Usability:	★★★★	Based:	UK
Product Range:	★★★	Express Delivery Option? (UK)	No
Price Range:	Medium	Gift Wrapping Option?	No
Delivery Area:	Worldwide	Returns Procedure:	Down to you

www.popbeauty.co.uk

Here's a new, young retailer offering a clever, well-priced range of cosmetics online, with names such as Sparkling Emerald Eye Glimmer, Dust Delux and Yummy Sugar Shine lip gloss, and all at accessible prices. The site also has some pretty gifts (which are not so inexpensive) but which arrive gift wrapped with a free make-up bag. This is a colourful and well put together website which I'm sure will prove to be extremely tempting to any make-up addict.

Site Usability:	★★★★	Based:	UK
Product Range:	★★★	Express Delivery Option? (UK)	No
Price Range:	Very Good Value	Gift Wrapping Option?	Yes, for some of the gifts
Delivery Area:	Worldwide	Returns Procedure:	Down to you

www.pout.co.uk

Pout is the perfect place for beauty junkies who want to enjoy and have fun with cosmetics. The whole range is clever and lighthearted through tongue-in-cheek product names such as 'Bite my Cherry' and 'Saucy Sadie'. Packaging is inspired by the founders' favourite items of underwear, gaining Pout the reputation as 'the underwear of make-up'. If this sounds slightly silly, don't be fooled – it's a gorgeous, cleverly packaged range of cosmetics, make-up bags, great gifts and excellent beauty accessories. Take a look round now.

Site Usability: ★★★★★	Based:	UK
Product Range: ★★★★★	Express Delivery Option? (UK)	Yes
Price Range: Medium	Gift Wrapping Option?	Yes
Delivery Area: Worldwide	Returns Procedure:	Down to you

www.powderpuff.net

Next time you want to buy one of your regular beauty essentials, have a look at this website, offering free delivery in the UK and a huge selection of products. It's been called 'the daddy of all beauty sites' and you'll find it hard to disagree. You'll find brand names such as Lancôme, Clarins, Clinique and YSL, plus GHD, Kinerase and Fudge, together with skincare, cosmetics and fragrance and mostly at very good prices. They'll also deliver worldwide.

Site Usability: ★★★★	Based:	UK
Product Range: ★★★★	Express Delivery Option? (UK)	Yes
Price Range: Medium/Very Good Value	Gift Wrapping Option?	Yes
Delivery Area: Worldwide	Returns Procedure:	Down to you

www.procosmetics.co.uk

There are four main brands available from this new skincare and cosmetics website: Nouba, with its excellent range of cosmetics and make-up brushes and bags, Algodermia for marine-based skincare, 3 Lab for specialist treatments and Lucky Chick for fun and well-priced spa treats (think Lucky Lips Vanilla Lip Shine and Foot Fetish Spearmint Foot & Leg Cream). Take a look now.

Site Usability: ★★★★★	Based:	UK
Product Range: ★★★★	Express Delivery Option? (UK)	No
Price Range: Medium	Gift Wrapping Option?	No
Delivery Area: Worldwide	Returns Procedure:	Down to you

www.spacenk.co.uk

Nars, Stila, Darphin, Laura Mercier, Eve Lom, Diptyque, Frederic Fekkai and Dr Sebagh are just some of the 60-plus brands on the website of this retailer, famous for bringing unusual and hard-to-find products to the UK. (So you don't have to go to New York any more to buy your Frederic Fekkai shampoo

– shame.) It is also an excellent place for gifts as it offers a personalised message and gift wrapping service and next-day delivery if you need it. It's a well-designed and easy-to-navigate website with clear pictures.

Site Usability:	★★★★★	Based:	UK
Product Range:	★★★★	Express Delivery Option? (UK)	Yes
Price Range:	Luxury/Medium	Gift Wrapping Option?	Yes
Delivery Area:	Worldwide	Returns Procedure:	Down to you

www.urbanapothecary.co.uk

Whether you're looking for a pampering gift or something for yourself, you'll almost certainly like this website, which is easy to use and well photographed. Choose from Beauty, Skincare, Haircare, Candles and Home Fragrance or Gifts and Accessories from brands such as Korres, Sohum or This Works. Alternatively shop by brand or by scent. Check out the site's recommendations or take advantage of free gifts and special offers. Whatever, you'll have a fun time browsing here.

Site Usability:	★★★★★	Based:	UK
Product Range:	★★★★★	Express Delivery Option? (UK)	Yes
Price Range:	Medium	Gift Wrapping Option?	No
Delivery Area:	UK	Returns Procedure:	Down to you

www.xen-tan.co.uk

If you want to know everything there is to know about the hot new self-tan product from the US, this is the website to visit. Read all about it, then choose from the Body Scrub, Tan Extender, Lotion, Mousse and Mist, plus the Perfect Bronze Compact. There's also an excellent Application section to help you get the perfect fake tan.

Site Usability:	★★★★★	Based:	UK
Product Range:	★★★	Express Delivery Option? (UK)	No
Price Range:	Medium	Gift Wrapping Option?	No
Delivery Area:	EU	Returns Procedure:	Down to you

Chapter 27

Natural and Organic Beauty

I have to confess that I'm a confirmed traditional and modern brand name fragrance and skincare person. I tend to steer away from natural and organic products, probably because I don't know enough about them. When I was researching for this chapter I was amazed at the beautifully presented websites I discovered and the enormity of the range of products available online, a range that's expanding all the time.

Some of the products here have been sourced from around the world – I hadn't heard of them before and you may well not have either. However, the love and care that have been put into bringing them before you and the amount of information that you'll be given on each and every one makes this a paradise for anyone who likes natural and/or organic beauty. I'm sure you'll find something here.

An area where I'm definitely tempted is aromatherapy. Some of the products – the fruit-scented essences, naturally fragranced soaps, fizzing soap bombs and candles – sound like perfect antidotes to the stresses of our everyday lives. You know what I'm talking about – children, husbands, dogs, work, mess, clutter.

Browsing round the specialist websites was full of far too many opportunities to buy (no, I'm not going to tell you whether I did or not). One thing I'm certain of. If you spend very long here, you'll be tempted too.

Sites to Visit

www.airandwater.co.uk

Here you can discover the properties of essential oils with their natural soaps, beauty products, aromatherapy boxes, carrier and massage oils. You can enhance your home with oil burners, incense, resins, candles and vaporisers and find Bach flower remedies and the Rescue Remedy range of herbal supplements. Suppliers include Edom Health and Beauty Products, Meadows Aromatherapy and Arran Aromatics.

Site Usability:	★★★★	Based:	UK
Product Range:	★★★★	Express Delivery Option? (UK)	Yes
Price Range:	Medium	Gift Wrapping Option?	No
Delivery Area:	EU	Returns Procedure:	Down to you

www.baldwins.co.uk

G. Baldwin & Co is London's oldest and most established herbalist. If you pay a visit to its shop you'll find yourself stepping back in time, encountering wooden floors, high, old-fashioned counters and shelves stacked with herbs, oils and ointments. You can shop online from the complete ranges of both Bach Flower Remedies and the Australian Bush Flower Essences, Baldwin's own-brand aromatherapy oils, natural soaps, creams and bath accessories and herbs, seeds, roots and dried flowers.

Site Usability:	★★★★	Based:	UK
Product Range:	★★★★	Express Delivery Option? (UK)	Yes
Price Range:	Medium	Gift Wrapping Option?	No
Delivery Area:	Worldwide	Returns Procedure:	Down to you

www.beauty-republic.com

Beauty Republic sources natural beauty secrets from all over the world. It offers a range of specialised products such as Black Palm Natural Soap, Hi Shine hair products, Lullaby Lavender, Kosmea natural skincare and Rainforest Remedies. For each and every product the site tells you what it does, what's in it and how to use it, so if you've never come across it before you may well be tempted to give it a try.

Site Usability:	★★★★★	Based:	UK
Product Range:	★★★★	Express Delivery Option? (UK)	Yes
Price Range:	Medium	Gift Wrapping Option?	Yes
Delivery Area:	Worldwide	Returns Procedure:	Down to you

www.bodyshop.co.uk

Alongside all the luxury skincare and cosmetic brands you can find online there's The Body Shop. Now with a beautifully laid out, fun-to-use website, it offers all the well-priced ranges of skincare, bath and body products and cosmetics, such as the Ultra Smooth Foundation, Aloe Soothing Night Cream and Relaxing Lavender Massage Oil. There are lots of gift ideas as well and you can trust Body Shop's mandate of shunning animal testing and protecting the planet.

Site Usability:	★★★★★	Based:	UK
Product Range:	★★★★★	Express Delivery Option? (UK)	Yes
Price Range:	Very Good Value	Gift Wrapping Option?	No
Delivery Area:	UK, but there are overseas transactional websites	Returns Procedure:	Down to you

www.freshsoapdeli.com

The handmade soap deli is a speciality soap, bath and body company producing a therapeutic range of products. It uses high-quality essential oils, tailor-made fragrances and herbal extracts to create a range which includes 'freshly cut off the block' soaps, wonderful Lemon Sherbert, Cherry and Lavender bath bombs, Mango Body Butter, Strawberry Body Polish and gifts such as the Tutti Frutti Soap Kebab. You'll definitely have fun choosing here.

Site Usability:	★★★★	Based:	UK
Product Range:	★★★	Express Delivery Option? (UK)	No
Price Range:	Medium	Gift Wrapping Option?	No
Delivery Area:	EU	Returns Procedure:	Down to you

www.fushi.co.uk

Fushi was established just over four years ago as a lifestyle-brand of holistic health and beauty products. Expanding on the philosophy that inner health promotes outer well-being, Fushi has developed a range of natural products including herbal remedies, cosmetic ranges and aromatherapy oils, most of which are organic. Use the product finder to treat specific ailments or select by product range. There's lots of information, so be prepared to spend some time here.

Site Usability:	★★★★★	Based:	UK
Product Range:	★★★★	Express Delivery Option? (UK)	No
Price Range:	Medium	Gift Wrapping Option?	No
Delivery Area:	Worldwide	Returns Procedure:	Down to you

www.highlandsoaps.com

On this attractive website you'll find a wide range of handmade soaps from the Highlands of Scotland. They come beautifully packaged and with names like May Chang and Lime, and Rosehip and Patchouli. Alternatively there's Mango Butter, Wild Nettle and Heather and exfoliating soaps with natural loofah (I'll definitely be trying one of those!). The site offers bath bombes, body cream and luxurious hand wash, plus gift boxes and bath accessories. Services include overseas shipping and gift wrapping.

Site Usability:	★★★★★	Based:	UK
Product Range:	★★★	Express Delivery Option? (UK)	No
Price Range:	Medium	Gift Wrapping Option?	Yes
Delivery Area:	Worldwide	Returns Procedure:	Down to you

www.loccitane.com

L'Occitane is another brand you're sure to have heard of, offering products ranging from personal care to home fragrance and all manufactured in traditional ways using natural ingredients, primarily from Provence. The range includes fragrance, body and hand care, bath and shower products, skincare, hair care and home fragrance, with Verbena Harvest, Eau d'Ambre, Lavender, Oranger and Green Tea forming the bases for eau de toilette, soaps, hand creams, shower gels and shampoos.

Site Usability:	★★★★★	Based:	UK
Product Range:	★★★★★	Express Delivery Option? (UK)	No
Price Range:	Medium	Gift Wrapping Option?	Yes
Delivery Area:	Worldwide	Returns Procedure:	Down to you

www.lovelula.com

There's a huge amount of information available here on Love Lula's organic apothecary website, from which natural products to buy for stress, acne, chapped lips and stretch marks to the online skincare consultation and 'Ask Lula' email option. There are lots of products to choose from, including gifts and special ranges for mother and baby, and everything's clear and easy to see.

Site Usability:	★★★★★	Based:	UK
Product Range:	★★★★★	Express Delivery Option? (UK)	Yes
Price Range:	Medium	Gift Wrapping Option?	No
Delivery Area:	Worldwide	Returns Procedure:	Down to you

www.mandala-aroma.com

Mandala Aroma is a luxury organic aromatherapy company set up by former fashion buyer and qualified aromatherapist Gillian Kavanagh. Here you'll discover bath oils, body treatment oils and aromatherapy candles, all under the headings of Wisdom, Love, Courage and Strength. Click on the item of your choice and you'll find out more about its ingredients and benefits.

Site Usability:	★★★★★	Based:	UK
Product Range:	★★★	Express Delivery Option? (UK)	No
Price Range:	Medium	Gift Wrapping Option?	No
Delivery Area:	Worldwide	Returns Procedure:	Down to you

www.musthave.co.uk

Musthave offers the best in natural and organic skincare, body care, fragrance and cosmetics sourced from suppliers around the world. You'll find REN, Paul & Joe, Anthony Logistics, Cowshed, Jo Wood Organics, Headonism Organic Haircare, Living Nature and Abahna alongside brands you probably already know such as Nailtiques, Phyto and Caudalie. The information is extremely clear here and written by professional beauty therapists. You can browse by brand, product type or skin and hair type.

Site Usability:	★★★★★	Based:	UK
Product Range:	★★★★★	Express Delivery Option? (UK)	Yes
Price Range:	Medium	Gift Wrapping Option?	Yes
Delivery Area:	Worldwide	Returns Procedure:	Down to you

www.mysanatural.com

Quite a lot of online retailers offering natural and environmentally friendly products think that we want to see them looking as natural as possible. Personally I don't think we do – buying lotions and potions online should always be a treat. Here at Mysa the natural and treat elements meet beautifully – think Pink Grapefruit Hand and Body Lotion, Ginger Loofah Soap or Sweet Jasmine Body Scrub and you'll get the idea. Packaging is chic and minimal and there are great gift sets too.

Site Usability:	★★★★★	Based:	UK
Product Range:	★★★	Express Delivery Option? (UK)	Yes
Price Range:	Medium	Gift Wrapping Option?	No
Delivery Area:	Worldwide	Returns Procedure:	Down to you

www.nakedbodycare.co.uk

Naked Body products are made using mainly naturally derived ingredients. The company claims that its products are 97% natural, with the other 3% being the preservatives and emulsifying agents. This isn't a huge range but it's extremely well priced and you can order all the hair, body, hand, bath and shower products online for next-day delivery.

Site Usability:	★★★★	Based:	UK
Product Range:	★★★	Express Delivery Option? (UK)	Yes
Price Range:	Very Good Value	Gift Wrapping Option?	No
Delivery Area:	Worldwide	Returns Procedure:	Down to you

www.naturalcollection.com

All the products on this website are seriously natural, from fairly traded laundry baskets to organic cotton bedlinen. There is also a Personal Care selection which includes brands such as Organic Options (natural soaps), Faith in Nature (aromatherapy body care) and Barefoot Botanicals (skin and body care). Together with lots of natural pampering products and gift ideas, in the Wellbeing section you'll find Sage Organics vitamins and minerals and Bath Indulgence Spa sets.

Site Usability:	★★★★★	Based:	UK
Product Range:	★★★★★	Express Delivery Option? (UK)	Yes
Price Range:	Medium	Gift Wrapping Option?	No
Delivery Area:	Worldwide	Returns Procedure:	Down to you

www.nealsyardremedies.com

This is probably one aromatherapy and herbal remedy retailer you have heard of. From the first shop located in Neal's Yard in the heart of London's Covent Garden, Neal's Yard Remedies has grown into one of the country's leading natural health retailers. On its attractive website you can buy a wide range of its products, from aromatherapy, body care, luxurious bath products and homeopathic remedies to attractively packaged gift sets.

Site Usability:	★★★★★	Based:	UK
Product Range:	★★★★	Express Delivery Option? (UK)	Yes
Price Range:	Medium	Gift Wrapping Option?	No
Delivery Area:	Worldwide	Returns Procedure:	Down to you

www.nicetouch.co.uk

Nice Touch offers REN, Aromatherapy Associates, Dermalogica, Trilogy botanical skincare, Xen-Tan self-tanning range, St Tropez, Pacifica soy candles and prettily packaged, earth-friendly baby products. The company prides itself on helping you make informed choices about the products that you put on your skin. There's all the information you need about each brand, including the ingredients of the products, their suitability for your skin type and the ethics of the companies which make them. It's an excellent website.

Site Usability:	★★★★★	Based:	UK
Product Range:	★★★★	Express Delivery Option? (UK)	No
Price Range:	Medium	Gift Wrapping Option?	No
Delivery Area:	Worldwide	Returns Procedure:	Down to you

www.origins.co.uk

You may well have heard of Origins, specialists in natural skincare. The company uses aromatic plants, earth and sea substances and other resources to make its products as close to nature as they can be. Now you can buy the full range online, including the luxurious Ginger Souffle Whipped Body Cream,

Jump Start Body Wash and Pomegranate Wash cleanser. You really do want to try them all.

Site Usability:	★★★★★	Based:	UK
Product Range:	★★★★	Express Delivery Option? (UK)	Yes
Price Range:	Medium	Gift Wrapping Option?	No
Delivery Area:	UK	Returns Procedure:	Down to you

www.potions.org.uk

Potions & Possibilities produces natural toiletries and aromatherapy products, ranging from soaps and bath oils to restorative balms and creams. Everything is blended and created using the highest-quality essential oils. You can find the award-winning products in Bloomingdales (in the US) and Fenwicks in the UK, among other stores, and, of course, online. Choose from bath sizzlers, bath and shower gels, shampoos, fragrance and gift collections.

Site Usability:	★★★★	Based:	UK
Product Range:	★★★	Express Delivery Option? (UK)	Yes
Price Range:	Medium	Gift Wrapping Option?	No
Delivery Area:	Worldwide	Returns Procedure:	Down to you

www.primrose-aromatherapy.co.uk

This attractively laid-out website is just about aromatherapy and the selection of essential oils is huge, with pictures of the fruits, flowers and herbs themselves rather than dinky little bottles. For each product there's a great deal of information on the properties and how to use them. They will ship all over the world and you need to contact them if you want courier delivery.

Site Usability:	★★★★	Based:	UK
Product Range:	★★★	Express Delivery Option? (UK)	Yes
Price Range:	Medium	Gift Wrapping Option?	No
Delivery Area:	Worldwide	Returns Procedure:	Down to you

www.pureskincare.co.uk

All of the products here are 100% natural and suitable for vegetarians. There's also brief information next to each brand name to show which brands are organic or contain organic ingredients, rather than those which are purely 'natural'. Brands available include Balm Balm, Akamuti, Aubrey Organics, Dr Bronner, Suki and Trovarno Organics. Products range from general skin and hair care to specialist skincare and travel sizes.

Site Usability: ★★★★★	Based:	UK
Product Range: ★★★★	Express Delivery Option? (UK)	No
Price Range: Medium	Gift Wrapping Option?	No
Delivery Area: UK	Returns Procedure:	Down to you

www.parseme.com

Based in Kensington Church Street, London, Parseme offers an exclusive range of natural home fragrance and bath and body care products including scented candles, shower gels, body oils and room sprays in fragrances such as Lavande, Vanille, Verveine and Gardena Blossom. They also make wonderful, simply and beautifully boxed Pot Pourri in Fleurs Sauvages, Symphonie de Couleurs, Champe de Lavande and Les Orangerais all of which would be beautiful gifts.

Site Usability: ★★★★★	Based:	UK
Product Range: ★★★★	Express Delivery Option?	(UK) Yes
Price Range: Medium	Gift Wrapping Option?	Yes
Delivery Area: Worldwide	Returns Procedure:	Down to you

www.rose-apothecary.co.uk

Here's a natural beauty website with a difference, as it offers lots of its own, different, prettily packaged products such as Rose Petal Bath and Shower Creme, Lavender Shampoo and luxurious gift boxes. You will also find J & E Atkinson, fragrances I Coloniali, Rice and Segreti Mediterranei, Yardley English Lavender, 4711 Cologne and Soir de Paris. The aromatherapy products, remedy oils and creams and massage oils are all blended in house.

Site Usability: ★★★★	Based:	UK
Product Range: ★★★★	Express Delivery Option? (UK)	No
Price Range: Medium	Gift Wrapping Option?	No
Delivery Area: Worldwide	Returns Procedure:	Down to you

www.theorganicpharmacy.com

The Organic Pharmacy is dedicated to health and beauty using organic products and treatments. Fully registered with The Royal Pharmaceutical Society of Great Britain, it chooses to specialise in herbs, homeopathy and organic skincare. It promises no artificial preservatives, colourings or fragrances and everything it offers is handmade in small batches. Look for cosmetics, skincare and gorgeously fragranced candles, plus mother and baby care.

Site Usability:	★★★★★	Based:	UK
Product Range:	★★★★	Express Delivery Option? (UK)	No
Price Range:	Luxury/Medium	Gift Wrapping Option?	No
Delivery Area:	Worldwide	Returns Procedure:	Down to you

www.youraromatherapy.co.uk

This is a clear and modern aromatherapy website, where you can immediately see all the products on offer, including essential and massage oils, aromatherapy kits, candles and accessories, vaporisers and ionisers and body care for all the family. There is a good gift section and an attractive selection of candles.

Site Usability:	★★★★★	Based:	UK
Product Range:	★★★★	Express Delivery Option? (UK)	No
Price Range:	Medium	Gift Wrapping Option?	No
Delivery Area:	Worldwide	Returns Procedure:	Down to you

Chapter 28

The Beauty Specialists

I f you're not into the 'superbrand' beauty products but prefer something a bit out of the ordinary, or there's a special product or brand that you've been using for some time that's hard to find on the high street, then take a look here. You'll find brands such as Dermalogica, Eve Lom, Decleor, Dermablend, Liz Earle and Dr Sebagh.

At the end of the day it's what works for you and your skin. Most of these brands you may well have come across in beauty salons, both here and overseas, and of course that's what's so great about the internet – you can now find them without any trouble. But – and there is a 'but' here – the products here are also quite expensive. Some are very expensive. Before you invest heavily, ask for a sample, or buy the smallest-size pot, just to make sure you like the results.

No doubt you've guessed that I'm speaking from experience. In the past I've bought into a new product range – partially because I liked the sound of it and partially because I liked the packaging – and then really not used it properly and even (horror) ended up throwing it away. You definitely don't want to go there.

Even so, there is a marvellous choice here and you can find almost every product you've ever heard of. It's just another trial of temptation. Sorry.

Sites to Visit

www.beautyandtheeast.co.uk

This is one of those online retailers offering a wide range of specialist products where, if you use one or more, you'll surely like to shop. On its attractive website you can buy Aveda, Blinc Mascara, Burt's Bees, Elemis, Fudge, Molton Brown and Dr Lewinn's Ultra R4 Restorative Cream. There's plenty of detail and clear pictures to help you choose if you want to try something new.

Site Usability:	★★★★	Based:	UK
Product Range:	★★★★	Express Delivery Option? (UK)	No
Price Range:	Medium	Gift Wrapping Option?	No
Delivery Area:	UK, but ask for overseas delivery	Returns Procedure:	Down to you

www.beautyexpert.co.uk

Here you'll find beauty products by Caudalie, Aromatherapy Associates, Fudge, L'Occitane, NV Perricone, Phytomer and Ren, plus lots more. Most of these are not ranges that you'll find in the shops but specialist products from salons and spas. There's lots of specialist advice on the Advice Line run by beauty therapists if you should have a query and an excellent selection of starter kits if you want to try a new product.

Site Usability:	★★★★	Based:	UK
Product Range:	★★★	Express Delivery Option? (UK)	Yes
Price Range:	Medium	Gift Wrapping Option?	Yes
Delivery Area:	Worldwide	Returns Procedure:	Down to you

www.beautyflash.co.uk

Beauty Flash offers the full range from Dermalogica, including masques and moisturisers, specialist treatments and treatment foundations (although you really need to know your colour before you buy these), spa body products and sun care. It has the Skin Doctors range of professional-strength skincare, with lots of information and advice, plus Fake Bake and St Tropez tanning products, Air Stockings and Dermablend Cover Creme.

Site Usability:	★★★★	Based:	UK
Product Range:	★★★★	Express Delivery Option? (UK)	No
Price Range:	Medium	Gift Wrapping Option?	No
Delivery Area:	UK	Returns Procedure:	Down to you

www.beautynaturals.com

This is a family-run business, inspired by Martha Hill, who launched her herbal-based, cruelty-free skincare products over 30 years ago. The site offers a comprehensive and affordable collection of high-quality, natural health and beauty products. The Beauty Naturals collection encompasses all aspects of natural beauty and includes skincare, cosmetics, hand and nail care and bath and body products, plus a wide range of specialist products by unusual and hard-to-find brands.

Site Usability:	★★★★	Based:	UK
Product Range:	★★★★★	Express Delivery Option? (UK)	Yes
Price Range:	Medium	Gift Wrapping Option?	No
Delivery Area:	UK	Returns Procedure:	Down to you

www.beautyxposure.com

Beauty Xposure is a Dermalogica skincare salon based in Hertfordshire. On its clear and cleanly designed website it offers three ranges for you to buy online: Dermalogica skincare system, Fake Bake (a great fake tan that will last up to a week and was recently voted best self-tanner in the New York Times) and the Nailtiques nail care system. If you're not sure which Dermalogica products you should order, just fill in the questionnaire and they'll give you lots of advice.

Site Usability:	★★★★	Based:	UK
Product Range:	★★★	Express Delivery Option? (UK)	No
Price Range:	Medium	Gift Wrapping Option?	Yes
Delivery Area:	UK	Returns Procedure:	Down to you

www.drhauschka.co.uk

You may well have read in the press about Dr Hauschka's natural skincare products through its celebrity connections. When you look at the products online you'll find that they're not overpriced and there's lots of information about each one, not just what it's for but how to use it and a full ingredients list. When you find something you like the sound of, check to see whether a trial/travel size is on offer before you splash out.

Site Usability:	★★★★	Based:	UK
Product Range:	★★★	Express Delivery Option? (UK)	Yes
Price Range:	Medium	Gift Wrapping Option?	Yes
Delivery Area:	UK, but there are international websites	Returns Procedure:	Down to you

www.espaonline.com

ESPA was created to bring together the best of ancient and modern therapies with the finest quality ingredients and skincare advances. This is a light and modern website offering the famous range of aromatherapy products, from specific beauty treatments to bath and body products and luxury gifts, with everything formulated from the highest-quality, organically grown plants. So if you're feeling stressed, this would definitely be a good place to start.

Site Usability:	★★★★★	Based:	UK
Product Range:	★★★★	Express Delivery Option? (UK)	No
Price Range:	Medium	Gift Wrapping Option?	No
Delivery Area:	Worldwide	Returns Procedure:	Down to you

www.evelom.co.uk

This is surely one of the most famous names in modern skincare, based on Eve Lom's belief that the best skincare is quite simply total cleansing using natural products and her famous polishing cloth. You may not be able to get to her for a facial, but at least now you can find her products to buy online. The range is small and definitely not cheap, but you'll know that you're buying the very best.

Site Usability:	★★★★	Based:	UK
Product Range:	★★★	Express Delivery Option? (UK)	No
Price Range:	Luxury	Gift Wrapping Option?	No
Delivery Area:	Worldwide	Returns Procedure:	Down to you

www.karinhertzog.co.uk

'We didn't just jump on the oxygen band wagon, we created it,' they say here, where you can order from this Swiss range of oxygen skincare. If you're not quite sure (and the products aren't cheap), go for one of the trial packs and kits, such as the Congestion Charge, which aims to help skin with acne and dull, excessively oily skin, or the energising Detox in a Box. There's a lot to read here and you may well be tempted.

Site Usability:	★★★★	Based:	UK
Product Range:	★★★★	Express Delivery Option? (UK)	No
Price Range:	Luxury	Gift Wrapping Option?	No
Delivery Area:	UK	Returns Procedure:	Down to you

www.laline.co.uk

Laline is new range of bath, body care and home accessories, handmade with natural oils and fragrances such as shea butter, aloe and citrus oils, all sourced in France and beautifully packaged. The range includes soaps, body creams and souffles, body oils and face masks, plus products for men, babies and home. Prices start from around £4.

Site Usability:	★★★★	Based:	UK
Product Range:	★★★	Express Delivery Option? (UK)	Yes
Price Range:	Medium/Very Good Value	Gift Wrapping Option?	No
Delivery Area:	EU	Returns Procedure:	Down to you

www.lizearle.com

Liz Earle has a beautiful website offering her 'Naturally Active Skincare', a pampering range of skin, body and sun care products. She's particularly well known for her cleanse and polish hot cloth cleanser, together with well-priced and excellent special treatments and moisturisers. Shimmer products for body and lips, vital aromatherapy oils and travel mini-kits from the wide range are just some of the temptations on offer and the lovely packaging is a bonus.

Site Usability:	★★★★	Based:	UK
Product Range:	★★★★	Express Delivery Option? (UK)	Yes
Price Range:	Very Good Value	Gift Wrapping Option?	Yes, everything is beautifully packaged
Delivery Area:	Worldwide	Returns Procedure:	Down to you

www.philosophy.com

You can find a good selection of these products at www.hqhair.com, but if you want to choose from the complete Philosophy range you need to visit its US-based website and order from there. Although the range appears whimsical, with its childish pictures and lighthearted wording, there are groundbreaking cleansers and peels here as well as excellent moisturisers and anti-ageing treatments. You will also find bath and body essentials, fab cosmetics and good beauty accessories.

Site Usability:	★★★★★	Based:	US
Product Range:	★★★★★	Express Delivery Option? (UK)	No
Price Range:	Medium	Gift Wrapping Option?	Yes
Delivery Area:	Worldwide	Returns Procedure:	Down to you

www.salonskincare.com

Some of the brands you'll find here, such as Elemis, Decleor, Gatineau and Phytomer, are not hard to find on the web, while others, such as luxury skincare brand Carita, Baxter of California, Max Benjamin (candles) and MD Formulations, are not readily available. Couple this with the extremely well-thought-out design and this website becomes an essential beauty destination if you like salon brand products. You can also buy Dermalogica, Fake Bake, Molton Brown and Nailtiques here, plus Klein-Becker Strivectin SD, the stretch mark turned anti-wrinkle wonder cream.

Site Usability:	★★★★★	Based:	UK
Product Range:	★★★★★	Express Delivery Option? (UK)	Yes
Price Range:	Luxury/Medium	Gift Wrapping Option?	No
Delivery Area:	Worldwide	Returns Procedure:	Down to you

www.skinstore.co.uk

What's great about this website is that you can access the online chat facility and 'talk' to an expert to help you make sure that what you're buying will be right for you. The site offers the latest anti-ageing treatments and innovative skin and body products such as StriVectin, MD Skincare, Rodan and Fields and Sovage. There's a huge range here, plus lots of information, so if anti-ageing is what you're looking for, you should definitely pay a visit.

Site Usability:	★★★★★	Based:	UK
Product Range:	★★★★★	Express Delivery Option? (UK)	No
Price Range:	Luxury/Medium	Gift Wrapping Option?	No
Delivery Area:	EU	Returns Procedure:	Down to you

www.thebeautyroom.com

You may well have come across the French salon brands Gatineau, Phytomer and Mary Cohr (or perhaps you haven't), but on this website you can order from the full ranges of skincare including anti-ageing creams, cleansers, toners, moisturisers and exfoliators, plus the Mary Cohr/Masters Colours extensive range of cosmetics. These are expensive products and this website will work best for those who have already tried them, although there's lots of information and advice if you want to invest in a new range.

Site Usability:	★★★★	Based:	UK
Product Range:	★★★	Express Delivery Option? (UK)	Yes
Price Range:	Medium	Gift Wrapping Option?	No
Delivery Area:	No	Returns Procedure:	Down to you

www.thisworks.com

Here you'll find soothing, natural and gently scented products for bath and body, with unusual names such as Energy Bank or Deep Calm Bath and Shower Oil, Muscle Therapy and Enjoy Really Rich Lotion or Hot Stone Essences, all created by Vogue beauty expert Kathy Phillips. The collection includes bath and shower gels, moisturisers, lovely gift ideas and an irresistible travel pouch designed by Orla Kiely containing eight miniature This Works products.

Site Usability:	★★★★	Based:	UK
Product Range:	★★★	Express Delivery Option? (UK)	No
Price Range:	Medium	Gift Wrapping Option?	Yes
Delivery Area:	Worldwide	Returns Procedure:	Down to you

www.timetospa.com

Time to Spa offers Elemis face and body products, La Therapie solutions for acne, scarring and hyper-pigmentation and Steiner Haircare. This is not a retailer so much as a beauty salon, where you can register for an online consultation on your beauty regimen by one of the team of therapists, find out about food and fitness for health and have your beauty questions answered. If you purchase from the online shop you'll find lots of gift ideas, excellent Elemis travel collections and gift wrapping.

Site Usability: ★★★★	Based:	UK
Product Range: ★★★	Express Delivery Option? (UK)	Yes
Price Range: Medium	Gift Wrapping Option?	Yes
Delivery Area: Worldwide	Returns Procedure:	Down to you

www.zelens.co.uk

You may not have heard of this line of hi-tech skincare products: Zelens is a small, expensive and specialist range of day, night and eye creams, formulated by leading skin-ageing and cancer specialist, Dr Marko Lens. There are two ranges – Skin Science, which is a natural cellular protector and rejuvenation cream, and Fullerene C60, an extremely potent anti-oxidant. There's a great deal of product information on the website, but if you want to know more I suggest you give them a call.

Site Usability: ★★★★	Based:	UK
Product Range: ★★★	Express Delivery Option? (UK)	No
Price Range: Luxury	Gift Wrapping Option?	No
Delivery Area: Worldwide	Returns Procedure:	Down to you

Chapter 29

Travel Products

I'm one of those people who like to keep a well-organised bag packed and ready for the moment someone comes along to whisk me off to the Bahamas (is anyone listening out there?). I'm also one of those people who wants to travel light and always fails miserably, taking far too many clothes that I don't wear ('in case' clothes, you know the sort). But I am really, really good in the travel skincare, cosmetics and spa products department.

First, of course, you need a good wash bag with compartments that you can hang up, so whether you're staying just for one night or for a fortnight you have everything at the ready. Take a look at www.hqhair. com and www.zpm.com where you'll find a good selection. Then I want to be able to take either miniatures of my favourite products or something different and special that's available in small sizes (and needless to say, I frequently take both).

There's a good selection of retailers here offering travel-sized ranges of everything from skincare to bath and body products. Get your bag packed now.

Sites to Visit

www.arranaromatics.com

Click on the 'Travel Size' button on the menu here and you'll immediately be taken to a range of the site's best-selling products, packaged in essential 50ml travel sizes. The prices here are extremely reasonable so you can order your favourites and experiment with a few new products as well. You'll also find travel sets and gift boxes within the different ranges.

Site Usability:	★★★★★	Based:	UK
Product Range:	★★★★	Express Delivery Option? (UK)	Yes
Price Range:	Medium/Very Good Value	Gift Wrapping Option?	No
Delivery Area:	Worldwide	Returns Procedure:	Down to you

www.crabtree-evelyn.co.uk

Well known and sold throughout the world, Crabtree & Evelyn offers a wide range of bath, body and spa products from classic fragrances such as Lily of the Valley to the ultra modern La Source. As well as the large-size versions you'll find travel-sized sets of all the major fragrances, perfect for your next trip away and also very good as small gifts.

Site Usability:	★★★★★	Based:	UK
Product Range:	★★★★★	Express Delivery Option? (UK)	No
Price Range:	Medium	Gift Wrapping Option?	No
Delivery Area:	Worldwide	Returns Procedure:	Down to you

www.jomalone.co.uk

As well as the irresistible products you'll find on her website, you can buy her indispensable travel sets, exquisitely packaged in cream or black. They're available in several different sizes, from the perfect In Flight Travel Bag, which contains everything you could need on board, to the Ultimate Travel Bag, which you customise with your essential products.

Site Usability:	★★★★★	Based:	UK
Product Range:	★★★★★	Express Delivery Option? (UK)	Yes
Price Range:	Luxury	Gift Wrapping Option?	Yes
Delivery Area:	Worldwide	Returns Procedure:	Down to you

www.lizearle.com

Liz Earle has cleverly packaged her skincare products into kits perfect for travelling, with names such as The Holiday Beauty Essentials Kit and Mini Bodycare Kit. So not only can you try out her products if you haven't used them before, but you can pack them up easily and take them away with you.

Site Usability:	★★★★	Based:	UK
Product Range:	★★★★	Express Delivery Option? (UK)	Yes
Price Range:	Very Good Value	Gift Wrapping Option?	Yes, everything is beautifully packaged
Delivery Area:	Worldwide	Returns Procedure:	Down to you

www.loccitane.com

Here's another collection of fragrance, bath and body products where there's a comprehensive range of travel-sized products, from the mini pure Shea Butter to the Orange Leaves Eau de Cologne. Often if you buy several products you can choose an extra one for free. The gorgeous soaps come in mini versions too, which are perfect for travel or for guests.

Site Usability:	★★★★★	Based:	UK
Product Range:	★★★★★	Express Delivery Option? (UK)	No
Price Range:	Medium	Gift Wrapping Option?	Yes
Delivery Area:	Worldwide	Returns Procedure:	Down to you

www.moltonbrown.co.uk

Molton Brown's travel sets vary from the Extravagant set which contains full-sized bottles in an elegant zip bag, to the New Age Traveller, a luxurious take-anywhere leather bag containing ten scaled-down products for skin, body and hair and which is far more suited to trips away, in my mind. The trouble is that I'd want to take several of the shower gels as well. Oh dear, more packing problems!

Site Usability:	★★★★★	Based:	UK
Product Range:	★★★★★	Express Delivery Option? (UK)	No
Price Range:	Medium	Gift Wrapping Option?	Yes
Delivery Area:	Worldwide	Returns Procedure:	Down to you

www.mujionline.co.uk

You must have heard of Muji, the Japanese-based company offering functional and marvellous value products for the home and office, including stationery, storage solutions, cookware, bags, luggage and accessories. Did you know that you can, on its online store, also order from the excellent range of tiny spray, flip-top and screw-top bottles waiting to be filled with your favourite products? Nylon vanity cases and Muji's hair and body care ranges are available as well.

Site Usability:	★★★★★	Based:	UK
Product Range:	★★★★	Express Delivery Option? (UK)	No
Price Range:	Very Good Value	Gift Wrapping Option?	No
Delivery Area:	Worldwide	Returns Procedure:	Down to you

www.penhaligons.co.uk

You need to pick the fragrance of your choice and click through to see whether the site does a travel version. Kits include Bluebell, Lily of the Valley and Quercus for her, and Blenheim Bouquet for him. They all contain eau de toilette, soap, shower gel and shampoo and come in beautiful packaging, so they'd be great for gifts.

Site Usability:	★★★★★	Express Delivery Option? (UK)	Yes
Product Range:	★★★★★	Gift Wrapping Option?	Automatic
Price Range:	Luxury/Medium	Returns Procedure:	Down to you
Delivery Area:	Worldwide		

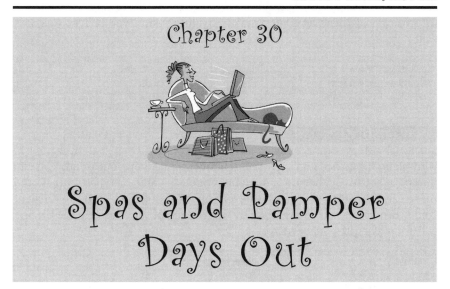

Chapter 30

Spas and Pamper Days Out

Doesn't it make you feel better just to think of getting on a plane and jetting off to somewhere warm and sunny, with soft sands, blue skies and someone waiting to massage all the stress away from your shoulders? It certainly does me. Even if we're not talking about long-distance spas but a day or two with friends or in relaxing solitude somewhere tranquil and stress free, with no one to bother you (provided you turn off your mobile, of course)?

Whether you want to spa (is that a verb? If not it should be) long haul or short or can spare only a day, take a look here, choose somewhere gorgeous, drop hints like mad or book for yourself and leave that phone at home.

Sites to Visit

www.leadingspasoftheworld.com

All you need to know here is when you want to go (did I say this was for a gift? I must have been mad), roughly where you want to go, i.e. which country, and you're away. Use the excellent search facility to find the most luxurious spas around the world. You can choose from spas with hydrotherapy, ayurvedic spas, spas with yoga, Pilates and tai chi, or somewhere gorgeous to just relax and be pampered. If you are going to give one of these as a gift, make absolutely sure you're free to go as well.

Site Usability:	★★★★★	Delivery Area:	Worldwide
Product Range:	★★★★★	Based:	USA
Price Range:	Luxury/Medium		

www.spabreak.co.uk

Spa Break offers comprehensive information on luxury spas all over the UK, with plenty of advice and pictures to help you make up your mind. You can purchase a gift voucher for a specific monetary value or type of break and these can be sent to you or whomever you want, together with the relevant colour brochure. You can see exactly where each of the spas is in the UK and call for advice if you need to.

Site Usability:	★★★★★	Delivery Area:	UK
Product Range:	★★★★	Based:	UK
Price Range:	Luxury/Medium		

www.spafinder.com

You can find a spa anywhere in the world through Spa Finder. This particular resource is for the UK only and is very easy to use – you just click on Spa Search to find the type of services you want, or use the Spa Guide first to narrow down your choice. You can order the worldwide Spa Directory here, check out day spa deals and group specials and buy gift vouchers to spas throughout Europe. Next time you need a bit of pampering, definitely take a look here.

Site Usability:	★★★★★	Delivery Area:	Worldwide
Product Range:	★★★★★	Based:	USA
Price Range:	Luxury/Medium		

www.thanksdarling.com

Yes, thanks indeed, here are some wonderful pampering spa breaks and days out, mainly in the south of England. On ordering, you (or your lucky recipient) are sent an open-dated voucher pack for the break you've chosen, whether it's a 'Special Chill Out Spa Break for Two' or a 'Luxury

Pamper Day'. You'll no doubt be extremely popular if you give one of these as a gift – and hopefully you'll be invited along.

Site Usability:	★★★★	Delivery Area:	UK
Product Range:	★★★★	Based:	UK
Price Range:	Luxury/Medium	Express Delivery Option? (UK)	No

www.thespasdirectory.com

Whatever you're looking for, whether it's a relaxing and pampering day out, a Pilates class or fitness advice, you'll find it here on the spas directory's advanced search facility. There's almost too much to choose from as the site covers the whole world. Does it make you feel better or worse to discover that the spa of your dreams is in Baja, Mexico? However, you'll surely find one nearer to home while you wait for your chance to leap on a plane. The site is clean and clear and there are full profiles with pictures on every spa listed, as well as a direct link through to each spa's website.

Site Usability:	★★★★	Delivery Area:	Worldwide
Product Range:	★★★★	Based:	UK
Price Range:	Luxury/Medium	Express Delivery Option? (UK)	No

Chapter 31

Pampering Gifts

There are so many wonderful websites where you can find all sorts of pampering gifts, from luxurious and unusual scented candles to pretty cosmetic bags and gorgeous bath and body products such as bath truffles, body shimmer and fragrance.

You're unlikely to go wrong here. Not only are the products attractive and often well-priced, but the retailers themselves are some of the best at pretty packaging, express delivery and often overseas shipping, making sure that what arrives is simply a joy to receive.

You'll notice that these online retailers are different from the others in the Pamper Yourself section, although most of those offer great gift ideas, so to make sure you have lots of choice you should take a look at those as well.

Sites to Visit

www.austique.co.uk

Here's an attractive and well-designed website offering a bit of everything: accessories, lingerie, Rococo chocolates, modern jewellery and unusual bathroom treats such as Limoncello Body Butter and Arnaud Chamomile and Lavender Bubble Bath. The range changes frequently depending on the season. The site offers gift wrapping, express delivery and international orders by special request.

Site Usability:	★★★★	Based:	UK
Product Range:	★★★	Express Delivery Option? (UK)	Yes
Price Range:	Medium	Gift Wrapping Option?	Yes
Delivery Area:	Worldwide	Returns Proce dure:	Down to you

www.bootik.co.uk

On this well laid out website you'll find lots of gift ideas, from pretty, well-priced jewellery set with semi-precious stones, beaded bags and attractive cosmetic bags to bath and body products, unusual cushions and tableware. There is also a small and very different (but not so inexpensive) collection of clothes. Most of the items here can't be found elsewhere, so it could be well worth having a look round.

Site Usability:	★★★	Based:	UK
Product Range:	★★★	Express Delivery Option? (UK)	Yes
Price Range:	Medium	Gift Wrapping Option?	Yes
Delivery Area:	Worldwide	Returns Proce dure:	Down to you

www.boutiquetoyou.co.uk

Boutique to You specialises in personalised gifts, gadgets and jewellery perfect for lots of different occasions. It has also been responsible for introducing some cult jewellery brands from the US, including Mummy & Daddy Tags, Lisa Goodwin New York and Fairy Tale Jewels. On its website there's a wish-list facility so you can send 'wish mails' to your nearest and dearest with hints of what you'd like to receive. The site is also introducing a loyalty scheme.

Site Usability: ★★★	Based:	UK
Product Range: ★★★★	Express Delivery Option? (UK)	No
Price Range: Medium	Gift Wrapping Option	Yes
Delivery Area: Worldwide	Returns Procedure:	Down to you

www.comptoir-sud-pacifique.com

Comptoir Sud Pacifique is a brand synonymous with escape, exotism and sun, so if you feel the need for an exotic change of scenery, just click through here and let your senses take you away. Choose from Vanilla, Spicy, Fruity, Woody, Floral and Fresh Waters fragrances and candles such as Muscade Orange, Vanille Apricot and Aqua Motu. You can order as you go round the website or from a list by clicking on Buy Online. All prices are in euros.

Site Usability: ★★★★	Based:	UK
Product Range: ★★★★	Express Delivery Option? (UK)	No
Price Range: Medium	Gift Wrapping Option	No
Delivery Area: France	Returns Procedure:	Down to you

www.cowshedproducts.com

Recognised for their quirky, bovine-inspired names such as Dirty Cow Hand Wash, Until the Cows Come Home Gift Set and Grumpy Cow uplifting candle, Cowshed products contain therapeutic blends of herbal infusions and high-quality pure essential oils from around the world. The names derive from the original Cowshed spa at Babington House in Somerset. There's a cute Baby Cow range here, plus attractively packaged candles and gift sets.

Site Usability: ★★★★★	Based:	UK
Product Range: ★★★★	Express Delivery Option? (UK)	No
Price Range: Medium	Gift Wrapping Option	No
Delivery Area: UK and US (separate site)	Returns Procedure:	Down to you

www.gorgeousthingsonline.com

This is a mixture of pampering gifts, including candles by Arco, bath melts and bath truffles by Di Palomo, Nougat London Body Shimmer and moisturising soap. There are also pretty bathroom accessories, throws and blankets and attractive cushions. Everything is beautifully photographed and extremely tempting and nothing is overpriced. They'll ship anywhere in the world and offer a gift wrapping service as well.

Site Usability:	★★★★	Express Delivery Option? (UK)	No
Product Range:	★★★★	Gift Wrapping Option?	Yes
Price Range:	Medium	Returns Procedure:	Down to you
Delivery Area:	Worldwide		

www.missgroovy.co.uk

There's a real mixture of products on offer here, from YSL Touche Eclat and Hollywood Fashion Tape to cosmetics by Girlactik, Duwop, Eyeko and Principessa, plus bath and body products, hair and nail care and lots of suggestions and advice. So if you're looking for something a bit different, this would be a good place to have a browse or to find an unusual gift. They'll ship worldwide and aim to despatch within a day.

Site Usability:	★★★★	Based:	UK
Product Range:	★★★	Express Delivery Option? (UK)	Yes
Price Range:	Medium	Gift Wrapping Option?	Yes
Delivery Area:	Worldwide	Returns Procedure:	Down to You

www.savonneriesoap.com

This is a beautiful website with a luxurious feel where you can buy exquisitely packaged handmade soaps (think Flower Garden and Honey Cake), bath and body products such as Geranium and Bergamot Oil, perfect gift boxes and The Naughty Weekend Kit. Take a look and you'll find out.

Site Usability:	★★★★★	Based:	UK
Product Range:	★★★	Express Delivery Option? (UK)	No
Price Range:	Luxury/Medium	Gift Wrapping Option?	No
Delivery Area:	Worldwide	Returns Procedure:	Down to You

www.serendipbeauty.com

Next time you're looking for a pampering beauty/gift website which is also a pleasurable and relaxing shopping experience, click on this new website.

Products on offer include Burt's Bees, Cowshed, Croft + Croft, Fruits and Passion, Jane Packer, Korres, Manuel Canovas and Tocca. If that's not enough there are lots of pretty gift sets to choose from, plus cute make-up bags and wash bags by Zoe Phayre-Mudge.

Site Usability:	★★★★★	Based:	UK
Product Range:	★★★	Express Delivery Option? (UK)	No
Price Range:	Medium	Gift Wrapping Option?	No
Delivery Area:	Worldwide	Returns Procedure:	Down to you

www.thehambledon.com

The Hambledon is a lifestyle shop based in Winchester, which has successfully transferred most of its gorgeous products online, on a pretty and easy-to-use website. You'll find fragrance and bath and body products by Miller Harris and Wickle, candles by Tocca and REN skincare. There's also a wide selection of gifts. Call them if you want overseas deliveries.

Site Usability:	★★★★	Based:	UK
Product Range:	★★★	Express Delivery Option? (UK)	No
Price Range:	Medium	Gift Wrapping Option?	No
Delivery Area:	Worldwide	Returns Procedure:	Down to you

Chapter 32

Beauty Buying Guide

uying beauty products on or offline is never an exact science unless you're going for something that you've used over and over again (in which case it may well be time to move on). Beauty companies are constantly trying to awaken our interest with new and ever more innovative – and ever more expensive – products to keep us looking younger, reduce lines and wrinkles, peel away the daily stress and introduce new radiance.

The trouble is, of course, that what suits one skin (not just one type of skin) doesn't necessarily suit another and you probably won't find out until you try it. The temptation is to go on buying new 'miracle' products, thinking they're going to make a huge difference, and either not bothering to use them properly or wondering why they're not working for you. In fact, the answer could simply be that it's winter and your skin is dryer than usual/it's summer and you need a different product anyway. Or it could be something as basic as not drinking enough water.

I'm not going to pretend to be a beauty expert, although I'm definitely an expert in buying beauty products and, of course, buying them online. My advice is this (and some of it is probably going to sound strange coming from me):

- Don't buy new and expensive skincare unless you've talked to an expert, either in a store or through an online retailer (lots of them have professionals waiting to talk you through the range).
- Buy all your tried and tested products online – it's quicker, easier, allows you more time to go out and try new things and, if you're lucky, it can be cheaper.
- Be careful when buying new 'coloured' products online: lipstick, blusher, eyeshadow and particularly foundation and powder. Colours online are not going to be as accurate as you almost certainly need them to be. In the same way, don't buy a new foundation or powder where you can see it only in artificial light and not in natural light. Artificial light will distort colour and unless you're with a real expert you can end up buying the wrong thing (I've done this too many times).
- If you do order something but when you open it it doesn't look quite right for you, pack it back up and return it. Don't even think of trying it or you won't get your money back – you chose it in the first place, after all.

Section 4
Useful
Information

Chapter 33

Top Tips for Safe Online Shopping

There are so many websites to choose from, for just about every product you can think of, not just fashion and beauty. Whether you're buying kitchen equipment, a new bed, cashmere knit or lipstick, the basic rules for buying online are the same. Here are the important things you need to know before you buy. Just keep them in mind before you start ordering and you should have no problems. Happy shopping.

- *Secure payment.* Make sure that when you go to put in your payment information, the padlock appears at the foot of the screen and the top line changes from http:// to https://. This means that your information will be transferred in code. To make sure you're clear about this, just go to www.johnlewis.com, put something in your basket, then click on 'Go to Checkout'. You'll immediately see the changes and those are what you're looking for each time. If they don't happen, don't buy.
- *Who are they?* Don't buy from a retailer unless you can access their full contact details. Ideally these will be available from the 'Contact Us' button on the Home Page, but sometimes they are hidden in Terms and Conditions. You should be able to find their email address, plus location address and telephone number. This is so that you can contact them in case of a problem. I get really annoyed by websites which hide behind

their email addresses – they need to be out there saying to you, the prospective customer, 'This is who we are and this is where we are, get in touch if you need us'. Sometimes they don't.

- *Privacy policy.* If it's the first time you're buying from this retailer you should check their privacy clause telling you what they'll be doing with your information. I suggest you never allow them to pass it on to anywhere/anyone else. It's not necessarily what *they* do with it that will cause you a problem.

- *Returns policy.* What happens if you want to return something? Check the retailer's policy before you order so that you're completely informed about how long you have to return goods and what the procedure is. Some retailers want you to give them notice that you're going to be sending something back (usually for more valuable items), others make it quick and simple – they're definitely the best.

- *Keeping track.* Keep a record, preferably printed, of everything you buy online, giving the contact details, product details and order reference so that if you need to you can quickly look them up. I also keep an email folder into which I drag any orders/order confirmations/payment details just in case I forget to print something. Then if you have a problem you can just click on the link to contact them and all the references are there.

- *Statements.* Check your bank statements to make sure that all the transactions appear as you expect. Best of all keep a separate credit card just for online spending which will make it even easier to check.

- *Delivery charges.* Check out the delivery charges. Again, some retailers are excellent and offer free delivery within certain areas while others charge a fortune. Make sure you're completely aware of the total cost before you buy. If you're buying from the US you will have to pay extra shipping and duty, which you'll either have to fork up for on delivery or on receipt of an invoice. My advice is to pay it immediately.

- *Credit card security.* Take advantage of the new MasterCard SecureCode and Verified by Visa schemes when they're offered to you. Basically they provide you with the extra facility of giving a password when you use your registered cards to buy online from signed-up retailers – a kind of online chip and pin. They're excellent and they're going to grow. For extra security, pay online with a credit rather than a debit or any other type of card as this gives you added security from the credit card companies on goods over £100 in value.

- *Shred the evidence.* Buy a shredder. You may think I'm daft, but most online and offline card fraud is due to someone having got hold of your details offline. So don't let anyone walk off with your card to a point where you can't see it and don't chuck out papers containing your information where they can be easily accessed by someone else. You have been warned.
- *Payment don'ts.* Don't ever pay cash, don't pay by cheque (unless you've got the goods and you're happy with them), don't ever send your credit card details by email and don't give your pin number online to anyone *ever.* I'm amazed at the stories I hear.
- *PC security.* Make sure your computer is protected by the latest anti-virus software and an efficient firewall. Virus scan your system at least once a week so that you not only check for nasties but get rid of any spyware.
- *Auction websites.* Be very careful using an auction website. Make sure that you know absolutely what you're doing and who you're buying from. This is not to say that everyone who sells on auction websites is waiting to get you, but some of them definitely are.
- *Fakes and replicas.* Be wary of anyone selling you 'replica' products – don't go there. If you're tempted to buy from someone selling you something that looks too cheap to be true, it probably is. If you're buying expensive products, always check on the retailer's policy for warranties and guarantees.
- *Additional information.* Don't give any information that isn't necessary to the purchase. You're buying a book, for goodness sake. Why do they need to know your age and how many children you have?
- *Take your time.* Don't buy in a hurry. Take the time to check the above before you click on 'Confirm Order'. If in any doubt at all, don't buy.

Have I managed to put you off yet? I assure you that's not my intention, but you really need to be aware of the above. Once you've carried out the checks just a few times you'll do them automatically. The internet is a marvellous place, but it's also a minefield full of unscrupulous people waiting to catch you out. Don't let them.

Chapter 34

Deliveries and Returns –

What to Look For and How to Make Them Easier

Deliveries

Deliveries from online retailers are getting increasingly better and more efficient. In many cases you can have your order tomorrow. Find a retailer you like who's stating the old 'within 28 days' policy and call them to find out if they're really that daft (being polite here). With most companies offering express delivery, who on earth is willing to wait for 28 days unless something is being specially made for them (in which case it may well take longer but at least you'll be aware before you order)?

Most companies offer the following:

- Standard delivery
- 24-hour delivery (for a small extra charge)
- Saturday delivery (very occasionally)
- EU delivery and sometimes EU Express
- Worldwide delivery and sometimes Worldwide Express.

The problem is that you very often don't find out about all these and the relevant charges until you've put something in your basket (note to online retailers: please make 'Delivery Information' a key button on your home page, it saves so much time). Yes, I have researched this information for you, but sometimes I had to practically place an order to discover a retailer's policies; ridiculous (are you listening out there)?

Returns

This is an area that often puts people off buying online (or from catalogues, for that matter). Well, don't be put off.

You will, of course, have read up on the company's returns policy before you bought, so you know how much time you have, but you might like to know the following:

- You are entitled to a 'cooling off' period (usually seven days), during which you can cancel your order without any reason and receive a full refund.
- You're also entitled to a full refund if the goods or services are not provided by the date you agreed. If you didn't agree a date, you are entitled to a refund if the goods or services are not provided within 28 days.

Having said that, and assuming that once you've started you're going to become a regular online shopper, the following will make your life easier:

- Buy a black marker pen, roll of packing tape and some different-sized jiffy bags (I use D1, H5 and K7, which are good for most things) just in case you want to return only part of an order and the original packing is damaged or too big.
- Keep these where the rest of the family can't get at them. (That tells you something about my family, doesn't it? Why doesn't anyone ever put things back?)
- Make sure that you keep the original packaging and any paperwork until you're sure that you're not sending stuff back and keep it somewhere easy to find.
- If you want to be really clever, go to www.vistaprint.co.uk and order some address labels. They're cheap and incredibly useful for returns, Recorded and Special Delivery postings and lots of other things.

- Don't be put off if a premium retailer wants you to call them if you're returning something valuable. It's essential that the item is insured in transit and this is something they usually arrange – for really expensive goods they may well use a courier service to collect from you.
- Rejoice when returns are free. Standard postage and packing is more and more frequently becoming free of charge from large online retailers. We'll be ordering far more when returns are free as well.

Chapter 35

Help If Something Goes Wrong

If something goes wrong and you've paid by credit card, you may have a claim not only against the supplier of the goods but also against the credit card issuer. This applies to goods or services (and deposits) costing more than £100 but less than £30,000 and does not apply to debit or charge cards.

Contact the retailer with the problem initially by email and making sure you quote the order number and any other necessary details. If you don't get immediate assistance, ask to speak to the manager. Normally this will end your problem. However, if I tell you that I ordered some expensive goods from a luxury store recently which didn't arrive when I expected them to, was treated rudely by the call centre assistant and then unbelievably rudely by the manager, you'll get the message that this doesn't always work. Ok, it's the company's fault for recruiting these people in the first place and not in-stilling in them the message that even if the customer isn't always right they should always be treated with the utmost care and politeness. What they're looking for is not your first order, believe me, it's turning you into a loyal repeat customer. Those types of customers are the most valuable of all.

Again it's not things going wrong that cause most of the trouble, it's how the company sorts things out. Do it right, make you feel really important and do that little bit extra and they've got you hooked. Handle things badly and they've not only lost this order but any future orders. Not only that but they've lost your goodwill with regards to recommending them to others. Stupid, stupid, stupid – are you listening out there?

In my case, and probably because I'm pushier than most people and didn't stop at the manager, I got what I wanted. (Note: push hard. Contact the company's owner if you can or press office if need be and tell them what's going on.) And no, I'm not going to tell you who my problem was with, sorry.

If after all of this you do not get a satisfactory result to your complaint, you can contact www.consumerdirect.gov.uk (for the UK) or call on 08454 040506 for what to do next. If your problem is with a retailer based in Australia, Canada, Denmark, Finland, Hungary, Mexico, New Zealand, Norway, South Korea, Sweden, Switzerland or the US, you can click through for help to www.econsumer.gov, a joint project of consumer protection agencies from 20 nations.

If (horrors) you find that someone has used your credit card information without your authorisation, contact your card issuer immediately. You can cancel the payment and your card company must arrange for your account to be re-credited in full.

Chapter 36

UK, European and US Clothing Size Conversions

H ere's a general guide to the clothing size conversions between the US, Europe and the UK. If you need size conversions for other specific countries, or other types of conversions, you'll find them all on the web at www.onlineconversion.com/clothing.htm.

To be as sure as possible that you're ordering the right size, check the actual retailer's size chart against your own measurements and note that a UK 12 is sometimes a US 8 and sometimes a 10, so it really pays to make sure.

Men's clothing size conversions

US	UK	EU
32	32	42
34	34	44
36	36	46
38	38	48
40	40	50
42	42	52
44	44	54
46	46	56
48	48	58

Women's clothing size conversions

US	UK	France	Germany	Italy
6	8	36	34	40
8	10	38	36	42
10	12	40	38	44
12	14	42	40	46
14	16	44	42	48
16	18	46	44	50
18	20	50	46	52

Women's shoe size conversions

UK	3.5	4	4.5	5	5.5	6	6.5	7	7.5	8	8.5
EU	36.5	37	37.5	38	38.5	39	40	41	42	43	43.5
US	6	6.5	7	7.5	8	8.5	9	9.5	10	10.5	11

Men's shoe size conversions

UK	7	7.5	8	8.5	9	9.5	10	10.5	11	11.5	12
EU	40.5	41	42	42.5	43	44	44.5	45	46	46.5	47
US	7.5	8	8.5	9	9.5	10	10.5	11	11.5	12	12.5

Chapter 37

Fashion and Beauty Trend Watch

I f you, like me, find it difficult to ascertain what's going on 'out there' from the catwalk pictures in the newspapers and glossies, take a look at these websites. They're really good at breaking down the trends into understandable bites, making it easy for you to decide which, if any, you want to go for this season.

Sites to Visit

www.handbag.com
Busy online stylezine handbag.com is the place to find out about what's really going on, whether it's what the celebrities are wearing this season or what you should be wearing in the next. It's fun and easy to read, with lots of features and advice, and covers everything from fashion to beauty and lifestyle.

www.mywardrobe.com
Another designer-led website that tells you (and right from the beginning of the season, with its 'sneak preview') about the key looks and pieces you should be buying.

www.net-a-porter.com

Even if you're not going to buy here as everything is expensive, you should take a browse round and get ideas about what's going on. Each week the site has a new feature for you to view, such as '10 Essential Ways to be Stylish for the New Season', and they make very good reading. The edited collections are also excellent.

www.style.com

The online home of US *Vogue* and *W* has everything you need to see and read about, from the full new season's trend reports to essential Top Ten Looks, making it an excellent resource.

www.vogue.com

Needless to say this is still very mainstream fashion oriented, but click through to 'Trends' on the top line and you can read about each of the trends for the new season, illustrated by catwalk shots. Start here. Also click on Beauty to look at the latest skincare and cosmetic trends, the latest products on offer and where to buy them.

www.warehouse.co.uk

Click on 'StyleWare' and be taken straight to the new season's essentials which won't break the bank. This is not so much a trend watch but it is a great place to let them help you buy into the trends.

Chapter 38

Top 20 Websites for Busy Women

I f you haven't yet quite had the time to browse through the 500-plus websites here, just take a quick look at the online retailers below, some of whom you'll almost certainly have heard of and some you probably won't have. These are the best of the bunch (as it were) and some of my favourites, all of which have beautifully designed layouts, an excellent product range and offer the kind of service that never (barring unexpected disaster) lets you down.

You'll notice that there's a wide range of products here, from US-based Abercrombie casual wear to your next set of contact lenses. The idea is that, from this small number of websites, you actually have a tremendous choice, so if you're in a hurry, you can shop here first.

Sites to Visit

www.abercrombie.com

This is where the young chic American denim brigade shop for their jeans, jackets and tees. The style is very 'Casual Luxury' and they even call it that. Take a look around if you can tear yourself away from the outstanding photographs of the most beautiful models (mostly men). Prices are good and delivery is speedy. The quality is excellent. Sizing is *small*, particularly for fitted items, so if in any doubt go up a size.

Site Usability:	★★★★★	Based:	US
Product Range:	★★★	Express Delivery Option? (UK)	No
Price Range:	Medium	Gift Wrapping Option?	No
Delivery Area:	Worldwide	Returns Procedure:	Down to you

www.aspinaloflondon.com

Here you'll find some beautiful wallets, vanity cases, make-up bags and travel document holders, plus the new range of handbags and travel bags. Each piece is handmade from high-quality leathers and beautifully lined and finished. Most items can be personalised and everything can be beautifully gift boxed and sent out with your personal message. This is a collection of elegant, sophisticated, classic and contemporary designs which you can have sent anywhere in the world.

Site Usability:	★★★★★	Based:	UK
Product Range:	★★★★★	Express Delivery Option? (UK)	Yes
Price Range:	Luxury/Medium	Gift Wrapping Option?	Yes
Delivery Area:	Worldwide	Returns Procedure:	Down to you

www.astleyclarke.com

New online designer jewellery retailer Astley Clarke has an attractive website, where you'll find the collections of New York- and London-based designers such as Coleman Douglas, Talisman Unlimited, Vinnie Day, Flora Astor and Catherine Prevost, some of which are exclusive to Astley Clarke. Prices for the precious and semi-precious jewels here start at around £100 and then go skywards. For gorgeous gifts or treats this is the perfect place, as everything arrives beautifully gift boxed and can be gift wrapped as well. There's also a collection for brides and bridesmaids.

Site Usability:	★★★★★	Based:	UK
Product Range:	★★★★★	Express Delivery Option? (UK)	Yes
Price Range:	Luxury/Medium	Gift Wrapping Option?	Yes
Delivery Area:	UK	Returns Procedure:	Down to you

www.beautique.com

Beautique is a new beauty and hair website, divided into three sections: Learn, where you can find tips and advice written by industry experts in all areas of beauty and hair; Buy, where you can order all the products offered; and Experience, showcasing treatments, spas and salons in the UK and around the world, with personal recommendations and reviews. Brands include Aveda, Bumble and Bumble, Carole Franck, Dr Hauschka, Guerlain and J C Brosseau. It's beautifully designed and well worth having a look round.

Site Usability:	★★★★★	Based:	UK
Product Range:	★★★★★	Express Delivery Option? (UK)	Yes
Price Range:	Luxury/Medium	Gift Wrapping Option?	No
Delivery Area:	UK	Returns Procedure:	Down to you

www.cologneandcotton.com

This is a very special website offering some unusual and hard-to-find bath and body products and fragrance by Diptyque (if you haven't already tried their candles you really should: they're gorgeous), Cath Collins, La Compagnie de Provence and Cote Bastide. There are also fragrances by Annik Goutal, Coudray and Rosine and for the bathroom there are lovely fluffy towels and bathrobes.

Site Usability:	★★★★★	Based:	UK
Product Range:	★★★★	Express Delivery Option? (UK)	Yes
Price Range:	Luxury/Medium	Gift Wrapping Option?	Yes
Delivery Area:	Worldwide	Returns Procedure:	Down to you

www.ctshirts.co.uk

Well known for its colourful and well laid out catalogue, now you can order all the shirts, handmade shoes, ties and other accessories online. The website is attractive and easy to navigate and the service is excellent. A range of shirt qualities and styles is available and there are frequently special offers. There's a good selection of casual shirts and knitwear, tailoring, ladies' shirts, cashmere knits and accessories and 'Tiny Tyrwhitt' clothing too.

Site Usability:	★★★★★	Based:	UK
Product Range:	★★★★★	Express Delivery Option? (UK)	Yes
Price Range:	Medium	Gift Wrapping Option?	Yes
Delivery Area:	Worldwide	Returns Procedure:	Down to you

www.escentual.co.uk

Escentual carries what is probably the widest range of fragrance for men and women in the UK. Choose a fragrance or fragrance-linked bath and body product, then search for it on this site – you're almost certain to find it. Bath and body products include Burberry, Bvlgari, Calvin Klein, Gucci, Guerlain, Rochas and Versace, plus Crabtree & Evelyn, Tisserand and I Coloniali. Delivery is free on orders over £30 and they also offer free gift wrapping.

Site Usability:	★★★★★	Based:	UK
Product Range:	★★★★★	Express Delivery Option? (UK)	Yes
Price Range:	Luxury/Medium/Very Good Value	Gift Wrapping Option?	Yes
Delivery Area:	Worldwide	Returns Procedure:	Down to you

www.figleaves.com

If you can't find it here, you may well not be able to find it anywhere else as this is definitely one of the best collections of lingerie, swimwear and sportswear available online. Almost every lingerie brand name is offered, from DKNY, Dolce & Gabbana and Janet Reger to Sloggi, Gossard and Wonderbra. And delivery is free throughout the world. All sizes are covered, from the very small to the very large, and there's a huge choice in just about every category.

Site Usability:	★★★★★	Based:	UK
Product Range:	★★★★	Express Delivery Option? (UK)	Yes
Price Range:	Luxury/Medium/Very Good Value	Gift Wrapping Option?	Yes
Delivery Area:	Worldwide	Returns Procedure:	Use their returns service

www.forzieri.com

Italian company Forzieri offers handbags and wallets by Dolce & Gabbana, Prada, Tods, Gucci and Burberry, plus superb leather and shearling jackets, a stylish shoe collection, gloves, leather travel bags and other accessories. There's also a wide choice of reasonably priced, high-quality Italian brands.

Very good descriptions are given about all the products, plus lots of different views so you know exactly what you're buying.

Site Usability: ★★★★	Based:	Italy
Product Range: ★★★★	Express Delivery Option? (UK)	Yes
Price Range: Luxury/Medium	Gift Wrapping Option?	Yes
Delivery Area: Worldwide	Returns Procedure:	Down to you

www.hqhair.com

If you haven't used it already you should try this fun and incredibly useful website. Along with funky beauty products and jewellery (and absolutely everything you could need for your hair, including Blax, Nexxus and Paul Mitchell products), you'll discover Anya Hindmarch, Kate Spade and Lulu Guinness exquisite cosmetic bags (perfect for presents and also for treats). There are also lots of beauty accessories, including high-quality make-up and hairbrushes.

Site Usability: ★★★★★	Based:	UK
Product Range: ★★★★★	Express Delivery Option? (UK)	No
Price Range: Luxury/Medium	Gift Wrapping Option?	No
Delivery Area: Worldwide	Returns Procedure:	Down to you

www.jimmychoo.com

Needless to say, the new Jimmy Choo website is beautifully and provocatively designed and makes you want to browse right through, even though the prices are quite frightening in most cases, to say the least. This is always a covetable collection, including diamante-encrusted sandals, killer-heel peep-toe slides, gorgeous boots and wonderful, right-on-trend handbags.

Site Usability: ★★★★★	Based:	UK
Product Range: ★★★★	Express Delivery Option? (UK)	Yes
Price Range: Luxury	Gift Wrapping Option?	Automatic
Delivery Area: Worldwide	Returns Procedure:	Down to you

www.johnlewis.com

John Lewis doesn't make it easy for you to discover the beauty products it offers, as you have to click on Fashion first. However, once you get there you'll see that you can buy Molton Brown, Elemis, REN, Philosophy, Neal's

Yard, Nougat and Gianna Rose Atelier (and more). I'm a huge fan of this website – there's an excellent range in all areas, you can see immediately what's in stock and the delivery service is just as you'd expect.

Site Usability:	★★★★★	Express Delivery Option? (UK)	Yes
Product Range:	★★★★★	Gift Wrapping Option?	No
Price Range:	Medium	Returns Procedure:	Call them to collect or return goods to
Delivery Area:	UK		store
Based:	UK		

www.kiarie.co.uk

Kiarie has one of the best ranges of scented candles, by brands such as Geodosis, Kenneth Turner, Manuel Canovas, Creation Mathias, Rigaud and Millefiori. There are literally hundreds to choose from at all price levels (this site is very fast, so don't panic) and you can also choose your range by price, maker, fragrance, colour and season. Once you've made your selection you can ask them to gift wrap it for you and include a handwritten message.

Site Usability:	★★★★★	Based:	UK
Product Range:	★★★★★	Express Delivery Option? (UK)	Yes
Price Range:	Medium	Gift Wrapping Option?	Yes
Delivery Area:	Worldwide	Returns Procedure:	Down to you

www.lensway.com

Lensway is one of the best online places to buy contact lenses (and I've tested them many times). The prices are just about the best you'll find online, the website is very easy to use and your lenses arrive incredibly fast. You can buy most types, from daily to monthly lenses by Johnson & Johnson, Acuvue, Bausch and Lomb and others.

Site Usability:	★★★★	Express Delivery Option? (UK)	No but fast delivery is automatic
Product Range:	★★★★★	Gift Wrapping Option?	No
Price Range:	Medium/Very Good Value	Returns Procedure:	Down to you
Delivery Area:	Worldwide		

www.mankind.co.uk

This is definitely one of the best men's websites. It's modern, easy to use and has a great range of products, showcasing the very best and most innovative shaving, skin and hair-care brands made for men such as Lab Series, Nickel and K2 and offering them in a way that makes buying simple, fast and fun. There are shaving products, skin basics and problem-skin solutions as well as gift ideas here.

Site Usability:	★★★★★	Based:	UK
Product Range:	★★★★★	Express Delivery Option? (UK)	Yes
Price Range:	Medium	Gift Wrapping Option?	Yes
Delivery Area:	Worldwide	Returns Procedure:	Down to you

www.mytights.co.uk

My Tights has a modern and easy-to-use website, offering the hosiery brands of Aristoc, Charnos, Elbeo, Gerbe, La Perla, Levante and Pretty Polly, to name but a few, plus maternity tights by Spanx and Trasparenze. So whether you want footless or fishnet tights and stockings, support tights, shapewear, knee highs or suspenders, you'll find it all here. Provided you order before 3pm you'll probably get it the next day.

Site Usability:	★★★★★	Based:	UK
Product Range:	★★★★	Express Delivery Option? (UK)	Yes
Price Range:	Luxury/Medium	Gift Wrapping Option?	No
Delivery Area:	Worldwide	Returns Procedure:	Down to you

www.net-a-porter.com

This is the über-fashionista's website, where you'll find the most impressive range of designer clothes and accessories available online and a retailer that's becoming increasingly well known for its clever buying, excellent service and attractive packaging. So if you're looking for something special with a designer label, such as Marc Jacobs, Alexander McQueen, Burberry, Roland Mouret, Alberta Feretti, Marni, Jimmy Choo or Paul Smith (the list goes on and on), you should definitely have a look here.

Site Usability:	★★★★★	Based:	UK
Product Range:	★★★★★	Express Delivery Option? (UK)	Yes
Price Range:	Luxury	Gift Wrapping Option?	Yes
Delivery Area:	Worldwide	Returns Procedure:	Free using their DHL service

www.shopatanna.co.uk

With stores based in London, Norfolk and Suffolk, Anna is an innovative boutique offering clothes and accessories by Betty Jackson, Seven, Issa London, Orla Kiely, Gharani Strock and lesser-known designers such as Day and Noa Noa. It's an eclectic and modern collection combining elegance and quirkiness and designers are being added all the time, so keep checking back.

Site Usability:	★★★★★	Based:	UK
Product Range:	★★★★	Express Delivery Option? (UK)	Yes
Price Range:	Luxury/Medium	Gift Wrapping Option?	Yes
Delivery Area:	Worldwide	Returns Procedure:	Down to you

www.thewhitecompany.com

The White Company's fashion and toiletry ranges increase with every season. Currently they include knitwear, nightwear and soft jersey daywear, in modern shapes and each new season's colours. For me, however, it's their bath, body and fragranced candles that win hands down every time. They're not overpriced, they are beautifully photographed, gorgeously packaged and perfect if you're looking for a gift or for something for yourself. Note that this is a great destination for presents for new mums and babies.

Site Usability:	★★★★★	Based:	UK
Product Range:	★★★★★	Express Delivery Option? (UK)	Yes
Price Range:	Medium	Gift Wrapping Option?	Yes
Delivery Area:	Worldwide	Returns Procedure:	Down to you

www.vivaladiva.com

This is an online store that's growing like topsy, with more and more styles and designers being added each season. You'll find couture shoes and boots by Beatrix Ong, Cavalli, Sergio Rossi and Lulu Guinness, the Boutique collection with names such as Amira and Carvela, plus much less expensive ranges like Schuh, Moda in Pelle and Converse. It's a fun website with a lot of attitude. The shoes are displayed very clearly and range from £25 to £300. Watch out for new designers being included.

Site Usability:	★★★★★	Express Delivery Option? (UK)	Yes
Product Range:	★★★★★	Gift Wrapping Option?	Yes/Automatic
Price Range:	Luxury/Medium/Very Good Value	Returns Procedure:	Free of charge by courier or Royal Mail
Delivery Area:	UK		

Index